Systemic Architecture

Marco Poletto and **Claudia Pasquero** are co-founders of ecoLogicStudio and Unit Masters at the Architectural Association.

ecoLogicStudio has built an international reputation for its innovative research combining systemic thinking with algorithmic design and large-scale prototyping. Completed projects include a public library, the "Lightwall" house and a large eco-roof prototype. ecoLogicStudio has presented installations at the most important Architecture Biennales, including Venice, London and Seville, Istanbul and Milan Fuorisalone.

Claudia and Marco lecture internationally and in 2012 will be Visiting Master tutors at the IAAC in Barcelona and Hans Strauch Visiting Critics at Cornell University in Ithaca, and will co-direct the new AA Visiting School in Milan, titled "Cyber-Gardening the City".

They live and work in London.

D1615002

This is a manual investigating the subject of urban ecology and systemic development from the perspective of architectural design. The authors set out with two main goals: to discuss the contemporary relevance of a systemic practice to architectural design, and to share a toolbox of informational design protocols developed to describe the city as a territory of self-organization.

Collecting together nearly a decade of design experiments by the authors and their practice, ecoLogicStudio, the book is organized into three design domains: "Environments", "Machines" and "Behavioural Spaces". The conversation touches disciplinary definitions, often perceived as oppositions, such as sustainable development versus ecologic urbanization, algorithmic (process-driven) versus critical (narrative-driven) architecture, bottom-up tactical versus top-down strategic design, space as patterns of use versus behavioural space, low-tech materiality versus high-tech design, and the boundary of the natural and the artificial realms within the city and architecture.

A new kind of emergent "real-time world city" is presented in the book in the form of an operational design manual for the assemblage of proto-architectures, the incubation of proto-gardens and the coding of proto-interfaces. These prototypes of machinic architecture materialize as synthetic hybrids embedded with biological life (proto-gardens), computational power, behavioural responsiveness (cyber-gardens), spatial articulation (ecoMachines and fibrous structures), remote sensing (FUNclouds) and communication capabilities (the Ecological Footprint Grotto).

With this manual ecoLogicStudio illustrates a form of know-how that constitutes the basis for its critical practice. Such a mode of practice is better understood through the actual application of the manual, by experiencing architecture as an experimental practice devoted to promoting a critical understanding of our society through the evolution of a personal architectural knowledge; a new individual *modus operandi* able to be shared and interconnected to trigger new appetites, new hungers in crafting a better environment.

Supporting the authors' own essays and projects are contributions from key innovators in contemporary architecture and urban design: Michael Batty, Andrew Hudson-Smith, Michael Weinstock and Patrik Schumacher.

Systemic Architecture

Operating Manual for the Self-Organizing City

Marco Poletto
Claudia Pasquero
[ecoLogicStudio]

Routledge
Taylor & Francis Group

LONDON AND NEW YORK

First published 2012
by Routledge
2 Park Square, Milton Park,
Abingdon, Oxon OX14 4RN

Simultaneously published in the USA and
Canada
by Routledge
711 Third Avenue, New York, NY 10017

*Routledge is an imprint of the Taylor &
Francis Group, an informa business*

*British Library Cataloguing in
Publication Data*
A catalogue record for this book is
available from the British Library

*Library of Congress Cataloging in
Publication Data*
Poletto, Marco.
Systemic architecture : operating manual
for the self-organizing city / Marco Poletto
and Claudia Pasquero.
  p. cm.
Includes bibliographical references and
index.
1. Architecture—Environmental aspects.
2. City planning.
I. Pasquero, Claudia. II. Title.
III. Title: Operating manual for the self
organizing city.
  NA9053.E58P5 2012
  711'.4—dc23
  2011021868

ISBN: 978-0-415-59607-7 (hbk)
ISBN: 978-0-415-59608-4 (pbk)

Designer: Alex Lazarou

Printed in Great Britain by
Ashford Colour Press Ltd

Contents

Preface vi

Thoughts 1

Discussions 13

Environments [b1] 24

Machines [b2] 112

Credits 260

Index 262

Preface *Systemic Architecture: Operating Manual for the Self-Organizing City* presents, in the form of a manual, nearly a decade of research projects and design experiments conducted by the authors, Marco Poletto and Claudia Pasquero, within a multiplicity of contexts, ranging from Central London to the informal barrios of Caracas, from the coasts of Sicily to Istanbul, from cultural events like the Venice Architecture Biennale to architecturally unexplored landscapes like the Rub Al Khali Desert in the Arabian Peninsula, and the submarine landscape of the World Lagoon in Dubai, UAE.

The definition of a systemic approach to architectural design, as well as the conception of the city as a territory of self-organization, which constitute the two defining topics of the book, have matured predominantly within the academic context of the Architectural Association School of Architecture, in London; while the testing beds and related projects presented in this operating manual are mainly part of the speculative work conducted by our practice ecoLogicStudio.

We are grateful to the network of people that constitute the unique cultural environment of the AA, to our students as well as our colleagues: Brett Steele, Mohsen Mostafavi, Simos Yannas, Susannah Hagan, Ciro Najle, Michael Weinstock, Charles Tashima, Hanif Kara, Eva Castro, Holger Kehne, Raoul Bunschoten, Eduardo Rico, Alex Haw, Jonas Lundber, Steve Hardy, Theo Spyropoulos, Vicente Guallart, Lucy Bullivant, Ivan Valdez, Marco Guarnieri, Juan Carlos Sanabria, Nick Puckett, Eva Sopeoglou, Abeer Shaheen Al Janahi, Jorge Godoy, Nilufer Kozikoglu. The book represents an effort to coherently capture and share the sedimentation of long hours of intense conversation on the "why" and the "how to" of a radical approach to the practice of architecture in this age of strong ecologic, economic and social turmoil; we have been debating the nature of a change of cultural sensibility in the practice of architecture that seeks to re-evaluate the social and cultural relevance of the architect, engaged in updating key disciplinary definitions, such as ecologic urbanism, algorithmic architecture, bottom-up or tactical design, behavioural space and the boundary of the natural and the artificial realms within the city and architecture.

The engagement with such disciplinary discourses has developed on two levels: by sharpening our critical and operational abilities through the coherent and systematic digitalization of our practice and of our toolbox, and by searching for challenging design scenarios or contexts; we have, in other words, evolved a form of know-how that constitutes the basis for our critical practice.

Such a mode of practice, perhaps more akin to that of a scientist, is reflected in the structure of the book, and in its conception as an operating manual: we feel that the best way to engage the readers in our research and in our critical trajectory is to share with them our know-how and to invite them to try it and test it directly: it is mostly through the application of the systemic design protocols presented here that the readers can establish a relevant connection with our research and evolve their own interpretation of its relevance in relation to a specific practice. Ultimately the ambition of the book is to stimulate, particularly students and young architects, to experience architecture as an experimental practice devoted to promoting a critical understanding of our society through the evolution of a new architectural know-how; a new individual modus operandi able to be shared and interconnected to trigger (in them) "new appetites and new hungers".

ecoLogicStudio is the place where this new modus operandi for architecture is developed and tested day by day thanks to the hard work and contagious enthusiasm of our team of architects and interns, to which we are extremely grateful; special thanks to Andrea Bugli and Alessio Carta for their support in collecting and editing the material for this book. The opportunity to develop a new know-how can only emerge within a context that shares the same wish to explore and to search for new exciting design possibilities: ecoLogicStudio has been privileged to work with curators, clients, consultants and sponsors which have commissioned and supported the projects featured in the book and which had the ability to create thriving conditions for their development: Paolo Brescia, Tommaso Principi, Alfredo Brillembourg, Hubert Klumpner, Guy Battle, Carlo Ratti, Pelin Dervis, Sandrine Von Klot, Melissa Woodford, Aaron Betsky, Emiliano Gandolfi, Marie Ange Brayer, Michele Latzinger, Pino Scaglione, Silvio and Felix Machetta, Luca Molinari, Simona Galateo, Federico Parolotto.

The first part of the book is dedicated to a series of speculative essays written by us and a pool of contributors, namely Patrik Schumacher, Michael Batty, Andrew Hudson-Smith and Michael Weinstock. Through their work they have been both a reference and a stimulus for the research presented here and their contributions provide an inspiring set of connected thoughts on the subject central to the book's conceptual thesis, which is the definition of a systemic practice of architecture and a clarification of its applicability in relation to a renewed notion of "real-time world city" which we call the self-organizing city.

The manual, which follows, is then organized into three domains: "Environments", "Machines", and "Behavioural Spaces". Each domain starts with a series of definitions of recurrent terms that we have used to name a specific component of our projects and with a short "About" section framing the type of case study presented.

The three domains are used to propose a systemic notion of architectural context,

aesthetic and space. The domain "Environments" engages with the scale of the landscape, presenting algorithmic techniques and socio-political protocols to engage the urban landscape and its social and material ecologies, harvesting their relevance as design drivers.

"Machines" focuses on exploring the aesthetic expressivity of material systems; installations are presented here as testing beds for a series of architectural machines articulating in space the structural behaviour of fibrous systems and the material articulation of biologic architectures.

"Behavioural Spaces" traces a relationship between the two previous domains, exploring architecture as a space of interaction, playfulness and participation; as architecture becomes a living body within the city the architects' role is questioned and perhaps evolves into that of a mediator or, in our terms, a "cyber-gardener".

Within the three domains each project has been framed as a case study to explore a specific aspect of systemic architecture, from engagement with the informal social systems of Caracas to the algorithmically defined new cities in the UAE; from the self-regulating material properties of STEM, to the self-organizing prototypes of the Metropolitan Proto-Garden, which proposes to connect the digital world of mapping and simulating to the material world of sensing and actuating by means of "a sort of Facebook for architecture".

Each project starts with a descriptive text and is completed by a "how to" section; these sections are key, as they describe each project as an algorithmic protocol, defining its applicability as a system for architectural action. They are the core of the manual, where we invite the reader to leave the book to one side and embrace experimental architecture as a wonderful adventure of playful discovery.

Thoughts on Systemic Architecture

Marco Poletto and Claudia Pasquero

The ecology of the self-organizing city
p. 2

The urban algorithm
p. 4

Coding as gardening
p. 6

Algorithmic diverseCity
p. 8

Architecture as systemic design practice
p. 11

THE ECOLOGY OF
THE SELF-ORGANIZING CITY

The operating manual of the self-organizing city incorporates into the design and planning of contemporary cities the bottom-up mechanisms found in nature as well as in the functioning of rural villages and post-industrial cyber-communities.

Intense urbanization is arguably one of the defining characteristics of our society; as capitalism reaches its terminal stage and the digital revolution shapes an instantaneous global world, cities are replacing national states as the social and economic centres of our new civilization. Spatial scales are transformed by the intensification of interscalar communication, influencing the relationship between the personal and urban realms. As Virilio points out:

> Home shopping, working from home, online apartments and buildings: "cocooning", as they say. The urbanization of real space is thus being overtaken by this urbanization of real time which is, at the end of the day, the urbanization of the actual body of the city dweller, this citizen-terminal.
>
> Paul Virilio, *Open Sky*,
> London: Verso, 1997, p. 20

Socially, urbanization is often perceived as an irresistible tendency, whereby the rural population urbanizes to fulfil the dream of a more comfortable life and a more rewarding career. However, with a more critical reading we find that migrations are often forced by the lack of investment into rural regions and into their informal market, or by the disappearance of the rural landscape itself. Such disappearance is both physical, as a result of property development, but mostly mental or psychogeographical, as a result of the emergence of a "real-time world city", whose spatio-temporal pull reduces to zero the perception of the journey across the nodes of the urban network:

> Today, when we are all so worried about the ecological balance of a human environment seriously threatened by industrial waste, would it not be appropriate to add to the concerns of green ecology those of a grey ecology that would focus on the postindustrial degradation of the depth of field of the terrestrial landscape?
>
> Virilio, *Open Sky*, p. 41

This loss of "depth of field" is exacerbated by a correlated process, the emergence of a new form of nomadic behaviour, whereby people leave their original settlements to search for more fertile pastures – richer markets; the material loss is replaced by a gain in economic value, a trading capacity that can grant this nomadic clan access to better services, including training and education. As the new nomads start their journey they inevitably break their symbiosis with their original land, losing their own mental interpretation of it as a productive landscape or, as landscape designer and philosopher Gilles Clement would define it, "a garden":

> If we look at the earth as a territory devoted to life, it would appear as an enclosed space, delimited by the boundaries of living systems (the biosphere). In other words, it would appear as a garden (the etymology of the word garden comes from the German garten, the etymological root for which is enclosed or bounded space). ... This statement impels every human being, in his transient existence on earth to commit to his responsibilities as guarantor of the living world that he has received for management. And here he is becoming a gardener.
>
> Gilles Clement, *Il giardiniere planetario*,
> Milan: 22Publishing, 2008, pp. 58–59,
> translation by Marco Poletto

Their original material practices are slowly forgotten, converted from rural and largely pre-industrial to urban and technologically mediated; they lose the ability to sustain their own community and become dependent on external provisions, even when these are of a lower quality. They stop contributing to the tending of our "planetary garden".

The current phenomenon of global urbanization therefore coincides with the weakening of the conception and perception of the landscape as a garden to nourish and to be nourished by. It is not just physical erosion of the natural land by urban structures, but a more fundamental loss of material practices and protocols and of their social meaning. As the global capacity to read the landscape as a "garden" disappears so does the ability to connect urban development with a sustainable relationship with the biosphere. From this perspective the global ecological crisis is a problem of the culture of urbanization; of loss of diversity of material practices; of transformation of the physical landscape in relation to the social one.

The self-organizing city is, instead, a new form of emergent "real-time world city": a conceptual and operational model of urbanization for promoting the re-structuring of endangered species of social, economic and environmental practices and organizations. The self-organizing city is described in this book by means of an operational design manual. Within each section dedicated protocols describe the assemblage of proto-architectures, the incubation of proto-gardens and the coding of proto-interfaces; these prototypes of machinic architecture materialize as synthetic hybrids embedded with biological life (see proto-gardens, in "Environments" and "Behavioural Spaces"), computational power, behavioural responsiveness (see cyber-gardens, in "Behavioural Spaces"), spatial articulation (see ecoMachines and fibrous structures, in "Machines"), remote sensing (see FUNclouds, in "Behavioural Spaces") and communication capabilities (see the Ecological Footprint Grotto, in "Behavioural Spaces").

If urbanization strongly correlates to global ecological stress, it is within the context of urban networks that we can effectively speak of ecological development: national states are limited by both their physical boundaries and their internal bureaucracies, while many international organizations lack operational focus. The emergent urban communities are dynamic, fluid and far from equilibrium, ideal incubators of new cultural networks;

they connect the main academic and research institutions to the self-organized clusters of creative development; they continuously develop new material practices or know-how by testing novel technologies or by recycling traditions; they fabricate new mechanisms to interact among themselves and with the surrounding environment.

By harvesting this inherent vitality the self-organizing city proposes a vision of urbanity that has interaction and a narrative of productive know-how as its constitutional protocols; as such the self-organizing city has no limits in either time or space, no beginning and no end, no fixed and final configuration, no permanent dweller, no single planner. Within the self-organizing city these forces generate diversity and cultivate differentiation as a means to evolve true novelty, to create new forms of material life on our planet.

Inhabiting the self-organizing city gives us the ability to play an active role in the making of an open future, turning destruction and erasure into potential for new originations, transformations and migrations; generative movements or trajectories of escape that become seeds for new virtual plots, new proto-gardens and new ecoMachines.

THE
URBAN ALGORITHM

In mathematics and computer science an algorithm is an effective method or procedure expressed as a finite list of logically defined instructions for calculating a function. Algorithms take in various *inputs* and after a series of transformations deliver an *output*; the relationship between input and output may not be deterministic or linear and may involve chance. We would argue here that the mathematical definition of algorithm needs to be reframed to encompass the coding of the "real-time world city" and to become what we will call an "urban algorithm".

Algorithms are traditionally conceived as "powerful problem solving machines" and as such have been used throughout history in various form. They require computation and computational power to run; in the past material or analogue computation was used extensively. Such a form of computation harvests the natural ability of materials to self-organize and "solve", for instance, problems of structural stability by means of a process of analogue form-finding; analogue computers were material assemblages able to multiply the effects of material computation, thus achieving sufficient problem-solving performance. Such computers were often large – in fact since antiquity many whole buildings have been conceived as architectural computing machines, a well-known example being the so-called "Nilometers" in Egypt. These beautifully ornamental structures were in fact large graduated tanks that, once connected by a complex network of pipelines to the river Nile, were able to measure the extent of each year's flood. This was then used to calculate the taxation rate to be imposed on the local farmers benefitting from the flooding. In good years, large flooding would make the ground more fertile and higher taxes could be imposed. In this example the river Nile's topography, its network of infrastructural canals, the cultivated landscape and the Nilometers operated together as a large analogue computer, embedded within the material substratum of the "garden" that it was designed to monitor and help to cultivate.

The digital revolution has dramatically increased the power versus size ratio of analogue computation; a computer as complex and large as the Nilometer system can now be reasonably well simulated by a 2 kg laptop processor. This progression has disconnected material computation from the fabric of our built environment and of our urban landscape; the architecture of computation is now beyond the scales of architectural and urban design. The discipline of architectural composition and urban design has evolved independently from any practice of analogue computation or, in other words, of material organization. So even if it's becoming possible to simulate complex organisms like our cities through the application of specifically customized algorithms, the main obstacle to their effective application to the design of our urban environment has been the need to overcome the conceptual difficulty of expressing urban and architectural design problems in the form of algorithmically solvable questions; or, in other words, to embed these algorithms in a coherent form of material organization.

Despite the rising use of algorithmic processes in design it is still necessary to overcome this conceptual shortcoming: a first step might be the expansion of the concept of algorithms as mathematical entities with strong disciplinary connotations and an almost exclusive applicability to the logical formulations typical of the scientific and engineering domains.

French philosopher Gilles Deleuze offers us some support here by providing an extended meaning of the term "machine" beyond the mechanical paradigm and towards a larger "machinic" framework. Such conceptual reframing can be adopted to expand the notion of algorithms as mere mathematical machines. For Deleuze the notion of machine exceeds the technical realm and includes abstract generative mechanisms that can be recognized in any organic or inorganic being and that operate across multiple realms and at multiple scales:

It makes no sense to think that an organism stands a chance of survival independently of the survival of its milieu; the milieu is a precondition for the organism's development; ... If we frame the organism plus milieu as a unit as Bateson suggests, than it is impossible to define it neatly as having a clear form, or limit.

Andrew Ballantyne, *Deleuze and Guattari*, Oxford: Routledge, 2007, p. 85

A simple example used repeatedly by Deleuze and Guattari is the relationship between the wasp orchid and the Thynnie wasp. The orchid flower has evolved parts that resemble very closely the female wasp; the seduced wasp male tries to mate with the flower and by doing so it pollinates the plant; the two have evolved so inseparably that even their appearance has become similar. Despite being an insect and a plant, the wasp is inherently part of the orchid so that it becomes very hard to draw a frame around its identity; however resisting doing so allows us to conceptualize the pair as a larger ensemble or machine, and their coupling as the process of reproduction of that machine.

In a similar fashion human beings can be defined as an assemblage of what Deleuze calls "desiring machines", thousands of mechanisms that without us noticing produce the desires that we *are* aware of. A similar machinic framework can be recognized in the formation and evolution of inorganic assemblages such as dunes and deserts: millions of sorting mechanisms create coherent patterns of sand distribution that travel in space and time until final dissolution.

The most important aspect of Deleuze's definition of machines, for our discourse, is that they cannot exist outside their "milieu", or environment; in other words, they are inextricably embedded in the environment within which they perform or are conceived: exactly like an animal and its habitat, or the Nilometer within the river Nile region, they form a "unit of survival". Following this line of thought we propose an evolved notion of algorithm, referred to as the "urban algorithm", a computational machine whose definition and evolution is inextricably embedded into its "milieu".

Two pioneering applications of an expanded notion of an algorithmic machine are provided by engineer Le Ricolais, working with models of structural analysis and behavioural simulations of structures observed during collapse, and by cybernetician Gordon Pask, who famously developed a series of artefacts, conceived in conversation with the surrounding environment as well as with the users, as testing beds for his theories on second order cybernetics:

Le Ricolais suggests that matter, material, construction systems, structural configurations, space, and place comprise a continuous spectrum rather than isolated domains. Such an understanding provides a model for organizing forces and their effects that is communicative, reverberating across scales and regimes.

Reiser + Umemoto, *Atlas of Novel Tectonics*, New York: Princeton Architectural Press, 2006, p. 110

It seems to me that the notion of machine that was current in the course of the Industrial Revolution – and which we might have inherited – is a notion, essentially, of a machine without goal, it had no goal "of", it had a goal "for". And this gradually developed into the notion of machines with goals "of", like Thermostats. Now we've got the notion of a machine with an underspecified goal, the system that evolves. This is a new notion, nothing like the notion of machines that was current in the Industrial Revolution, absolutely nothing like it. It is, if you like, a much more biological notion; maybe I'm wrong to call such a thing a machine; I gave that label to it because I like to realize things as artefacts, but you might not call the system a machine, you might call it something else.

Gordon Pask quoted in Mary Catherine Bateson, *Our Own Metaphor: A Personal Account of a Conference on the Effects of Conscious Purpose on Human Adaptation*, New York: Alfred A. Knopf, 1972

It is along these lines that the definition of algorithm inherited from mathematics and computer science can be re-defined to formulate the "urban algorithm" as a computational design protocol embedded in its extended milieu.

CODING
AS GARDENING

"Urban algorithms", as defined in the previous short chapter, possess a rather peculiar nature which makes coding specific to a certain milieu, be it the ecology of a landscape or an architectural material system. This peculiarity can be exemplified by comparing the methods of a chemist synthesizing artificial tissues in a lab with those of a gardener reviving a patch of dried land; while both are running generative protocols, the first requires a perfectly controlled and refined testing ground for her procedures to acquire general applicability while the second needs to consider the unexpected fluctuation of the ecology of his garden.

The chemist, within the controlled setting of the lab, can trigger a series of reactions and morphogenetic processes and slowly grow coherent and therefore potentially functioning tissues; if all the variables are well controlled and managed the final outcome can reproduce with enough precision the results predicted by early computer simulations of specific scenarios of development; a little unexpected mistake or variation in the testing bed and the final results would become unpredictable, incoherent and often lose their applicability. The gardener, instead, operates within a very different framework; his testing bed is by definition very differentiated and partially unpredictable in its daily or seasonal fluctuations; his operational protocols need to consider these fluctuations and differences in their formulas. As Gilles Clement points out in his beautiful description of the "moving garden", the gardener operates through a process of intensification of difference; his only chance to reconcile his desire for beautification and the natural expressivity of living processes resides in movement, intended in its biological and physical sense. The formalization of the garden becomes for Clement a process of formalized transmission of biological messages or, in our terms, of algorithmic coding; algorithms are for the gardener machines for breeding biodiversity.

Differences in slope, insulation, soil moisture and so on are registered and then exploited by the algorithm to promote the growth of different arboreal species; also the growth, being itself a variable and partially unpredictable process, needs to be read, assessed and then considered in the formulation of future actions, or in the future lines of the gardening code. The garden grows and beautification progresses in loops; each step generating more difference and local complexity that can be in turn recognized and bred; the management of this generative process is what makes the garden a potentially beautiful and healthy organism. In Clement's words:

> Reality is entirely contained within experience. Uniquely. Without gardening there is no garden.
>
> Gilles Clement, *Il giardiniere planetario*,
> Milan: 22Publishing, 2008, p. 66,
> translation by Marco Poletto

Coding here is based on experience and "know how"; with no gardening there is no garden. The gardening code is embedded in its milieu.

In algorithmic design both models of development, the laboratory and the garden, can be used. We favour the second, which we have been defining as the "urban algorithm", where coding becomes a form of "gardening". The reasons to prefer this model are multiple – Clement suggests an eco-political one:

> How can we oppose the brutality of these so-called modern techniques, with a handling [of the earth's biosphere] that is sensitive, diverse and therefore really contemporary? By bending the technological know-how to planetary ecological needs rather than, as we can still observe in all the rich countries, enslaving it for the exclusive benefit of the lobbies.
>
> Clement, *Il giardiniere planetario*, p.71

The urban algorithm responds to the systemic and ecological sensibility of our times as opposed to the mechanical productive logic of the twentieth century; today we seek to cherish and cultivate our biosphere, to understand how we can develop it or transform it in tune with its own vital cycles and the generative processes of life. Just like an "urban algorithm", life proliferates by breeding potentials of intensive differences; it is constantly opportunistic and open to the actualization of new material organizations. We seek to intensify these mechanisms while rescuing them from the conforming force of modern technology. In his book *The Three Ecologies* Félix Guattari suggests related technological and social reasons to adopt the machinic model:

> So, wherever we turn, there is the same nagging paradox: on the one hand, the continuous development of new techno-scientific means to potentially resolve the dominant ecological issues, ... on the other hand the inability of organized social forces and constituted subjective formations to take hold of these resources in order to make them work.
>
> Félix Guattari, *The Three Ecologies*, New York: Continuum, 2008 (originally published in France, 1989), p. 22

Machinic protocols embed technology into material organizations that become part of everyday ecological practices of planetary cultivation of the biosphere, operating at multiple interconnected scales. Unlike the dominant technological protocols, the "urban algorithms" do not need the production of problems, or catastrophes, to be able to fabricate meaningful solutions; they operate on the self-organization of social forces by means of technological augmentation and their usefulness emerges out of daily material experimentation within the milieu of the "real-time world city"; in relation to this technological paradox Guattari adds:

> Social ecosophy will consist in developing specific practices that will modify and reinvent the ways in which we live as couples or in the family, in an urban context or at work, etc. ... Instead of clinging to general recommendations we would be implementing effective practices of experimentation, as much on a micro social level as on a larger institutional scale.
>
> Guattari, *The Three Ecologies*, p. 24

The successful survival of the "real-time world city" requires participation and exchange at the various social levels and material scales; a code that incorporates participation must be able to grow as the network grows, it cannot be defined a priori in a controlled or predetermined environment. "Urban algorithms" co-evolve within their milieu, the articulation of their structure increases in relation to the complexity and diversity of the urban network they serve. "Urban algorithms" are the necessary coding logics for the self-organizing city.

ALGORITHMIC
DIVERSECITY

What are, then, the key features of the "urban algorithm" and how does it encode the self-organizing city? First of all, as mentioned above, in order to become a systemic design instrument the "urban algorithm" must be embedded in its milieu; its set of instructions cannot be generic but need to be referred specifically to the "algorithmic plan". In the design phase of the self-organizing city we propose the algorithmic plan to be a parametric relational model diagrammatically representing the output of the algorithmic simulation; as Ciro Najle has suggested in his manual for the machinic landscape, the plan will constitute a pre-urban medium:

> a technically controlled sieve that acquires consistency as it integrates a multiplicity of determinations in a medium of production, virtualizing potentials by constantly oscillating between management of information, programming of responses, generation of organizations, evaluation of performance, coordination of collaborations, scripting of protocols, coding of communication, engineering of materials, modulation of expression and fine-tuning of inflections.
>
> Ciro Najle, *Landscape Urbanism*,
> London: AA Publications, 2003, p. 39

Running a new line of code will generate a new pre-urban algorithmic plan; any following lines of code must operate in the plan generated by the previous one and recognize the potentials it has produced. As the code evolves the plan differentiates and generates novel potentials or breeding grounds; the recognition of such potentials generates in turn new specific lines of code, thus evolving the algorithmic machine as a whole. As a consequence the "urban algorithm" cannot be defined a priori, or outside of the algorithmic plan.

The solutions of each line of code influence the formulation of the following line; this process

has the inherent tendency to branch, that is, to generate multiple solutions; the "urban algorithm" is therefore generative by definition; each branch leads to increased internal diversity and articulation. As a result, a second feature of the "urban algorithm" is nonlinearity; the algorithm doesn't treat growth as a linear chronologic sequence, rather it establishes horizontal connections in the plan, it relates circumstances, nodes of attraction, organizations of power promoting growth as a nomadic propagation; as a consequence its ramifying structure will not resemble the centralized branching of a tree but rather, as Deleuze suggests, a rhizome.

The growth of the algorithm is related to the growth of a proto-representation of the self-organizing city and is defined by its articulation and differentiation. Growth is therefore not merely a linear process of geographical expansion but rather one of complexification of its network of internal links; a good example is the process of evolution of a forest. Organisms like forests are extremely diverse, or bio-diverse; this biodiversity has been generated in thousands of years of constant differentiation; all the species that inhabit forests have adapted and in turn have evolved into lineages composed of many instances; the algorithm of the forest must include all the algorithms that regulate each species within it; as such it is extremely articulated and diverse.

Biodiversity can also decrease, as is often the case when human action intervenes or as an effect of globalizing forces; as such cities, like forests, can shrink, perhaps not so much in terms of physical boundaries but in terms of bio-social-diversity and internal articulation. The case of post-industrial Detroit is emblematic, with its inner plots reverting to countryside or abandoned wasteland. Artist Kyong Park has re-inhabited this post-industrial terrain through a choreography of signs and messages able to re-code the emergent gaps as part of a new network of urban proto-spaces. His experimental practice has, in turn, encountered and perhaps even stimulated the vitality of the local suburban dwellers, now turned into urban gardeners of a form of network agriculture:

Artistic behavior, then, once considered characteristic of small, excluded, marginalized and unpredictable social groups once viewed as foreign to the business world, has now gained a new centrality in the social economy. ... This is then a "buzz economy" that follows discontinuous flows of an energy that is more relational than productive.

Andrea Branzi, *Weak and Diffuse Modernity*,
Milan: Skira, 2006, pp. 39, 50

Such socio-economic models require urban designers to map emergent network spaces in real time and to promote urban transformation through the re-coding of urban gaps. In this circumstance the "urban algorithm" enables them to operate through a proto-representation of the city, turning the algorithmic plan into a device of urban incubation able to map the potential for social interaction and to promote the emergence of urban life. Another key feature of the "urban algorithm" is therefore its ability to deploy technology as a means to activate the vital forces of the self-organizing city:

The metropolis of the information age is not, then, the capital of technology; it is rather the land of the humane, in all its ability to connect its own DNA with that of business, disseminating its own genes in a tight network of parental and entrepreneurial relations.

Branzi, *Weak and Diffuse Modernity*, p. 24

As we said before, each "urban algorithm" is unique; it belongs to its milieu and from this specific interaction, it grows articulation as well as its specific traits and qualities. This makes it very different from a classic optimization algorithm whose applicability is generic; the mode of operation of the "urban algorithm" is local, it operates by exploiting local difference or constraints; it turns constraints into generative opportunities for the specification of new infrastructures and urban spaces:

Every little dissimilarity is an event, a useful landmark for the construction of a mental map composed of points (particular places), lines (paths) and surfaces (homogeneous territories) that are transformed over time. The ability to know how to see in the void of the places and therefore to know how to name these places was learned in the millennia preceding the birth of nomadism.

Francesco Careri, *Walkscapes*,
Barcelona: GG, 2002, p. 42

A city will never emerge in a neutral and controlled environment such as that of the lab or the virtual space of a computer; existing complexities, topographic irregularities, political boundaries or social lines of conflict are always present. Traditional algorithms have been applied in multiple site conditions by considering constraints to be external interferences; as such constraints are often problematic and non-generative and the temptation is to try to remove them. "Urban algorithms" instead grow out of a productive manipulation of these constraints; they use these differences to breed new diversity and to slowly produce higher levels of efficiency in the milieu. This process has an inherent economy of means as it works with the local conditions rather than against them; this recalls the metaphor of the gardener, and his ability to promote the colonization of the garden by various animals and insects as part of the process of beautification. Negotiations, rather than weakening the algorithm's efficiency, actually contribute to its evolution and to the richness and beauty of the algorithmic plan:

Architecture would thus become part of a wider ranging activity, and like the other arts would disappear in favor of a unified activity that sees the urban environment as a relational ground for a game of participation.

Careri, *Walkscapes*, p. 116

The urban environment, its socio-cultural-economic context and the "urban algorithm" itself are interconnected parts of the same machinic assemblage. This relationship materializes in a multitude of architectural and urban prototypes; the "urban algorithm" is the working protocol of such a design apparatus as described in the algorithmic plan. Eventually, design intentions, technological media as well as local constraints will co-evolve and become inextricably part of the urban machine:

> Public spaces must have a prototypical character; they are instruments of change for a society. ... [it only gradually became] clear that in fact this combination between form – specially diagrammatic form – and the operational mechanism of a prototype together is the link between architectural space and urban dynamics.
>
> Raoul Bunschoten, *Public Spaces*,
> London: Black Dog, 2002, p. 5

The "urban algorithm" as well as the city is never complete or finished; the design, construction and evolution of a city can be all conceived algorithmically as a continuum. The regulatory body of the city and its inhabitants become part of the design apparatus as they begin to influence the coding of the design algorithm generating the self-organizing city.

ARCHITECTURE AS
SYSTEMIC DESIGN PRACTICE

A Deleuzian (extraordinary) diagram is an abstract machine that is valued precisely because its downstream implications are totally open. The crucial difference between ordinary and extraordinary diagrams does not reside within the graphic or digital object itself, but in the patterns of its use.

Patrik Schumacher, The Autopoiesis of Architecture,
London: Wiley, 2010, p. 350

The limits of our design language are the limits of our design thinking. The medium of representation delimits the domain of architecture and implicitly defines what architecture is. How we represent architecture determines how we anticipate (design) architecture.

Schumacher, The Autopoiesis of Architecture,
p. 330

One of the transformations that took place in architecture in the 1990s is the abandonment of the ideology of form and the advance towards establishing what we could call "the ideology of the process", based on the exploration of potential patterns of use of new diagrammatic representations supported by emerging digital design technologies. Ideology here is not intended as political but refers instead to the infrastructure of a general knowledge regime which forms the base for a professional practice. Before the introduction of algorithmic design processes it was common to define architecture as a line of autonomous practices, related one to the other in linear fashion, creating a sort of hierarchy.

The architectural system of production was based on the illusion that it was the determiner of the final form of what was imagined during the expressive phase of activity within the studio of the lead architect. As work was carried out with a repertory of forms totally dependent on Euclidean geometry, it was easy to believe this illusion. Each mathematical expression represented a single constant form that, when represented in design, was easily associated with the real form of the final product.

Algorithmic design demonstrates the illusory nature of this association. One of its key initiators, Gregg Lynn's work on animate forms can be considered the first manifesto of a new knowledge regime of production which declared the end of the era of predictable forms that started with the Renaissance. As Schumacher argues:

Algorithmic design techniques allow us to conceive form as an emergent effect in a design process; the initial design actions or sketches merely define starting points within a process of creation or production and cannot determine what the final result will be like. What emerges from this are architectural practices implemented by the continuous going back and forth within the process, which we call "systemic design practices". The old hierarchy of expertise is now being replaced by a new, possibly more democratic, production process where the efficiency of the design solution is built up through revisions which consequently incorporate intelligence and performance. This is a process where the initial decision of form can be repeatedly re-described by another decision taken on another level of the urban algorithm; it is a process where all practices are the indivisible parts of an emergent whole:

The truly innovative architects' designs swarm architecture for an open source in real time. Building components are potential senders and receivers of information in real time … People communicate. Buildings communicate. People communicate with people. People communicate with buildings. Buildings communicate with buildings. Building components communicate with other building components; all are members of the swarm, members of the hive.

Kas Oosterhuis, Hyperbodies,
Basel: Birkhäuser, 2003, pp. 5–6

While complex algorithmic procedures can be developed in order to predict a final form, this is not vital for their existence; they are virtual multiplicities held by a mathematical formula with infinite possible geometric solutions that can be made to evolve and interact within the milieu and in real time. Form is then the product of an algorithmic procedure of material organization applied in a specific space and time:

> Mies's constraint of matter by ideal geometry is based on an essentialist notion: that matter is formless and geometry regulates it. ... When freed from such essentializing conception, matter proves to have its own capacities of self-organization. As an analogue computer, it can perform optimizing computations that have been shown to be trans-scalar; ... it becomes a model not only for dealing with structure but for dealing with the feedback that occurs between multiple forces at work on a building.
>
> Reiser + Umemoto, *Atlas of Novel Tectonics*, New York: Princeton Architectural Press, 2006, p. 88

Geometry does not domesticate material; rather it operates as a tympanum against which material properties resound. As novel spatial effects emerge, so structural behaviour evolves as a consequence of this dynamic exchange of intensive and extensive information; structural design logics are then also transformed. Empirical calculations representing a building's structural behaviour on a two-dimensional plane, depicted within the context of formulas which are the universally valid results of previous experimentation, are no longer relevant. Systemic design practices do not operate within such a strict polarity; there is no such yes/no solution; a particular structural behaviour is always modelled in real time, defining an area of efficient possibilities within an almost chaotic whole, generating design solutions which evolve iteration after iteration:

> The sedentary space is striated by walls, enclosures and routes between the enclosures, while the nomadic space is smooth, marked only by strokes that are erased or shift with the journey. ... The nomadic city is the path itself, the most notable sign in the void ... The points of departure and arrival are less important, while the space in between is the space of going, the very essence of nomadism, the place in which to celebrate the everyday ritual of eternal wandering.
>
> Francesco Careri, *Walkscapes*, Barcelona: GG, 2002, p. 38

Systemic design practices suggest a different spatial logic exemplified by the smooth space of the Fibrous Room; this architectural apparatus does not prescribe form, rather it describes an informational protocol, an experimental "derive" in the field of architectural prototyping, concrete structural design and material ornamentation guided by strictly defined rules of information. The experiment works as a sort of training session in material disorientation; how wide a series of relevant possibilities can we create in the context of designing, calculating and building a concrete structural prototype? Certainly there is no guarantee that all these possibilities will become useful in the future; all the same it is worth trying, because what creates the future is the experiment itself, the practice of experimentation which has no definitive end:

> So that is another rule for the whole nature of architecture: it must create new appetites, new hungers – not solve problems, architecture is too slow to solve problems.
>
> Cedric Price, *Re: CP*, ed. by Hans-Ulrich Obrist, Basel: Birkhäuser, 2003, p. 57

Discussions on Systemic Architecture

with

Patrik Schumacher
Michael Batty and Andrew Hudson-Smith
Michael Weinstock

On systemic architecture
p. 14

The liquid city
p. 18

Ecology and material culture
p. 21

ON SYSTEMIC ARCHITECTURE

Claudia Pasquero (CP) and Marco Poletto (MP)
in conversation with Patrik Schumacher (PS)

CP Ecological processes always include a component of unpredictability; do you think architecture can be conceived as an experimental practice able to engage unpredictability as a generative/creative force?

PS Yes! The use of non-linear, unpredictable processes delivers creativity. One might even define creativity in terms of unpredictability. Radical innovation depends on radical newness as one of its conditions. The task is to go beyond familiar forms of spatial organization, to expand the search space for viable solutions. However, rather than just harnessing pure randomness (subject to intuitive selection and post-rationalization) one might try to simulate processes of self-organization that embody a certain performative rationality, via constraints or even via (relative) optimization. What I said so far pertains to the design process in advance of construction. A master-plan, by contrast, often evolves in parallel to phased construction. A "master-plan" today is no longer a master-plan but only viable as a temporary hypothesis. As a parametric system it might offer a range of solution possibilities on a number of dimensions. The market can choose. If the ranges offered are insufficient, the plan must be recalibrated or even radically expanded to adapt to developments that were not anticipated. The plan can evolve without losing its identity only if key principles and criteria have been stated that guide the plan's adaptation. It is in this way that I would like to interpret your concept of the self-organizing city made up of "virtual plots". Beyond this we can still rely on the heuristics of Parametricism to guarantee ongoing continuity within an evolving plan that continues to adapt to radical shifts in market conditions and shifts in political impositions. Thus although not predictable in its detailed form, the urban future can be expected to follow a certain paradigm.

Within the paradigm of Parametricism local unpredictability can be creatively harnessed or absorbed while maintaining a global frame of principles. We should not think that we could invent an urban system that could automatically, on its own account, react to and resolve such unpredictable contingencies. This can only be the result of the reflective application of a historically pertinent heuristics, i.e. via creative work within a historically pertinent style or design research programme.

MP The foundation of cities was often a response to opportunities found in the landscape and in the local ecological systems; do you think the notion of the contemporary metropolis should be re-evaluated in systemic terms by including all the relevant global systems that are co-defining its actual state?

PS You talk about the contemporary metropolis as eco-social landscape. That's pertinent. However, the architect has certainly no control over all systems that co-define the actual state of the contemporary metropolis. He cannot even evaluate these systems, far less re-evaluate them. Within functionally differentiated society all societal subsystems – the economy, the political system, the mass media, engineering/science, architecture etc. – evaluate and regulate themselves according to their own unique criteria of success. These systems co-evolve. They observe and irritate each other, as demands and constraints, and then adapt to each other. They depend on each other and must serve each other without being able to control each other. I think you point to this when you define urban space as "the product of processes of co-evolution of multiple agents behaving as a coherent assemblage". Architecture has the universal, exclusive competency and responsibility for the adaptive innovation of the built environment as ordering frame and interface for social interactions of all kinds: economic, political, recreational, etc.

The engineered infrastructures, traffic, land values, investment opportunities and other economic parameters are so many constraints and/or demands upon architecture's adaptive, organizational and articulatory repertoire and intelligence. In this sense architecture must take account of all systems that co-define the actual state of the contemporary metropolis, but it cannot re-evaluate or re-define these. That's not within architecture's competency.

MP Do you think ecologic problem solving can define a contemporary architectural agenda?

PS The ecological challenge is confronting all subsystems of global society, the economy, the political system, science/engineering and also architecture/design. So, ecological sustainability is on the agenda of architecture. Initially, the demand for environmental sustainability is just one more constraint that burdens architecture's ability to deliver on its societal task: the framing of social interaction/communication. However, Parametricism is able to take this constraint and turn it into an architectural opportunity by utilizing environmental parameters as occasions to differentiate envelopes accordingly, on the basis of sun exposure, wind, rain, etc. Environmentally adaptive differentiation can become an orienting articulation. In this way an engineering constraint is transformed into an architectural pursuit.

CP Simulating the city is the new mantra of urban design; is it an illusion or is it actually possible to simulate the behaviour of a city? What can we understand from urban behavioural simulations? Can urban forecasting influence or even stimulate a new form of emergent, real-time urban design model?

PS I think our capacity to develop sophisticated models that are able to take on and simulate more and more aspects and factors of the urban process is increasing by the day. However, there is indeed an inherent dilemma

and limitation in all modelling and forecasting. The very fact that the model/forecast is available and communicated becomes a new, potentially important factor that immediately changes the situation. The forecast thus defeats itself as relevant actors adapt their expectations and behaviours in response to the forecast. But this defeats the forecast only as forecast. If we understand it as a platform of constructing emergent collectives it can work. Then it's not about prediction but about construction. One of our teams at DRL constructed such a scenario of real-time online participatory planning/developing/selling with regards to a residential community.[1] You also talk about "ecologic feedback, participation and social self-organization". You note that "urban self-organization requires the definition of an operational medium that generates responses out of urban stimuli". Perhaps it is the new social networking media that can be harnessed here somehow.

MP Should architecture reconsider its traditional Vitruvian canons to redefine its materiality in relation to the flows of information, matter and energy crossing its boundaries?

PS Architecture has already shifted its canons a number of times since Vitruvius. The last great shift was the shift from Historicism/Eclecticism to Modernism, and now we are finally moving beyond Modernism after 25 years of experimental explorations plus 10 years of cumulative design research under the auspices of the new paradigm of Parametricism. The flows of information, matter and energy are more complex and dynamic. What is more important though is the increasing density, complexity and intensity of social communication and interaction. This is what ultimately drives and justifies the new paradigm, whether this is always fully understood or not.

MP Our society is obsessed with control; can architecture mature a critical role by deploying novel design techniques and computational sensibilities to challenge this contemporary obsession of our society?

PS Yes, there seems to be an obsession with control. However, this does not lead to an increase in control. Rather I see this obsession as a rear-guard reaction to self-organizing societal dynamics which are impossible to control. As Luhmann has noted contemporary society is a world society with no control centre. It is a society of global, co-evolving subsystems. The computational techniques of contemporary architecture – generative and genetic algorithms, agent-based modelling, etc. – are congenial to a world that can no longer be controlled or predicted. This world invites everybody to co-evolve within the evolution of society. Architecture joins this dynamic co-evolution.

CP The style of Parametricism vs. the non-figurative architecture of Andrea Branzi, Cedric Price, John Frazer, etc. Are these two discourses, as it appears, mutually exclusive or should reconciliation between the stylistic and the machinic/systemic be an ambition for the future?

PS Yes, I think that Parametricism will have to absorb the innovations proposed by the strand of the avant-garde you allude to. I would also count Bernard Tschumi and Rem Koolhaas in this group. They are all concerned with charting and advancing the programmatic/software side of the built environment. Formal and programmatic research needs to converge and be synthesized within a new, comprehensive paradigm. Parametricism as it currently presents itself empirically has not yet risen to this challenge. However, both my general theory of architecture's autopoiesis and my special theory of Parametricism accommodate this requirement as my theory moves from the descriptive into the normative mode. My normative reconstruction of the concept of style and of Parametricism demands and formulates both a formal and a functional heuristics as definitory requirements of a mature style/Parametricism. So, what you call the machinic/systemic, as well as the programmatic/functional, as well as the formal/aesthetic is included in my enhanced concept of style. The concept of style deserves to be reinstated on this comprehensive, ambitious level because it has a history of giving the defining stamp on an epoch. It's not only about appearances, it's much deeper than that. However, we should also be aware that the appearance of the built environment matters enormously. The built environment functions through its appearance, via its legibility and its capacity to frame and prime communication. The built environment is not just channelling bodies. It is orienting sentient, socialized beings who must comprehend and navigate ever more complex urban scenes.

CP The more urbanized our society becomes, the more technologically mediated it will need to be; technology is the necessary instrument in developing a more effective and sustainable relationship with the biosphere. However a very small effort is devoted to the spatial and material integration of such innovations within the fabric of our cities and landscapes. Should architecture claim a new role in the evolution of this urban machine? Should architects participate in the development of new technologies by evolving their spatial, temporal and material framework?

PS Yes, architects are in charge of the overall organization of the built environment, in as much as it is interfacing with social communication. What is underground or under the hood is engineering business. But as Piano + Rogers have demonstrated with their Centre Pompidou, architects might bring the technological systems into view and let them become part of the task of articulation. Tom Wiscombe has picked this idea up within the style Parametricism. I think this is a fascinating proposition. To reveal the technological systems and networks can play an orienting role that enhances the legibility of our built environment. If you want to find the big auditorium, just follow the biggest ductwork. The same attitude that allows architects to opportunize on the differentiated structural systems for the differentiated articulation of space can be applied to the mechanical systems as well as to the passive environmental systems. Close collaboration with engineers allows architects to harness the articulatory potential of material technical systems. That's what has always been called tectonics. This could also be scaled up into an urban tectonics. In this way the city fabrics you envision to include a lot of environmental technology can become an architectural project.

MP Machines have been always part of the history of architecture; however recently the "machinic" in architecture has acquired a new meaning, expanding the mechanical significance it has acquired during the Industrial Revolution. What relevance do you think the notion of the machine can acquire in redefining architecture and its relationship with technology?

PS There are a number of avenues to consider here. "Machinic" sometimes means nothing other than avoiding preconceived ideas by harnessing blind material or computational processes. This is certainly a powerful heuristic. I also like your insistence on a new conception of materiality where the matter of architecture is freed from the essentialist conception that considers it as a formless entity regulated by transcendental geometric rules, and it becomes an active, generative force instead. I also would subscribe to your concept of the ecoMachine.

Concerning machines proper: on the side of production/fabrication a new era is dawning that requires design research. Here the AADRL a.o. has taken the lead with the attempt to seed design projects with the invention of fabrication machines and processes that allow for the fabrication of complex geometries without the aid of moulds. The idea here is to harness the self-computing, form-finding capacity of material systems. This paradigm was pioneered by Frei Otto and lies beyond the mechanical paradigm. It's part of a new paradigm of material self-organization. The second great arena of post-mechanical technology within architecture is the investigation of electronically augmented, responsive environments that respond to both environmental variables as well as to social occupation and event parameters. Again the AADRL a.o. has moved into this arena with its three-year agenda Responsive Environments.

CP Is the communication of architecture evolving from a figurative narrative to a more direct immersive and interactive language of smart materials and embedded electronics?

PS I think the potential of embedded electronics (responsive environments) is exciting. However, it provides augmentation rather than substitution. That's the way we treated it at the AA Design Research Laboratory (AADRL). Complex spatial configurations and complex geometries were the premise of our responsive environments. (This made the introduction of kinetic capabilities much more difficult.) The variable, transformative parts of the built environment will always be the smaller part. The fixed figurations remain decisive. What we were interested in was to achieve strong reconfigurations – Gestalt-catastrophes – with a minimal amount of kinetic investment. Thus we had to build in perceptual ambiguity/latency. I termed this ambition "parametric figuration". For me this is one of the more exciting research agendas within the overarching paradigm of Parametricism. It introduces observer parameters in addition to object parameters into the parametric set up.

1   Patrik Schumacher, "Autopoiesis of a Residential Community", in Brett Steele and RAMTV (eds), *Negotiate My Boundary: Mass-customisation and Responsive Environments*, London: AA Publications, 2002.

Patrik Schumacher is Partner at Zaha Hadid Architects and Founding Director at the AA Design Research Laboratory. Schumacher studied philosophy and architecture in Bonn, London and Stuttgart, where he received his Diploma in architecture in 1990. In 1999 he completed his PHD at the Institute for Cultural Science, Klagenfurt University. He joined Zaha Hadid in 1988.

THE LIQUID CITY

Michael Batty and Andrew Hudson-Smith

Cities are machines for connecting people. Until some 200 years ago, when energy began to be widely exploited to move people and materials over greater distances, their size and functions were largely limited by how far one could walk. The largest cities, invariably capitals of empires, were limited by the resources that could be used to control distant places and rarely grew to populations of more than one million, a size that was difficult to sustain. The internal combustion engine changed all that. First railways, then cars, perhaps planes, enabled cities to spread out physically but in parallel; the shift from energy to information, from "atoms to bits" as Negroponte has so eloquently phrased it, is now changing cities in ways that are no longer immediately visible. The telegraph and the phone dramatically changed the extent to which cities could link with one another in terms of trade and this forced globalization, but the transition of these information technologies into computable form and their miniaturization into digital devices now means that everyone has access to these technologies. The effects of such communication at a distance, globally, means that cities are beginning to merge into one another, if not physically, then digitally. We will all be connected in a giant urban cluster by the end of this century, which will be the physical manifestation of an intricate global nervous system created by a world of information technologies.

The digital revolution is creating multiple layers or skins of communications media, some visible but much invisible, some substitutable for traditional physical media but most complementary to it. This is building complexity. At the same time, much of this digital media is being embodied into material infrastructures with the prospect of real-time control of cities using online sensing from the bottom up. The process of constructing the built environment is fast moving from traditional top-down actions to notions about growing physical structures from the bottom up, but structures whose growth is only possible through embedded digital media and information systems. All this is changing the rate at which we can engender change. When information is instant, from anywhere, anybody and at any time, things in cities begin to be different. Cities are becoming considerably faster in their response to new information, to innovation, to physical change. Populations with more information are able to make decisions ever more coherently at faster and faster rates. In this sense, cities manifest a new liquidity of action, a confluence of light and speed, which we term the "liquid city": a place where physical desires, face to face contacts, and digital deliberations provide a new nexus of innovation. Flows, networks, connections rather than inert buildings dominate this physicality as infrastructure comes to represent this new liquidity which is built on layer upon layer of flux and flow.

Our new understanding of how cities function is predicated on action from the bottom up. Cities are built by actions exercised by individuals on behalf of themselves or larger collectivities, agencies and groups mainly configured as local actions. Global patterns emerge, best seen in how different parts of the city reflect the operation of routine decisions which combine to produce order at higher and higher scales. Cities are fractal in their form and function, as many of the insights in this book suggest. In the main, they self-organize from the bottom up where local actions are successively done, undone and transformed as individuals adapt to what is locally optimal. This is design the way nature intended, and as cities enable more and more of their populations to indulge in positive decision-making, they are becoming more and more organic. Traditional planning and design that fights against such self-organization will fail and in this, the best principles for design must reflect organization from the bottom up: the metaphor is evolution, the way nature works its magic.

The exemplar par excellence is the network. The various examples which we show here illustrate network structure at many levels where the hierarchy is implicit in the volumes of flows. This kind of structure reflects growth around a series of market centres and other hubs or cores in the urban landscape. Networks spread out to capture consumers and producers who come together at the core to buy and sell in the market: the traditional function of transportation in cities is to connect people in economic exchange. Flows of people to work and to markets to produce or consume through trade and exchange are the outward manifestations of the most obvious flows of energy which form the glue that keeps the components of the city together. Networks to channel these flows cannot develop everywhere so they spread out, tree-like, as if reaching out into the air or the soil, the way a tree grows out in search of energy to sustain it in the most economical way. The capacity of these networks increases according to the population that can be sustained by each of its nodes, and when a node reaches capacity, new ones appear, as in edge cities that are rapidly changing the dominant form from the monocentric to the polycentric city. The way cities fill their space is intimately related to the way we try to use space efficiently, in two and three dimensions, and the form that results is the product of many decisions that grow structures from the bottom up. Plans that do not account for such structures and are imposed from the top down are bound to falter for we cannot exercise the degree of control necessary to contain the diversity of individual actions by the many that might conflict with the more grandiose schemes of the few that reflect homogeneity of structure. Plans, in so far as they impact on naturally growing urban structures, occur in short bursts and are rapidly absorbed into the urban fabric which continues to mirror social structure, culture and the predominant technology, regardless.

Such rudimentary theories of how cities grow and evolve help us understand the enormous changes that are being wrought on the city by new information technologies. Although the emergence of mass physical transportation in the form of the car has provided an order of magnitude change in our opportunities to communicate at a distance, the now almost universal use of devices that enable us to capture, share and create information that can be manipulated at a distance is providing countless new ways of producing, consuming, thinking,

innovating, entertaining and so on. All of these are likely to have a profound impact on the way we use cities and we are already beginning to see this in the way we use information to direct our physical movements and interactions. For the first time, we are beginning to see how the economy is underpinned by transactions as much of this is now online, how we communicate in various ways with friends and social groups, how we search for information about others which changes our behavioural responses to the decisions and actions we continue to make across a wide spectrum of activities. What is much harder to second guess is how all this information technology is making an impact on the physical form of the city, particularly at the level of the built environment. The issue is complicated by the fact that the very information technologies that we are using to provide a new sense of how we use the city are also being embedded in the very physical infrastructures that actually compose the city.

Cities are becoming their own sensors at their most elemental level, as their physical fabric is being automated in ways that enable us to monitor their performance and use. But these combined material and digital forms are also being overlain with digital skins that seek to enable populations to use the city in countless different ways, such as figuring out in real time what services are located in different places, where friends and acquaintances reside, and what physical means of transportation there are to move oneself to distant locations. When we combine this with more basic sensors that reflect the way buildings are working, we are augmenting our reality in ways that have not been possible hitherto. At higher spatial and temporal scales, our ability to sense the city remotely offers new insights into how they are growing or declining, how they are being used over longer periods than in real time, and how we might identify problems that emerge at a more global scale than those that are more associated with individuals operating in real time.

All of this offers enormous opportunities for a new age of urban design that takes account of the city as a self-organizing system. In any age, we always know less than we need to know to develop the best designs for the future. Our knowledge is always incomplete and this is a time when so many new developments are pushing us from a world built on life styles and chances that constrain us to single places to ones that enable us to embrace many places. Cities are still largely fashioned around physical styles and behaviours that reflect medieval or even ancient cities, and we may look back and see the era in which we are currently living as one of a great transition from the city as a village to the city as a global metropolis where space and time act very differently. In this sense, our designs in the future are likely to reflect the fact that cities will be so complex that it will be essential that their continued evolution be based on self-organizing behaviours with respect to how the environment is created and how we use it. What is very clear is that the future form of the city must and will reflect a multitude of interaction patterns which suggest that cities will be used much more intensively for many different purposes over much longer diurnal and seasonal time spans than cities in the past. Multi-functional land use will once again, as in the medieval city, become the norm as information technologies embedded in ourselves and in our buildings enable us to coordinate many new and different ways of using the environment. Design based on self-organization where buildings are reconfigurable, in ways that we have barely begun to imagine, is likely to become the norm and for this, we require much more than the rudimentary theories about how cities form and evolve that we have at present. These are in the making as we have implied here and this book contains a glimpse of what we might expect in this future.

Michael Batty is Bartlett Professor of Planning at University College London where he runs the Centre for Advanced Spatial Analysis (CASA). Previously (1990–1995) he was Director of the NSF National Center for Geographic Information and Analysis (NCGIA) in the State University of New York at Buffalo, and from 1979 to 1990 he was Professor of City and Regional Planning at the University of Cardiff. His research work involves the development of computer models of cities and regions (see www.complexCity.info/).

Andrew Hudson-Smith is Director and Deputy Chair of the Centre for Advanced Spatial Analysis (CASA), he is Editor-in-Chief of *Future Internet* journal, an elected Fellow of the Royal Society of Arts and Course Founder and Director of the MRes in Advanced Spatial Analysis and Visualisation at University College London. He is author of the Digital Urban Blog with 5200 daily readers and has been at the forefront in CASA of developing digital geographical technologies that support design professionals working in the built environment.

ECOLOGY AND MATERIAL CULTURE

Michael Weinstock

There are no ecological systems on the surface of the earth that have not been modified in some way by the effects of the extended metabolisms of human societies. The emergence and subsequent development of human settlements and cities, of interlinked systems of cities, of imperial systems and the evolutionary development of the global system that we now inhabit has extended the metabolic systems of civilization across the face of the earth. City forms originally emerged from the extended networks of smaller settlements, from which they condensed. Cities expanded and proliferated, developing in size and complexity, variations arising as adaptations to the dynamic changes of climate and ecology within which they were situated. Until quite recently cities extended their metabolic network across their immediate local territory, and linked systems of cities across whole regions. As the systems of civilization developed in complexity, cities became less dependent on their immediate surroundings, and today few cities draw their energy and materials from their local territory. Cities now extend their metabolic systems over very great distances, so that the territory of a city and its geographical "place" are often completely decoupled. Humans have always modified ecological systems and the topography of the earth, and have done so at a variety of spatial and temporal scales.

The growth and vitality of many cities is no longer dependent on the spatial relationship with their local territory but on the regional and global flows of resources. Cities and extended urban conglomerations across the world will continue to expand in the coming decades as populations rise. Europe already has 80 per cent of its population living within cities or extended urbanized areas. Conurbations are common right across Europe, consisting of several overlapping city territories that extend urban fabric across a range of scales, often coterminous with agricultural, industrial and energy generation territories. The most densely populated regions of Asia, Europe and North America now consume biological materials at more than twice the rate at which the ecological systems of their own regions can regenerate. They are now dependent on resources from distant regions to meet the deficit in the flow of energy and materials required to support their preferred patterns of consumption. In turn, the increased demands on other regions limit their capacity to expand their own populations. More than half of all the fuel energy consumed in the USA and Europe today is imported from other regions, and the dependence on energy imports in Asia is accelerating.

There are many indicators that suggest that the global system of civilization is poised at the critical threshold of stability and is consequently very sensitive to social, climatic and ecological changes. It is clear that the current metabolic system of the world, with its accelerating informational complexity, extreme velocity and volumes of fuel and food energy flowing across continents and oceans, and high but inequitable energy and material consumption, exhibits similar characteristics. Despite the high-density flow of information and the high proportion of the population engaged in regulating and administering the energy and material flows, the global system is now highly vulnerable to disruption and perturbation.

INFORMATION FLOW

Information transmission has always been an essential characteristic of human culture, although the means of transmission were slower in the past than they are today, with less immediate effects. The transmission of detailed information concerning material practices and architectural forms has been accelerated exponentially several times, with the sequential emergence of large trading networks, mathematical notation, writing and drawings systems, printing, shipping and worldwide navigation. As printed images and text opened up an exchange of knowledge, strong geographical separations between cultures were weakened:

people, materials and artefacts were no longer bound to their place of origin. Until very recently the working methods of architects were determined by the basic pattern of the late-nineteenth-century drawing systems of engineering industries. These were the product of what was then a new practice of industrial drawing, which had acquired a central role in the production of ships, railway carriages and engines and, later, motorcars and aeroplanes. The hierarchy of designers and draughtsmen set an increased distance between the origination of the design and the execution of its construction. Embedded in the discipline were the concepts of industry, particularly standardization and accurate repetition, functional instruments of control with an emphasis on the interchangeability of parts, standardization of forms, and "management" of design, materials and fabrication.

The conceptual apparatus of architecture has always given a central role to the relations of mankind and nature. The human body has been a source of harmonious proportions and the shapes of many living organisms have been adapted for architectural use. Architecture's current fascination with nature is a reflection of the availability of new modes of imaging the interior structures of plants and animals, of electron microscopy of the intricate and very small, together with the mathematics of biological processes. The new emerging architecture, that relates pattern and process, form and behaviour, with spatial cultural parameters, offers new behaviours and adaptations to the changing ecologies and climate of the natural world.

The transference of material knowledge by spoken, graphical and numerical languages constitutes a system of information transmission that is distinct from the biological system of transmission, the genome. Culture acts to transmit complex, social and ecologically contextualized rules for material practices laterally between local populations and vertically down through time. It is clear that material culture is inherited by descendents, there is descent with modification, and that the material forms of buildings and even cities can be grouped into morphological taxonomies. There are, however, significant differences between the mode of operation of material cultural evolution and of biological evolution. Such differences include the mode of inheritance, which in culture may be horizontal or oblique, as cultural practices concerned with material construction diffuse between distinct social groups. Perhaps the most significant difference between biological and cultural evolution lies in the "selection" of forms that survive to pass on their genes or information to their descendents.

The substantial recent changes to culture, climate and energy economies construct a new regime of "natural selection" that has destabilized the prior relationship of the material, cultural and physical ecology within which architecture is produced and inhabited. Material practices are at the beginning of a substantial reconfiguration, and our future practices are to be located in the intersecting fields of knowledge and data flows. The interaction of computational systems, the transmission of information by the internet, and the emergence of a worldwide network of rapid transit systems have each acted in turn as a positive feedback on cultural transmission and diffusion, and collectively they have produced a marked contemporary tendency to the convergence of architectural forms and material practices right across the world. This is as true of motorcars and mobile phones, of clothes and computers as it is of skyscrapers and shopping malls.

Architecture has begun a systemic change, driven by the changes in culture, science, industry and commerce that are rapidly eroding the former boundaries between the natural and the artificial. The complex interaction between the form, material and structure of natural material systems has informed "biomimetic" industrial processes, generating "artificial" materials that can be manufactured with specific performance characteristics. Such new materials have radically transformed everyday consumer products, motor vehicle and aerospace design. Manufactured cellular materials, especially metals and ceramics, offer an entirely new set of performance and material values, and have the potential to reinform and revitalize the material strategies of architectural engineering and construction. Biomimetic strategies that integrate form, material and structure into a single process are being adopted from the "nanoscale" of material science for the design and construction of very large buildings, and new cities.

ARCHITECTURAL CULTURE
AND ECOLOGY

The material practices of contemporary architecture cannot be separate from this paradigm shift, as the context in which architecture is conceived and made has changed. In the natural world change is normal, but its intricate choreography is now further accelerated and perturbed by human activities. Global climate change is upon us, and its effects will be local and regional – more energy trapped in weather systems produces emergent behaviour and consequences that are not entirely predictable. So too, the emergent behaviour of local economies and cultures, now connected and interlinked globally, are substantially reconfigured.

The cultural parameters of the emerging regime of selection that is driving the evolution of a new architecture are clear. There is a growing cultural fascination with the new understanding of nature and of natural form both living and non-living. The architectural and material manifestations of fluidity and dynamics, of networks and new topologies, are at the centre of architectural discourses and innovations. The materiality of the boundaries between interior and exterior space, between public and private territories, is no longer so relentlessly solid and opaque. The increasing transparency of such boundaries is accompanied by less rigid territorial demarcations. Programmes are not so strictly confined within the building envelope, and connections and co-existence are enhanced. The experience of being in spaces that flow one into one another, with "soft" transitions between private and public domains, and between interior and exterior space, is increasingly recognized as an essential characteristic of contemporary life. The largest public spaces, for example in the concourses of transit spaces such as airport terminals, ports and railway interchanges, have boundaries that are achieved less by rigid walls than by extended thresholds of graduated topographical and phenomenological character, enhancing spatial connectivity and coded communication. This form of spatial organization is not confined to transit systems, but is increasingly found in many architectural forms that range from the scale of the apartment or house, through the largest high-rise buildings to new urban configurations and spaces.

New working methods of architectural design and production are rapidly spreading through architectural and engineering practices, as they have already revised the world of manufacturing and construction. They include computational form-generating processes based on "genetic engines" that are derived from the mathematical equivalent of the Darwinian model of evolution, and from the biological science of evolutionary development that combines processes of embryological growth and the evolutionary development of the species. New architectural and infrastructural forms will emerge, with structural and material behaviours derived from the logics of biological systems. They will proliferate across the world as constructed material artefacts that are more closely and symbiotically related to the ecological systems and processes of the natural world.

Michael Weinstock is an architect, currently Director of Research and Development, and Director of the Emergent Technologies and Design programme in the Graduate School of the Architectural Association School of Architecture in London. Born in Germany, he lived as a child in the Far East and then West Africa, and attended an English public school but ran away to sea at age 17 after reading Conrad. Weinstock spent years at sea in traditional wooden sailing ships, with shipyard and shipbuilding experience. He studied Architecture at the Architectural Association from 1982 to 1988 and has taught at the AA School of Architecture since 1989 in a range of positions from workshop tutor, Intermediate and then Diploma Unit Master, Master of Technical Studies and through to Academic Head.

eco-social frameworks

[b1:1.1]
Messina 2012: A Regional
Proto-Garden
p. 30

[b1:1.2]
Regimes of Slowness
Caracas: Operational
Landscapes
p. 48

eco-social landscapes

[b1:2.3]
The Systemic Favela: Design
Algorithms for a Social Free-
Zone in the Arabic Peninsula
p. 68

[b1:2.4]
The World Dubai Marine
Life Incubators
p. 94

Virtual plots

1. One of the main conceptual as well as material components of the self-organizing city: virtual plots are the organizational units of the city, the measuring block of its spatial and temporal articulation. **2.** The word "virtual" does not refer to a negation of the real urban plots or to a simulated version of their subdivision as in a form of virtual reality. Rather it describes an alternative model to represent the city, one that refers to the past and the present configuration of the city

> as pregnant not only with possibilities which become real, but with virtualities which become actual. Unlike the former, which defines a process in which one urban structure out of a set of predefined plans acquires reality, the latter defines a process in which an open urban problem is solved in a variety of different ways, with actual forms emerging in the process of reaching a solution.
>
> Gilles Deleuze, *Bergsonism*, New York: Zone Books, 1988, p. 97

The conceptual difference leads to a vision of the future that could be defined as "advanced determinism", based on the non-linear and circular causality of the feedback loop, where the effects of an action react back onto its causes. **3.** Each virtual plot of the city becomes therefore a unit of urban problem solving, within which multiple actors and agents are able to self-organize, giving rise to novel local structures and prototypes. The form of these structures can vary greatly and locally, sometimes re-describing the existing plots while on other occasions operating within or across their boundaries.

Operational fields

1. The representation of diagrammatic pre-urban structures developed in order to allow cross fertilization and loading of different types of informational field and urban stimuli within a coherent urban plan. **2.** Such coherent spatialization of multiple stimuli is a precondition for the development of protocols for the occupation of new territories or the redevelopment of existing urban landscapes; within this operational framework ecologic feedback, participation and social self-organization become possible. In fact we shall argue that urban self-organization requires the definition of an operational medium that generates responses out of urban stimuli; it scans the landscape defining resolutions, scales, regimes of sensitivity, rhythms, and renders fields of material accumulation and informational exchange. **3.** Operational fields require a diagrammatic kind of representation and given their machinic nature depend on the development of dedicated design mechanisms; associative and algorithmic modelling techniques are at the core of this diagrammatic urban machine.

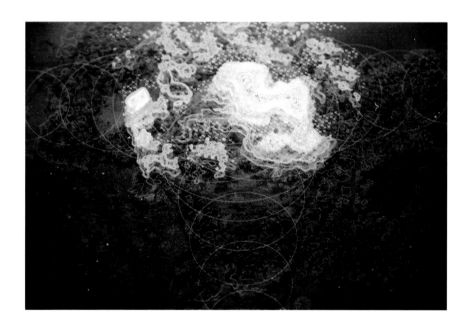

The World Dubai
Marine Life Incubators:
model of artificial island
formations

About ...

The eco-social frameworks of this part of the book are two research projects unravelling the tight relationship existing between the ecology of the local landscape and the related social practices in Messina, in the Sicilian Stretto, and in Caracas, the Venezuelan capital city.

The projects have a strong analytical and methodological character and have been instrumental in setting the ground for the synthesis of new eco-social landscapes.

Both contexts are rich in social complexity and both present a particular case of ecologic stress or rupture between local residents and their own land; the consequences are suffered by the ecologic systems and the social groups alike, with pollution, landslides and desertification matched by poverty, violence and grief.

Following a systemic method of investigation of the site, the eco-social frameworks start by mapping the local topographic regions and related operational fields. An operational medium is produced, able to generate responses out of urban stimuli. Such a design device affords the architect a more comfortable and productive platform to breed his or her design arguments; through correlation of variables it is then possible to develop from a critical understanding of landscape processes to an engagement with the multiple related social conflicts. The resolution of ecologic tensions becomes therefore a strategic technique to resolve parallel social conflicts, thus setting the ground for processes of social reconnection to develop and self-regulate.

In Messina the framework extends to the entire region of the Stretto, to what has been named a Regional Proto-Garden. In Caracas the framework has more intimate connotations, involving a form of domestic operational landscape; a manual of landscape consolidation and phyto-depuration is passed on to the local community to empower the cultivation of this new domestic resource through a slow process of material and psychological remediation.

The intense experiences provided by these projects in such charged environments have proved important tests for the development of a method of urban ecologic design that could span scales and regimes and could be deployed in "*tabula rasa*" scenarios, where urban life is absent and architecture is asked to incubate urban life intensity. Examples of such scenarios exist on the outskirts of Dubai and Al Ain, UAE.

Here **eco-social landscape** projects operate as urban life incubators; the landscape itself provides the substratum for the incubation of living mechanisms able to generate a new abundance of sustainable resources and support interaction among new social groups.

The challenges posed by these two project scenarios are widespread and constitute a clear point of interest for the contemporary architect operating on a global scale. In Dubai the artificial World Lagoon was left unfinished by the financial crash, leaving desolation, marine life devastation and a damaged local fishing industry; with any plan of conventional development non-viable, some alternative strategy is necessary to avoid the deterioration of the environmental conditions of a site that has no form of balanced ecology.

In Al Ain, a magnificent and wild desert wadi, or valley, at the outskirts of the city has been subjected to development pressure. In contrast to Dubai, the design brief here calls for the development of a new city from zero, devoted to research on renewable technologies and open to a population of Westerners as well as local academics.

Both projects have a contradictory nature, that seems to be one of the inevitable consequences of the influence of the current global socio-economic system onto urban development. The resolution of such contradictions is necessary to promote a sustainable future for our society; however this requires architects to stop being complacent about the system and start equipping themselves with the intellectual and methodical resources necessary to promote valid design alternatives.

In Dubai such an alternative appears in the form of a coral garden, an artificial reef where multiple processes of mineral accretion, sand sedimentation and water depuration have been imagined. Characterized by very low initial investment and a slow self-propelling growth, this design solution will transform the lagoon into a living reef able to attract researchers and visitors, and with them investing institutions with interests in global ecology. Such programmatic intensification will be supported by the material substratum that, on reaching maturity, will provide a stable ground for construction, avoiding the need for expensive consolidation works.

The protocol of development derived from our experience in Caracas is adopted more tactically here, an algorithmic form of planning that is able to choreograph the territory, without prescribing any rigid final arrangement; such an open and co-evolving framework is necessary to cope with the accidents of the future and embrace their vital powers.

In Al Ain this protocol is more literally deployed as a normative system for the new city, a cyber-favela where the informal logic of shanty town developments is coupled with the possibility offered by ubiquitous environmental sensing and energy-producing technologies. What emerges is a form of rhizomatic village, where tight social groups opportunistically colonize the landscape while at the same time nurturing it, in a delicate dynamic equilibrium; as trading emerges among the groups so does urban life and social diversity.

Community meeting and presentation of the land remediation protocol, Barrio La Vega, Caracas

b1: **Environments**

[b1:]

Messina 2012:
A Regional
Proto-Garden

CATEGORY: b1 Environments
PROJECT TYPE: b1:1 Eco-social
               frameworks
PROJECT #:   1
LOCATION: Messina, Italy
YEAR: 2007

pp. 30–31
Fishing harbour and beach
on the Stretto

this page
Local fisherman's stall
on the shores of the
Ganzirri Lake

Introduction   The complexity of the socio-ecologic setting of the Stretto di Messina stands in sharp contrast to the linearity of the planned bridge linking Sicily to Italy's mainland. Such a contrast is evident among the local inhabitants, many of whom have been protesting against political and mafioso business interests and have opposed the bridge project since its inception. The ambition of the Regional Proto-Garden proposal is to engage with the problem of increasing regional connectivity while highlighting and debating the conflict the bridge project has generated.

Ever since Homer's *Odyssey* first described Scylla and Charybdis, the creatures that sank any ship that tried to pass through, the furious currents of the Stretto have had a mythical status. Its geomorphological singularity has created a magnetic effect on the surroundings, attracting throughout history multiple routes, from commercial trading to bird migration to water current. The Stretto can be seen as a zone of perpetual passage and transition.

This has given the Stretto the status of "liminal body"; looking at it as a body allows one to discard the common acceptance of it as a divider between Sicily and Italy's mainland and to consider instead the multiplicity of living processes and socio-ecologic organs that contribute to its life and define its identity. From such a perspective the intention of connecting the two sides of the coast facing the Stretto has to be understood as the process of intensification of the multiple flows of living matter, information and energy that feed the Stretto's body.

Such flows create a network of paths and trajectories, a diffused meshwork of relationships that stitch the territory into a large urban region. The landscape, including the submarine one, represents an element of continuity rather than separation, as it materially supports and defines this meshwork as a whole, a unique body within the Mediterranean that has been able to evolve increasing prosperity and richness.

The Regional Proto-Garden project starts therefore from the intention to nourish this landscape, to turn it in fact into a new kind of large-scale regional garden. Such an intention implies the restoration of the network of relationships that connects the land and the social structure it supports and from which it gains vitality; the Regional Proto-Garden aims at creating a new identity for the landscape within the local population by building up new mechanisms of interaction and cultivation.

As such the Regional Proto-Garden is the anti-bridge project; it turns the bridge's imposing concrete structure into a diffused, resilient, embedded and self-supporting web of structuring landscape components, such as birds' nesting beds, sand sedimentation piers or bio-digesting parks; it replaces the bridge's transportation infrastructure with the strengthening of weak social relationships and their ability to develop local empowerment and participation; finally it opposes the bridge's financial mechanism of large public investments, notoriously a source of corruption

Satellite view of the
Stretto di Messina

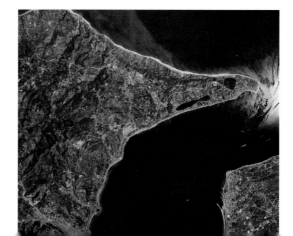

and waste, with the proliferation of micro-credited private enterprises aimed at the re-evaluation of the local potential of land and ecology-related businesses.

This design ambition was developed by means of an international workshop, conducted with landscape and urbanism specialists Ivan Valdez and Jorge Godoy. The proposed solutions took the form of four proto-gardens, pilot projects for the city region of Messina (in Sicily) and Reggio Calabria (on the mainland). The result was the generation of a large urban co-action plan, the so-called "Regional Proto-Garden" for the Stretto City Region.

The MIGROTYPE Proto-Garden occupies a particular lagoon located on the tip of the Sicilian side of the Stretto and internationally known as a stepping stone along the migratory routes of many species moving from Africa to northern Europe. This gives the lagoon the status of a natural conservation area; however this title has scared off private investors and has contributed to the lagoon's current state of neglect. The project proposes the local community-driven management of the migratory flux of birds together with mussel cultivation to promote the emergence of a new concept of natural reserve ecology. This includes a management network that will connect the local communities along the migratory routes, turning ecologic conservation into an opportunity for investment, networking and economic return.

The BATHYMETRIC TISSUE Proto-Garden deals with the deep waters of the Stretto channel; rich in natural features and archaeological pockets, the deep waters have recently suffered from water pollution, a deterioration of the local fishing economy/ecology and erosion problems due to intense traffic in the channel. The bathymetric tissue is a connective fabric of flexible membranes anchored to the seabed and able to adjust and fluctuate with the current; these membranes can turn the dynamic water body of the Stretto into a ground for touristic and scientific research activity. The project also coordinates a set of new technologies operating as platforms for direct interaction, energy generation, sensing, fauna and flora feeding and erosion management.

The ECO-TOURISTIC LOOM Proto-Garden provides a planning framework for the development of eco-touristic settlements. It operates across two realms: the management of the relationship between productive-agricultural and consuming-leisure programmes and their spatial articulation along the dynamic coastal edge of Casa Bianca. The mechanism of the loom is deployed as an urban machine for the interweaving of productive and consuming functions – the productive component seeks to enhance existing crops and fertile plots while the touristic one inhabits the beautiful sandy dunes; the eco-settlement derives inspiration from tent cities and campsites for their ability to self-organize and adapt to the shifting dune landscapes.

A BIO-DIGESTING BELT has been proposed along the ravines region, connecting the inner valleys of Messina to the Stretto. Streams flow along the valleys, bringing water from mountain catchment areas to the sea, and in many cases have been channelled when they reach the urban settlements of Messina. These channels are often clogged with rubbish, causing them to explode. The bio-digesting belt prototype brings together the logic of the green belt, a zone of controlled access and restricted development, with the integration of waste differentiation and processing technologies. Waste production, reuse, recycling and conversion is coordinated through a network of specialized processing stations. The typologies of linear park, piazza and recycling station are re-described into a synthetic matrix for the "digestion" of pollution and the social re-appropriation of beautiful valleys and their urban streams.

Percentage of vegetation
cover of virtual plots in the
area around the Ganzirri
Lake

● 100%
● 80%
● 60%
● 40%
● 20%
  0%

how to 1 : Frame topographic regions

{

      // The topographic regions have been identified to allow the
      // scanning of the territory of the city-region and the
      // identification of areas of common geologic origin and ecologic
      // behaviour. Such areas are likely to require common operational
      // frameworks.

      1.1 {Map the entire region surrounding the Stretto, including the rivers'
            watersheds discharging in the Stretto seawaters} ❶

      1.2 {Identify and list regions of different topographic character, for
            example: ravines and mountain cords, waterfronts, marine basins
            and the lagoon areas}

      1.3 {Frame each region with dedicated managerial sectors; name and
            label each sector individually} ❷

      1.4 {Consider ecologic systems and habitats within each sector, and
            define ecological stresses for each system}

}

❶

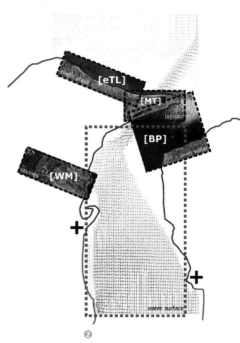

❷

how to 2 : Define operational fields

{

    // In each region specific operational fields have been developed,
    // and the local ecological stress has been defined as the main
    // triggering condition for intervention.

    2.1 {Ecological stress manifests itself as an imbalance able to drift the
        dynamic processes of a region out of equilibrium; from the point of
        view of the city-region these conditions are readable as emerging
        patterns of social tension or conflict, loss of economic potential,
        environmental devastation or pollution. Define each stress as an
        operational field within each managerial sector}
        Refine → 1.3 Sectors' boundaries
    2.2 {Connect each operational field with potential pilot projects,
        prototypical ecologic interventions able to influence local dynamic
        equilibria and trigger urban phase transitions}
    2.3 {Trace multiple connections and influences among operational
        fields and pilot projects; successful projects are likely to be the
        ones that have multiple levels of influence across many sectors}
    2.4 {Trace interconnections between pilot projects and their
        subsystems or subcomponents. Systemic prototypes are unlikely to
        function in isolation} ❸

}

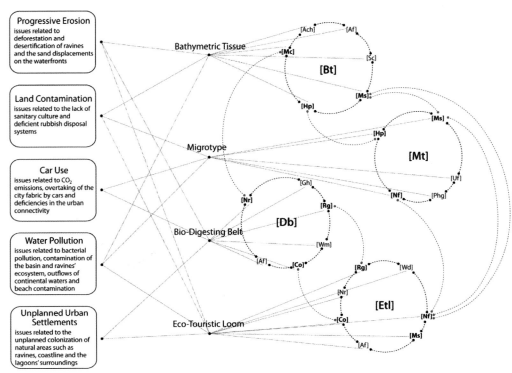

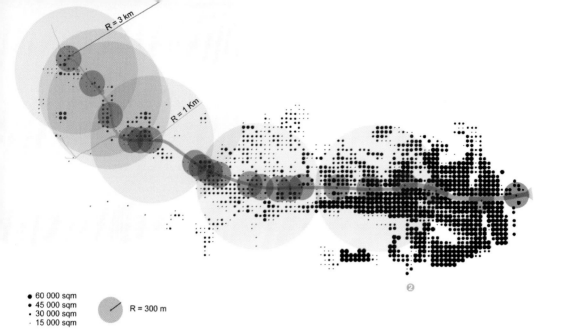

- 60 000 sqm
- 45 000 sqm
- 30 000 sqm
- 15 000 sqm

R = 300 m

how to 3 : Diagram operational fields
{

// The application of diagrammatic machines [developed by means of parametric
// and algorithmic design tools] allows the systematic scanning of the urban
// landscape and the definition of design resolutions, regimes of sensitivity, rhythms
// and the simulation of fields of material accumulation and informational exchange.

3.1 {Set a scanning resolution and sensitivity for each specific ecological stress
     within a sector or topographic region}
3.2 {Define appropriate descriptor parameters to map each stress and identify data
     maps containing the necessary level of information}
     Affects → 2.1 Definition of operational fields
3.3 {Develop an algorithmic process to scan the region, read input data and
     generate output drawings representing the operational field for the specific
     descriptor within that region} ❶
3.4 {Rescale, normalize and/or adjust output information to become visually
     manifest and use line colour, line type, line width, etc., to hold information and
     render it visible} ❷
     Regulates → 3.1 Resolution and sensitivity
3.5 {Be accurate and consistent across the entire region}
     Affects → 1.3 Regional frames

}

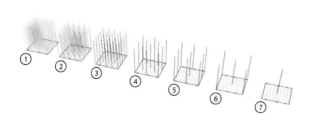

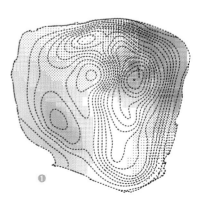

how to 4 : Urban prototyping and proto-gardening

{

    // Our analysis led us to believe that a social disconnection between
    // urban development and the understanding of the local landscape was
    // taking place with evident negative repercussions on both realms. As
    // a consequence the design has developed a catalogue of proto-gardens,
    // pilot projects stimulating reconnection and intensifying co-action
    // between socio-economic groups and their immediate surrounding landscape.

    4.1 {Define social groups operating locally}
    4.2 {Define potential involvement of each group or individual within the group
         in the setting-up, development and management of the proposed pilot
         projects} ③
         Affects → 2.2 Definition of pilot projects
         Affects → 6.2 Action plan of pilot projects
    4.3 {Define mechanisms of revenue and co-action among groups}
         Affects → 2.4 Interconnection and co-action among pilot projects

}

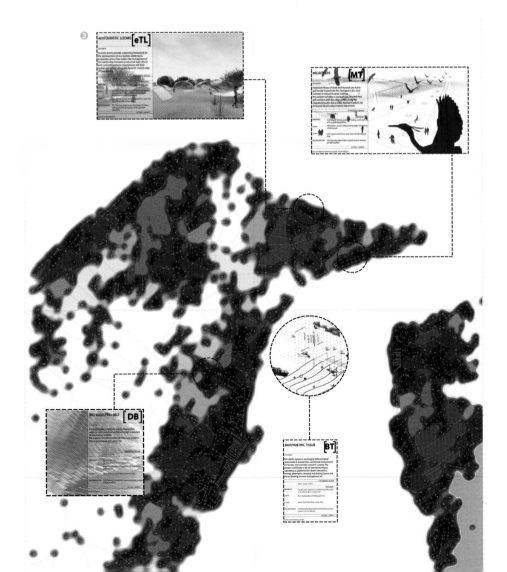

}

// Each pilot project is articulated spatially and materially through the
// development of specific material systems and architectural or urban prototypes.

5.1 {Define available technologies for the actualization of the pilot project}
5.2 {Develop prototypical material organizations and test integration of
technological performance} ❶
<example> The bathymetric tissue operates as a connective fabric of flexible
membranes anchored to the seabed and able to adjust and fluctuate with the
current; the membranes are differentiated in fields of various densities, length
and rigidity and can function as mechanisms of sedimentation, safety nets for
divers and fishermen, hideouts for marine life and filters for large polluting
objects such as plastic bags </example>
5.3 {Test pilot project on site with embedded sensing and data logging devices} ❷
Affects → 5.1 Choice of technology
Regulates → 5.2 Material organization rules
5.4 {Map and relay in real time the behaviour of the pilot projects on site}
Affects → 2.2 Definition of pilot projects

}

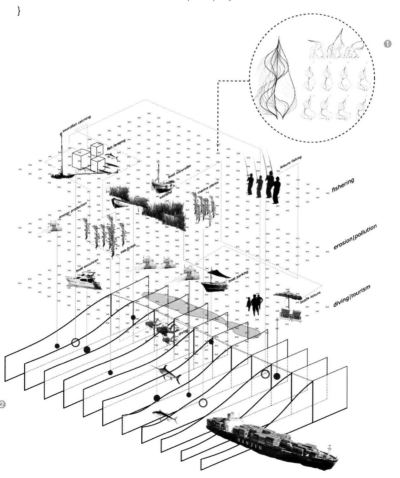

how to 6 : Action plans and subcomponents
{
      // Each pilot project grows in structure and complexity with time and
      // requires multiple specialized subcomponents to function; action plans define
      // functioning protocols and relational rules for actors and subcomponents.

    6.1 {Define potential subcomponents of the pilot project}
    6.2 {Define the protocols for the functioning of each subcomponent and for
        the rules of interaction among subcomponents} ❸ <overleaf>
        Affects → 5.1 Definition of technologies
        <example> Four subcomponents articulate the migrotype: the phyto-
        gardens, the nesting fields, the lake blast and the migro-network.❹ An
        urban furniture system of piers, poles and floating platforms constitute
        the main built infrastructure. An action plan regulates the multiple
        feedbacks between subcomponents, promoting systemic growth, material
        differentiation and intensification of relationships among the systems of
        fauna (air and lake), flora (lake and lakeside) and touristic/food trading
        (lakeside) </example>
    6.3 {Define roles and regulations for the actors and social agents within each
        pilot project}
        Affects → 4.1 Definition of actors and agents
        Go to → 5.3 Test pilot project on site
}

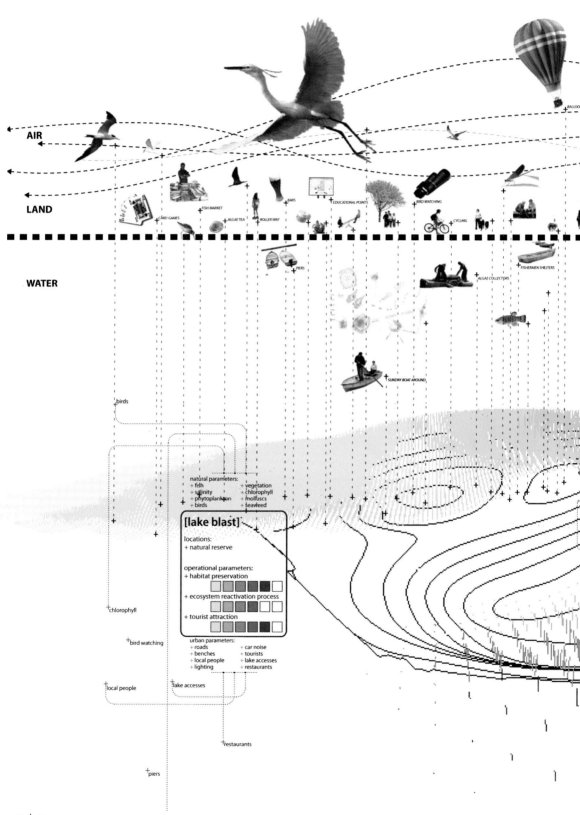

AIR

LAND

WATER

CARD GAMES   FISH MARKET   ALGAE TEA   ROLLER WAY   BARS   EDUCATIONAL POINTS   BIRD WATCHING   CYCLING

PIERS   SUNDAY BOAT AROUND   ALGAE COLLECTORS   FISHERMEN SHELTERS

birds

natural parameters:
+ fish   + vegetation
+ salinity   + chlorophyll
+ phytoplankton   + molluscs
+ birds   + seaweed

[lake blast]

locations:
+ natural reserve

operational parameters:
+ habitat preservation

+ ecosystem reactivation process

+ tourist attraction

chlorophyll

bird watching

urban parameters:
+ roads   + car noise
+ benches   + tourists
+ local people   + lake accesses
+ lighting   + restaurants

local people   lake accesses

restaurants

piers

46 | 47

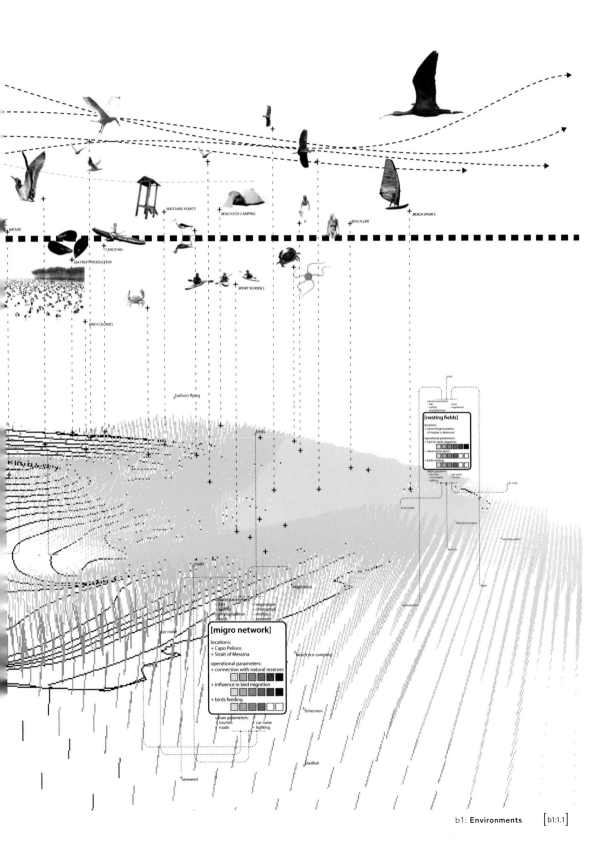

NATURE

SEA FRUIT PRODUCTION

CANOEING

WATCHING POINTS

BEACH ECO-CAMPING

BEACH LIFE

BEACH SPORTS

SPORT SCHOOLS

BIRD COLONIES

balloon flying

birds

[nesting fields]

natural parameters:
+ fish   + birds
+ salinity   + vegetation
+ phytoplankton

locations:
+ where fragmentation
  of habitat is detected

operational parameters:
+ halt for birds migration

+ observation point

+ birds nesting

urban parameters:
+ benches   + car noise
+ local people + hostess
+ lighting

local people

educational point

watching points

car noise

roads

vegetation

natural parameters:
+ fish   + vegetation
+ salinity   + chlorophyll
+ phytoplankton + molluscs
+ birds   + seaweed

car noise

[migro network]

locations:
+ Capo Pelloro
+ Strait of Messina

operational parameters:
+ connection with natural reserves

+ influence in bird migration

+ birds feeding

urban parameters:
+ tourists   + car noise
+ roads   + lighting

beach eco-camping

fishermen

phytoplankton

shellfish

seaweed

[b1:1.2]

Regimes of
Slowness Caracas:
Operational Landscapes

CATEGORY: **b1 Environments**
PROJECT TYPE: **b1:1 Eco-social
frameworks**
PROJECT #: **2**
LOCATION: **Caracas, Venezuela**
YEAR: **2003**

pp. 48–49
Meeting the community in
Barrio La Vega

this page
Formal and informal
settlements negotiating the
slopes of La Vega

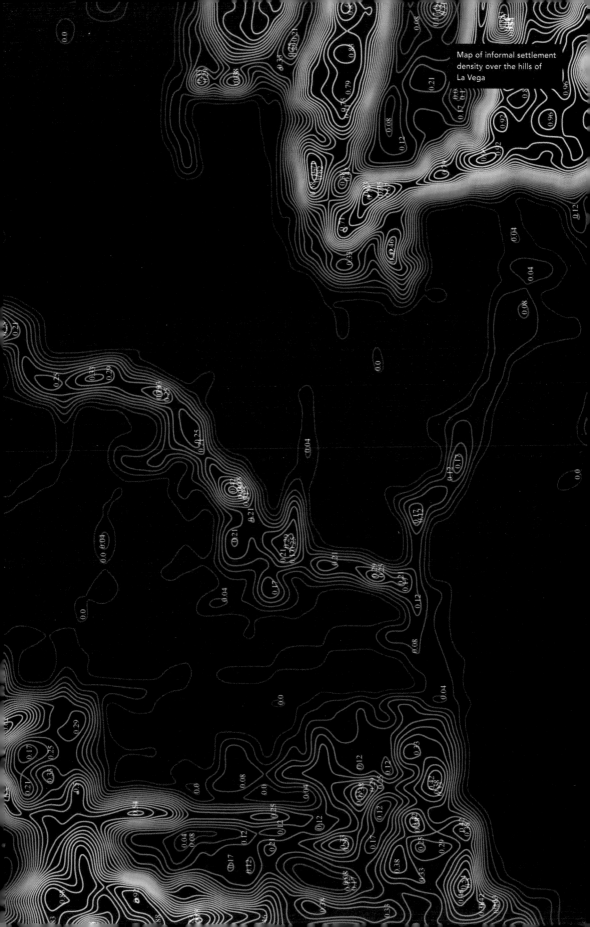

Map of informal settlement density over the hills of La Vega

Introduction   Venezuela has developed a pathological dependency on the oil economy. What could be logically seen as an immense richness has in fact turned out to be its ruin. During the oil boom thousands of people moved to Caracas hoping to join the new wave of prosperity; they left their houses and "ecosystems" to become "parasites" of the new global city. The country abandoned its productive activities and started to import even the most basic goods from abroad. The complex net of consequences of this process is visible everywhere; in the incredible socio-political contrasts as well as in the environmental threats (landslides, lack of water, land contamination, etc.).

Parasitism in architecture   "Parasites" is a recurrent term when describing the nature of Caracas' growth; we believe this is an effect of the visual impression that the "barrioscapes" (Caracas' huge shanty towns) convey when looked at from a certain distance: an unstoppable fluid made up of micro-units seems to digest hills and plains, and like a lava flow it seems to fill the gaps dividing modernist towers and unfinished urban complexes. Beyond the metaphorical meaning of the word, however, it can be useful to consider whether the properties of real parasites in any way reflect this informal practice of urbanization.

The first interesting notion connected to parasitism is the one of relationship: every description of parasitism involves the definition of a host and a guest. A second important consideration is the nature of this relationship; in this respect there are two categories of parasites. A first group is constituted by a relationship of exploitation: the guest uses the host's resources until its death and then it migrates to colonize another host. A second group instead creates a symbiotic relationship with or within its host and the coexistence lasts the entire lifetime. This second case is particularly interesting because it involves the co-presence of actions of transformation and of maintenance. The addition made by the new guest's presence is a first transformation; this is immediately followed by a second transformation with the aim of ensuring the host's maintenance. Such a relationship can only be imagined in cybernetic terms of action/reaction; that involves the consideration of the combined effect of space and time and the resulting dynamic. Moreover these actions cannot be conceived in isolation but as a feedback loop between guest and host; molecular biologists have in fact devised a series of techniques based on the analysis of the guest–host dynamic system, on the definition of parameters called descriptors, and on the use of computer modelling techniques to simulate possible dynamic scenarios for different values of the descriptors.

Satellite map of informal
settlements over the hills
of La Vega

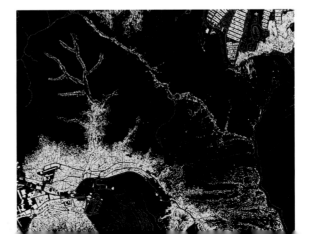

The buoneros case   Going back to the use of the word "parasites" to define Caracas' urban dynamic the phenomenon of the buoneros (street vendors) deserves attention. Street vendors proliferate along infrastructures such as highways. They constantly negotiate their position in relation to the cars, inducing controlled modifications of the environment in which they operate; they construct their own edge conditions which are the spatio-temporal result of their feedback relation with the site. They don't distribute evenly along the highway because in certain sectors of it the speed of the cars is too great to make any interaction possible. They occupy a limited amount of space and carry a limited amount of material to avoid obstructing the flow of cars upon which their activity is based. They interact with each car for a limited amount of time depending on the driver's reaction (insistent behaviour can irritate the driver, thus reducing the future possibility of accomplishing their selling task) and on the number of slow cars. They drift along their high probability trajectory for a distance dependent on the timing of a traffic light, for example, and on the number of cars involved. Other descriptors may be identified for specific locations, but what is important to notice is that the relationship involved in the street vendors' dynamic exhibits all the characteristics of symbiotic parasitism, which means that street vendors are actually able to insert a new urban programme into a public infrastructure. At the same time it is evident that a figurative analysis would be totally incapable of capturing the nature of the phenomenon and to represent its constituent links.

The barrio case   If we consider the reality of the barrios from which our discussion of parasitism started, we immediately recognize that some of the characteristics described above are missing. The new guests plug themselves into the existing infrastructure but they don't actually create any sort of feedback interaction with it. Their edge conditions might be internally negotiated (mainly to guarantee access to each property) but the relationship with the site of insertion is totally unidirectional and their external boundaries are defined by physical impossibility (gravity or space saturation). It is interesting to notice that while this analysis applies to the architecture of the barrio units a very different story should be told about the social dynamics related to the barrios' development which, by contrast, exhibit traits of symbiotic interaction. The little barrio units often discharge waste water in the ground, creating the conditions for self-destruction or damage of neighbours' areas (land collapse and erosion). Waste is thrown down the slope, producing soil and water contamination with the potential for epidemic outbreaks. Water and electricity are stolen from the grid, leading to an irregular supply and social friction with the rest of the population which has a duty to maintain an overloaded system.

Contradictions   An interesting question emerges: why the same guests have created such different kinds of relationship with their hosts in the case of the flow of cars and people in the street infrastructures and with the flow of water, waste and electricity within the potable water, waste disposal and electricity infrastructures. Why, moreover, are traditional techniques related to the transformation of locally available renewable resources (palm leaves transformed into screens or hats for instance) and able to incorporate difference and instability within their structure not entering the realm of architecture and landscaping?

Building techniques and the culture of formality   The questions could have multiple answers for different domains of investigation but here we concentrate on what we believe is one of the main reasons for this double behaviour: housing and water, waste and electricity infrastructures strictly belong to the domain of architecture and building engineering. If we extend our analysis to building units located in the centre of Caracas we will perceive a similar unilateral relationship of exploitation of the site, but on a much larger scale. The consumption of water of a tower block per surface unit of plot is one order of magnitude bigger than in a barrio unit; the same happens for its waste production. Little attention is paid to the use of natural renewable sources; solar energy, wind energy and cooling effects, and rainwater are very rarely exploited even though they are generously present in the Caracas microclimate. The architectural culture of the formal city, developed mainly during the oil boom, is one of unilateral exploitation of the surrounding environment as a condition to implement audacious master-plans and to erect iconic architectures and urban environments. The Universidad Central de Venezuela (UCV) campus is a wonderful exception, where agile concrete structures joke with gravity and play with light and wind to create sensible and ever-changing spaces. In too many other cases the emptiness of huge concrete cathedrals just reminds us of the excitement of a period in which everything seemed possible but which the subsequent economic crisis has erased, most probably forever. The people from the barrios initially left their previous lives behind to join that urban excitement. Working as builders they poured that concrete; they like to say that they built the formal city from which they are now systematically excluded. In fact they mastered the building technique to such an extent that they were able to build their own barrio units in the same way and without the need for architectural and engineering support. Their houses are irregular because no big excavations were made to found them and their arrangement is the product of a slow process of growth constrained by a series of local negotiations within neighbours; but the technique is the same: concrete frame and red terracotta blocks for the walls. Only the ranchos, the first stage of construction, are different but they are considered provisional, to be totally rebuilt as soon as possible.

Hypothesis   Our research hypothesis has been that this building technique and the cultural background within which it evolved in Caracas have constrained the potential for creative solutions to emerge from the dynamic of such an unplanned system; they have almost prevented the potential for the formation of the previously described symbiotic guest–host relationship. A natural ambition to be included in the formal city, to become real citizens, has pushed most of the barrio dwellers to reject their old rural habits of cultivation of the landscape and of symbiotic growth to replicate within their small plots what they see as the real urban model of living. The result has been the progressive failure of the informal city system, leading to an uncontrolled modification of the guest/host equilibrium (the host in this case being the landscape that feeds Caracas).

Contextualization   Considering the state of environmental emergency (in 2003, when this research was conducted, the dryness of the Camatagua Lake was keeping almost half of the city without water while a single storm was able to destroy 100 cars by transforming one of the highways of Caracas into a wild river) we all agreed on the need for alternative solutions. Moreover those solutions had to be effective at the large scale (to cope with the size of the problems), adaptable in time and space (to be long-lasting in such an unstable environment) and with low starting investments (to have any chance of implementation). In other words, the need was for solutions able to grow symbiotic relationships between the city and its artificial and natural structures, such that from the proliferation of starting seeds new large-scale organizations could emerge and the self repairing mechanisms of the biosphere could be enhanced to promote a sustainable equilibrium.

Since the so-called informal structures of the city were the only ones showing such properties and since the scientific-systemic approach was the only one able to describe their behaviour we will combine a further description of the barrios' social reality with an operational approach to architecture and engineering to seek new design possibilities.

Social dynamics in the informal city   Concentrating on the issues that are relevant for the current discussion leads us to investigate the link between social practices and the processes of production, within which we can include construction.

The barrios of Caracas are currently undergoing a process of stratification which has its practical implementation in the assignment of land titles to the families occupying the lots. Beside the socio-economic relevance of the transition it is interesting to notice that the process involves the formation of the so-called "comities de tierra", which are the formal expression of a movement of communitarian organizations. Within these organizations a number of issues are under discussion and education is one of the most deeply debated. At one end of the scale they are formulating new strategies for the first level schools: here the aim is to teach kids the culture of the barrio with all its practical rules which are the result of years of sedimentation of daily life experiences. At the other, the discussion touches access to higher education and together with it to a higher level of expertise and, as a consequence, to institutional roles. The impossibility for the barrio people to access universities (mainly due to the costs) means a further level of dependency on institutions and on the technical experts related to them. For instance, when a problem of soil stability threatens the safety of a barrio's slope, its solution fully depends on the action of an engineer of the relevant Alcaldia (Mayor's Office) who has to visit the site, understand the problem and formulate a solution able to solve the problem within ranges of safety (which are totally open to discussion) and ranges of economic feasibility. This process forces the barrio people into inactivity and dependency and puts the solutions of the problems in the hands of the totally inefficient (not to mention often corrupt) institutional system.

A member of the local community actively engaged in the dry sanitation project

Social empowerment as design tool   In this respect the word that seems to unify opposed parties is "empowerment". Everyone agrees on the positive effect of empowering people's ability to better shape their own reality and the reality of the society in which they live. In systemic terms it is about increasing the diversity of solutions and therefore the heterogeneity and ultimately the robustness of the system by reducing its dependency on a centralized source of decision making. But if we consider the instruments of empowerment in the architectural and engineering domains we have to face again the question of the nature of expertise. The figurative approach still dominant in architecture and the relative independence of building engineering make it impossible for processes of empowerment to take place. This project, therefore, promotes a non-figurative approach to architectural design based on the construction of a meta-plane of intervention whereby expertise from different fields and bottom-up individual action can be coordinated and co-evolved.

Testing bed: La Vega   As a testing bed for this approach we chose to look at the revitalization of La Vega, one of the biggest, oldest and possibly most socially active barrios in Caracas. While the lower part of the barrio has evolved into a consolidated high-density urban village, the higher part still consists of shacks precariously hanging from the unstable hillside; rainwater, sewage and litter flow down the mountain virtually uncontrolled, provoking slides and soil contamination that endanger the lives of not only the residents of the higher part of the barrio but also the ones living in the lower part.

So far the situation has been addressed formally: communities from the lower part of the barrio have asked for intervention by municipal experts. This intervention, based on the introduction of traditional retention walls and drainage systems in the areas of major land collapse, has failed to address both the complexity of the social system of the barrio and the dynamics of its landscape; finally it has stopped due to the lack of economic resources.

Operational fields   Our approach has applied the lesson learned from the informal street vendors; first we chose specific descriptors, which were the relevant parameters for the description of the ecologic problem. For land instability infiltrations are a main cause and so we could start to map the amount of black water discharge per surface unit of slope (mc/sec.sqm); that gave us an idea of the soil and water contamination problem and its distribution; if we look at surface instability erosion is the dynamic process we are trying to capture; ground steepness (per cent), vegetation density (per cent), urban crust porosity (per cent), rainwater flux on ground (mc/sec) can be the relevant descriptors. We used them to generate a spatio-temporal map of opportunities or as we call them ecologic operational fields. These opportunities are possible relationships that can be created to promote symbiotic coexistence.

A typical rancho on the
heights of La Vega hills

Moreover, as we have noticed, the problem of land instability is linked to cycles of an apparently different nature such as water, waste and ecology; engaging one problem will automatically involve triggering responses at multiple levels. In other words, our solution could incorporate other variables, negotiate their instability, grow in complexity and diversity and finally become more robust.

We first considered bio-engineering soil stabilization techniques by means of bamboo plantations and did define a family of variations of the same model; each member of the family hold a rule that relate the pattern of planting (number/sqm on square grid) with the steepness of the slope (per cent). The techniques differ for type of plant and modalities of construction but they all relate to the slope through their own rule. The rules are formulated on the base of performances; time-based simulations had to be run to establish rules and their applicability. Rules and performances can drive processes of actualization where raw material gets transformed into a structured system. Technical reports containing this kind of information can become instruments of empowerment: they are not rigidly dependent on metrical properties and therefore they are able to negotiate accidents and to liberate creativity.

As different types of bamboo plants have a different capacity to absorb nitrogen from the soil and therefore a different decontamination power, the stabilization system could incorporate this potential of phyto-depuration of the soil by diversifying its planting type and by negotiating its cleaning power with the stabilization one.

Water run-off is a main cause of surface soil erosion and lack of water is a current threat for Caracas: it is easy to imagine opportunities for a rainwater-capturing system which will tackle both problems: drainage channels will negotiate their inclination and distance with steepness (per cent) and surface water flow (mc/sec).

In our final proposal the soil stabilization and filtering system could incorporate water retention potential further enriching its operational possibilities and its capacity to sustain life.

Operational landscapes   The rancho type of house, typical of the highest neighbourhoods of La Vega, is usually constructed onto a terrace built with a primitive cut and fill process; this creates a section of steep slope of unstable soil behind and in front of each house. Our *soil stabilization–rainwater collection–filtering system* was then actualized as a new urban prototype defined by its set of rules of negotiation and by its operational possibilities in relation to the position of the houses and the related slope.

Described both through drawings and a simple rule-based operational protocol the prototype was then passed into the hands of the local community through a series of lectures and open practice sessions on a set of testing beds around the barrio.

This set of protocols are the empowering tools for the synthesis of a population of operational devices with the ability to promote a symbiotic relationship between inhabitants and landscape; the variability within this population will reflect and stimulate the cultural richness of the social environment within which it has evolved, transforming the barrios into inhabitable operational landscapes.

how to 1 : Analyse the informal landscape of La Vega

{

   1.1 {Choose relevant descriptors of the ecological stress fields}
       <example> For land instability infiltrations are a main cause; the amount
       of black water discharge per surface unit of slope (mc/sec.sqm) is a
       relevant parameter. For surface instability issues, erosion is the dynamic
       process to capture. Relevant descriptors include: ground steepness (per
       cent), vegetation density (per cent), urban crust porosity (per cent),
       rainwater flux on ground (mc/sec) </example>

   1.2 {Map the operational fields} ❶ ❷
       <example> Mapping black water discharge per surface unit of slope gives
       an idea of the soil and water contamination problem and its distribution in
       space and time </example>

   1.3 {Define possible new relational rules to promote symbiotic coexistence
       between the landscape and human development}

}

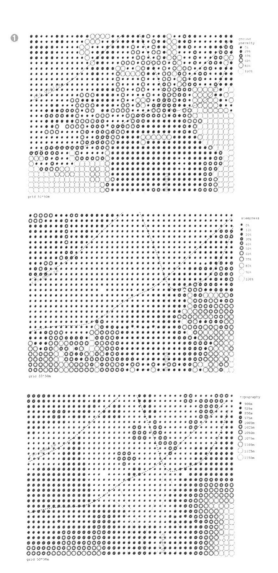

❷ >

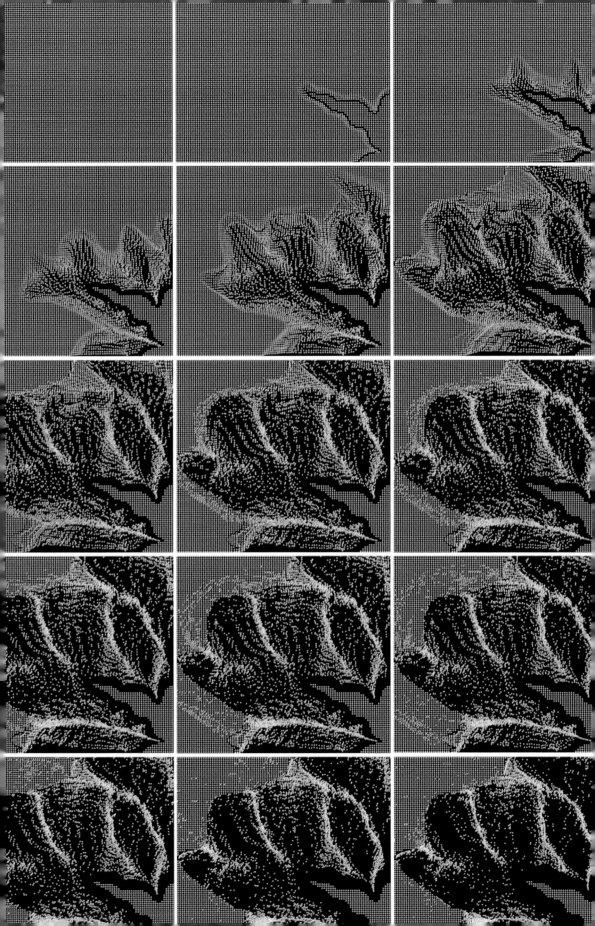

❶

how to 2 : Define an operational protocol of systemic design
{

// The problem of land instability ❶ is linked to cycles of different natures such as
// water, waste and ecology; however these cycles are all interconnected processes
// that have common causes and effects within the local socio- and biospheres.
// Engaging one cycle will automatically involve triggering responses at multiple
// levels. In other words, our design solution can grow by successive incorporation
// of variables; by negotiating their instability, it grows in complexity and diversity
// and becomes more robust.

2.1 {List operational fields}
2.2 {List relevant descriptors}
     Refer to → 1.1 Descriptors maps
2.3 {List bio-remediation technologies}
2.4 {Develop interconnection matrix among technologies and operational fields} ❷
2.5 {Choose technologies for prototyping based on maximum number of
     interconnections}
     Affects → 1.3 Rules of symbiotic coexistence

}

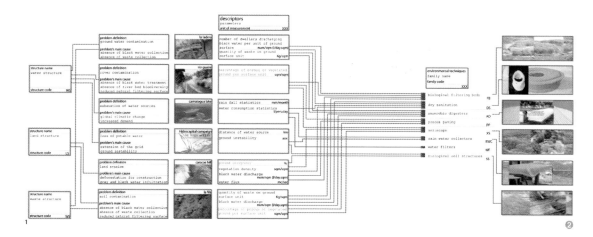

❷

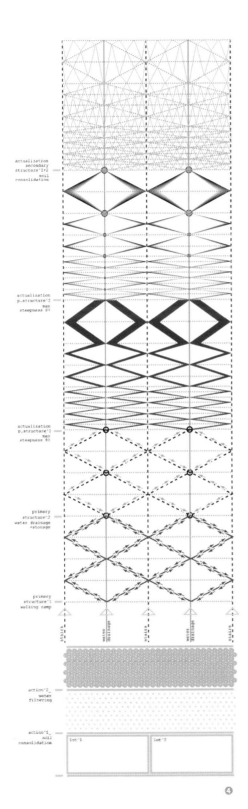

how to 3 : Design the material system

{

    3.1 {Consider bio-engineering soil stabilization
        techniques, for example by means of bamboo
        plantations} ❸

    3.2 {Define a family of variations of the same
        model; each member of the family holds a rule
        that relates the pattern of planting (number/
        sqm on square grid) with the steepness of the
        slope (per cent)}

    3.3 {Adjust the planting rule and the related
        techniques to the different types of plant and
        to the modalities of construction} ❹

    3.4 {Test system's performance and adjust the
        rule: time-based simulations have to be run to
        evolve rules and their applicability}
        Refine → 2.3 List of bio-remediation
        technologies

    3.5 {Compile a material system protocol: describe
        raw materials, each planting rule and related
        techniques to empower local community
        groups in the development and management
        of the material system}
        Affects → 4.3 Prototype diagram of
        subsystems' relationships

}

❹

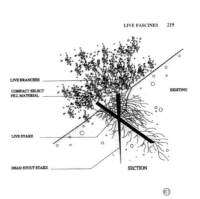

LIVE FASCINES   219

LIVE BRANCHES

COMPACT SELECT
FILL MATERIAL

EXISTING

LIVE STAKE

DEAD STOUT STAKE   SECTION

❸

how to 4 : Design the prototype's operating manual

{

// The prototype's operating manual can become an instrument of
// empowerment; as it is not rigidly dependent on metrical properties, it is a
// design instrument able to negotiate accidents and to liberate creativity.

4.1 {Negotiate the material system with multiple operational fields and
develop the prototyping manual}
<example> As different types of bamboo have a different capacity to
absorb nitrogen from the soil and therefore a different decontamination
power, the stabilization system could incorporate this potential of phyto-
depuration of the soil by diversifying its planting type and by negotiating
its cleaning power with the stabilization one </example> ❶

4.2 {Articulate the material system into a landscape prototype, including the
subsystems and their performative relationship}
<example> Water run-off is a main cause of surface soil erosion and lack
of water is a current threat for Caracas: it is easy to imagine opportunities
for a rainwater-capturing system which will tackle both problems:
drainage channels will negotiate their inclination and distance with
steepness (per cent) and surface water flow (mc/sec) </example>

4.3 {Develop the prototype diagram of subsystems, its naming and coding}
<example> The soil stabilization and filtering system could incorporate
water retention potential, further enriching its operational possibilities
and its capacity to sustain life </example> ❷
Affects → 5.4 Final operating protocol

}

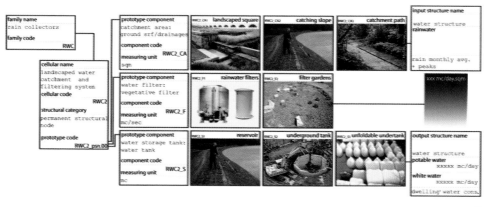

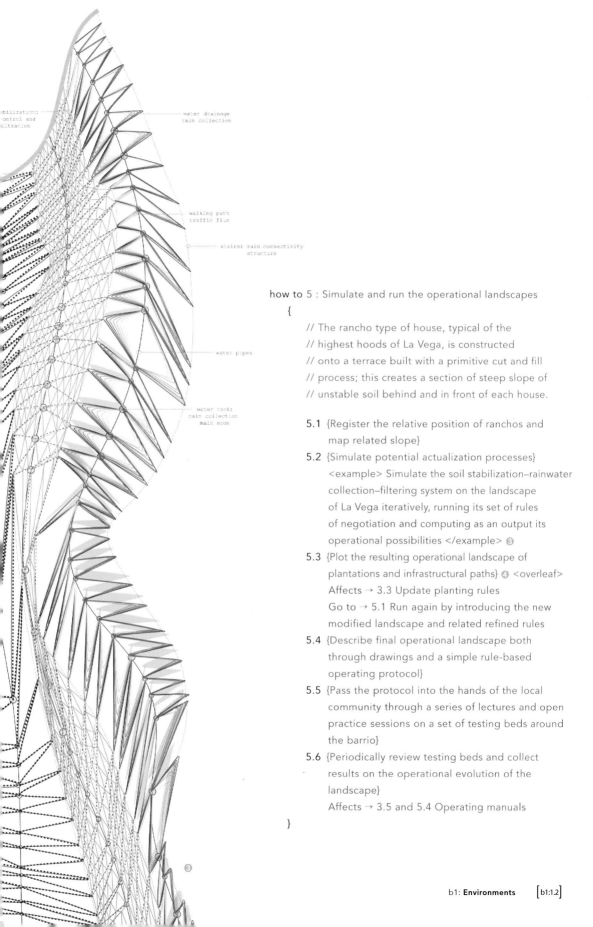

stabilization:
control and
filtration

water drainage
rain collection

walking path
traffic flux

stairs: main connectivity
structure

water pipes

water tank:
rain collection
main node

how to 5 : Simulate and run the operational landscapes
{

// The rancho type of house, typical of the
// highest hoods of La Vega, is constructed
// onto a terrace built with a primitive cut and fill
// process; this creates a section of steep slope of
// unstable soil behind and in front of each house.

5.1 {Register the relative position of ranchos and
map related slope}
5.2 {Simulate potential actualization processes}
<example> Simulate the soil stabilization–rainwater
collection–filtering system on the landscape
of La Vega iteratively, running its set of rules
of negotiation and computing as an output its
operational possibilities </example> ③
5.3 {Plot the resulting operational landscape of
plantations and infrastructural paths} ④ <overleaf>
Affects → 3.3 Update planting rules
Go to → 5.1 Run again by introducing the new
modified landscape and related refined rules
5.4 {Describe final operational landscape both
through drawings and a simple rule-based
operating protocol}
5.5 {Pass the protocol into the hands of the local
community through a series of lectures and open
practice sessions on a set of testing beds around
the barrio}
5.6 {Periodically review testing beds and collect
results on the operational evolution of the
landscape}
Affects → 3.5 and 5.4 Operating manuals

}

③

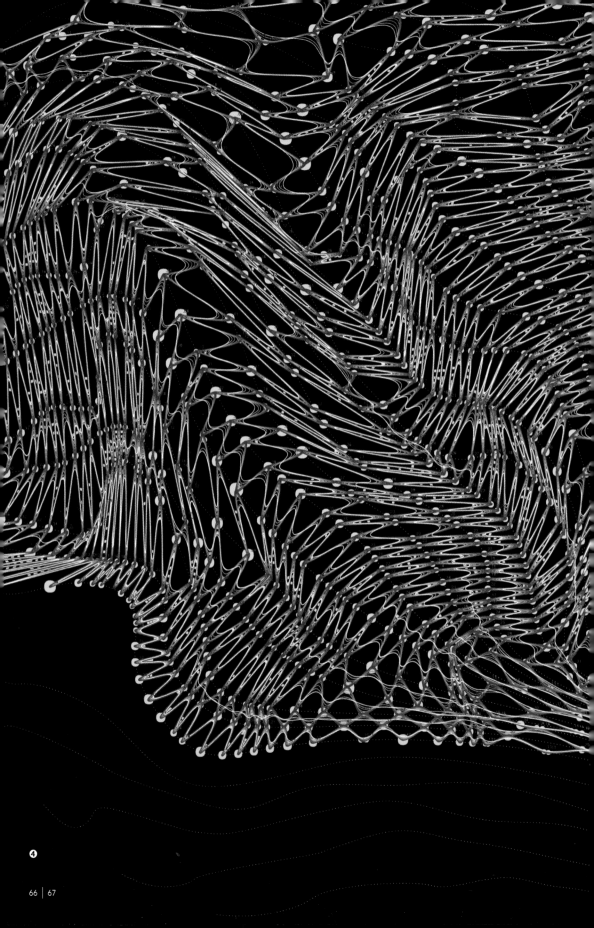

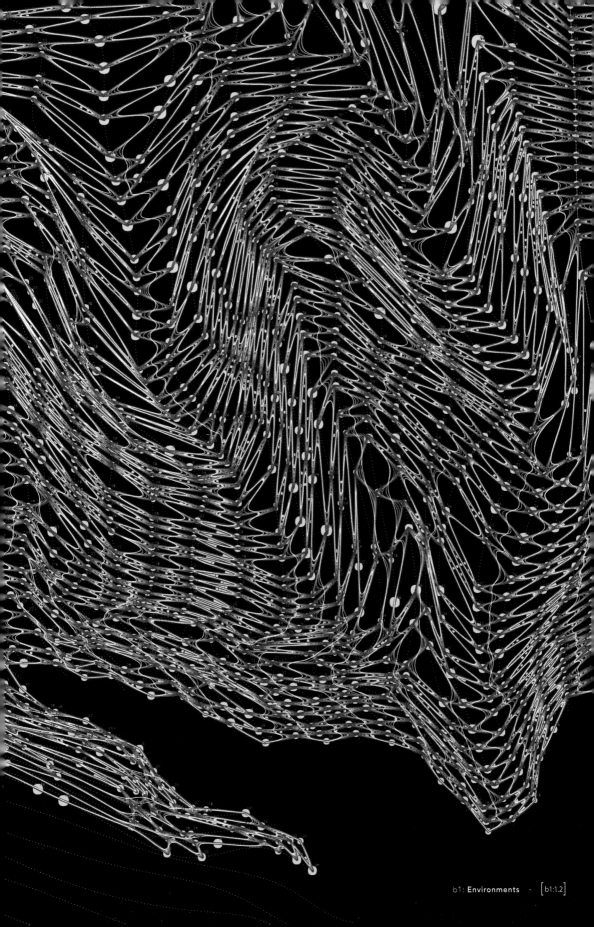

The Systemic Favela: Design Algorithms for a Social Free-Zone in the Arabic Peninsula

CATEGORY: b1 Environments
PROJECT TYPE: b1:2 Eco-social landscapes
PROJECT #: 3
LOCATION: Abu Dhabi, UAE
YEAR: 2010

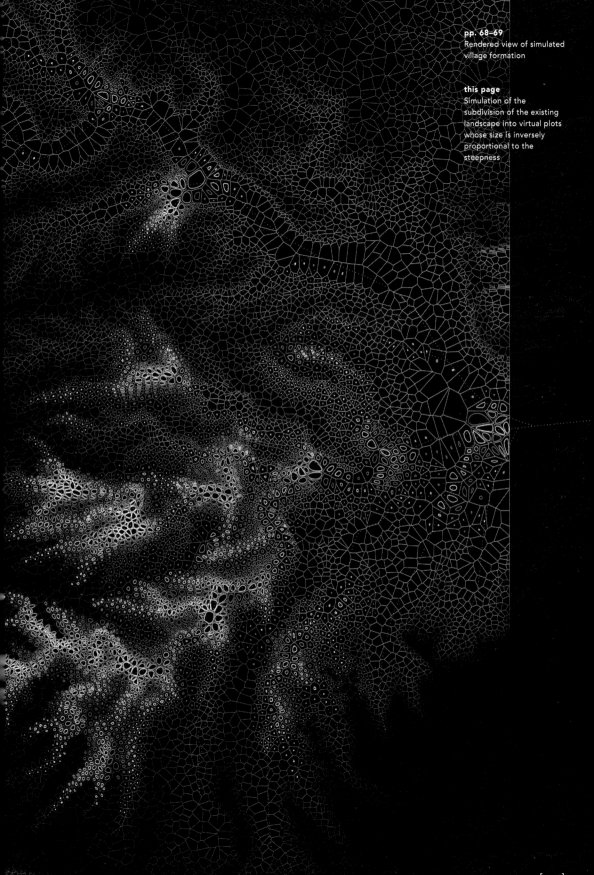

pp. 68–69
Rendered view of simulated
village formation

this page
Simulation of the
subdivision of the existing
landscape into virtual plots
whose size is inversely
proportional to the
steepness

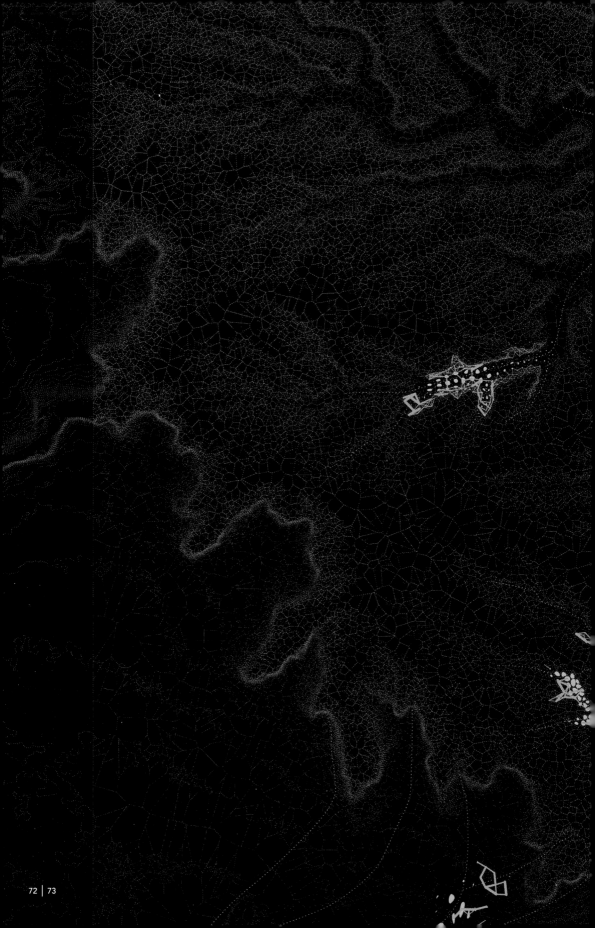

City-making simulation
showing the virtual plots'
occupational patterns and
the emergent network
system of connections

Introduction   The research conducted with the AA Inter10 unit at the Architectural Association, as well as the collaboration with the American and British University in UAE, was the opportunity to confront the master-plans for future urban development issued by the Emirate of Abu Dhabi with the traditional social and ecological practices of the region. The rupture is evident particularly if we consider the unique relationship with the landscape of the Bedouins who roamed the region up until 25 years ago and are now ruling the country from their new urban palaces. Such disconnection manifests itself in extravagant briefs that call for the development of a series of new eco-cities from zero, to be erected on various locations in the Emirati desert and designed to host populations of about 20,000 to 30,000 people.

The brief   The briefs trace the lines of what is called a clean-tech village, a model not far from American technology campuses. As we learned, in the Emirates it is not unusual to look at West-ern models of development; the local rulers have begun to realize the importance of diversifying their economy and investing in what is now globally recognized as the business of the future, re-newable energies and clean energy technologies. The ambition for these new cities is to become the world's leading centres in the testing of new models of urban living in symbiosis with the biosphere. Contrasting this progressive attitude is the socio-cultural conservatism of many of the countries of the Arabic peninsula, regions still strongly organized around a traditional social struc-ture and governed with a fair amount of control over the adoption of new "Western" lifestyles.

   This scenario led us to speculate on the conception of the new city as a new form of social free-zone, deliberately positioned away from the main cities and sunk in a stunning valley a few kilometres from Al Ain/Al Buraimi Oasis, at the foot of the mountain range which has been feeding the aquifer for centuries supporting the evolution of the extraordinary oasis city of Al Ain. The mechanism of the social free-zone would attract a multitude of social groups, from the increasing crowds of refugees, to unemployed construction workers, to scientists and explor-ers of cultural and ecological diversity; all would migrate to inhabit this remote location and experiment within a new urbanity founded on premises of social self-organization and energetic self-sufficiency.

The steep wadi slopes
eroded by the action of
water and wind

The urban mechanisms   The city experiment would be regulated by an algorithmic protocol based on two systemic mechanisms:

–   By borrowing the concept of economic free-zone, the project re-describes the city as a social free-zone, where mechanisms of open social participation and self-organization are allowed to operate as engines of evolution of a new social system; the algorithm is intended to be substitutive of Sharia Law within the boundaries of the city and to become the regulator for the development of the urban fabric and its own related independent social structure.
–   By developing a mechanism of reverse sustainability, the new settlement would evolve its own artificial ecology, able in time to reverse the local conditions back 10,000 years, to when at the end of the glacial age the region was covered in fertile pastures and rivers. This model is intended to work by amplification of environmental differences and real-time incubation of potentials towards the production of new local microclimates.

The social free-zone algorithm and the microclimatic transformation machine are co-evolving processes. Within the new emerging civilization social diversity will stimulate increasing biological diversity and as a result introduce increasing complexity in the codes of the social algorithm and the related articulation of the urban fabric; a systemic favela will emerge, embedded on a site that will transform and from which it will be transformed. This model of self-organization will constantly seek reconciliation between the self-sustaining role of nature and the new emergent tribal organizations of the global nomads of this late stage of capitalism. Such reconciliation is possible within the augmented reality of the new city because of the possibilities offered by its algorithmic code and real-time self-regulating capabilities; a co-networking city able to evolve as a self-sustaining "favela" of the digital age.

The infrastructural systems   This algorithmic city will spread onto the site symbiotically exploiting all the nutrients it can find, conjuring a new artificial landscape intertwined with the natural. Productive spaces thread continuously through the inhabited areas, optimizing water recycling in real-time, and providing oases of rich microclimatic articulation. Lower in the wadis, careful xeroscaping strategies generate a "dotted" landscape of dams, aquifer wells and pockets of vegetated park.

The algorithmic machine iteratively generates urban form from the very nutrients of the site, adapting to or carving into its contours, emerging from the social as well as geographic climate.

The design machine produces a "reversed" city, overturning conventional relationships, reversing destructive energy patterns: while accessible from the desert plane, the city itself develops in the shade, nested on the slopes and microclimatic niches near the top of the wadis.

A connective rhizomatic infrastructure materializes as the tangible manifestation of the emergent local social ties among inhabited cells and research labs that will populate, and finance, the expansion of the city. The infrastructure integrates supporting beams and pile foundations with vital energy modules, threaded with systems and services for nourishing and optimizing the city.

It will grow organically, layer by layer, encouraging different types of solar technology to be installed as they become available in the future, casting the city as a living laboratory.

The water and energy systems will be controlled by a unique ITS infrastructure. The soft-grid built into the infrastructure offers not only futuristic networking systems, but provides complete control of urban processes, reducing inefficiencies and greatly improving performance, ensuring the smooth movement of on-demand public transportation and assessing the usage of water, drop-by-drop in real time. It offers the dynamic support system for a real-time self-organizing city, leveraging the algorithmic design to evolve organically, reconciling the self-sustaining role of nature with the city's emergent social configurations.

The algorithmic protocol   The social free-zone and reverse sustainability algorithms at the core of the new favela city model develop from a set of simple questions, that will be first asked during early occupation:

– Where will be the best spot to locate the city starting nuclei?
– How will the city grow and to what size?
– How dense will it be?
– Where will the city get its energy and water from?
– How can we predict, regulate or frame its future developments while embedding the necessary degree of adaptability to face any possible social scenario?
– How can the city be a testing bed of technological innovation while functioning as an efficient urban system?

The mesh of virtual plots   Given the extraordinary nature of the site's environment, the abundance of solar energy and the relative scarcity of water, the algorithm is first deployed as a sieve, a filtering engine able to scan the landscape for sweet spots favourable for life. The first question is then answered by breeding a mesh of virtual plots, each terraced, surfaced and wrapped into a volume proportional to the life it can initially sustain. Not a single spot for growth then, or a series of starting nuclei, but a distributed mesh of possibilities, each with its own weight and attractiveness.

Scenarios of growth can then be run on this virtual ground by means of specific evaluation machines; given different sets of economic and technological conditions different portions of the landscape could be developed, giving rise to neighbourhoods and villages, high- to medium-density patches.

this page
City-making simulation with maximum virtual plot coverage and a fully developed network system

opposite
Satellite view of the wadi's erosional plains near Al Ain

The soft city   The simulation of the city's patterns of growth is turned into a problem of communication: the algorithm is used as a tool of communication allowing access to the generative code of the city and its founding parameters; a soft real-time city allowing planners, developers, prospective citizens and the Ruler himself to communicate via multiple simulated scenarios.

Algorithmically there is no optimal solution to urban form finding; no computer can compute the perfect city. However, logical ways to access the virtual plots can be computed generating minimal paths and road networks as well as related crossroads, junctions, corners, piazzas and galleries. These features become the main agents of urban form making, turning the traditional courtyard urban block into a population of new prototypical urban cells.

Differentiations and hierarchies   Starting from the definition of the main access points to the wadi the algorithm facilitates a sedimentation process; each design decision triggers the emergence of urban structures that influence the development of new algorithmic rules and related decisions. The courtyard cells are processed and organized in unexpected and differentiated assemblages, in turn becoming breeding grounds for programmatic and social differentiation. A typical example being the negotiation of Arabic and Western lifestyles on the same village, or the organization of ornamental and productive urban landscapes.

The endless algorithm for the endless city   In the new city this process is never-ending, embedded in the very fabric of the city it will become its way of living; an algorithmic city is a city in real time, in constant self-organization, where the urban norms and regulations are open source and adaptive, being themselves new rules in the urban algorithm. As in a cyber-favela the city operates as an open urban laboratory of inventions and individual contributions, registered and implemented collectively, producing ever more resolution and diversity.

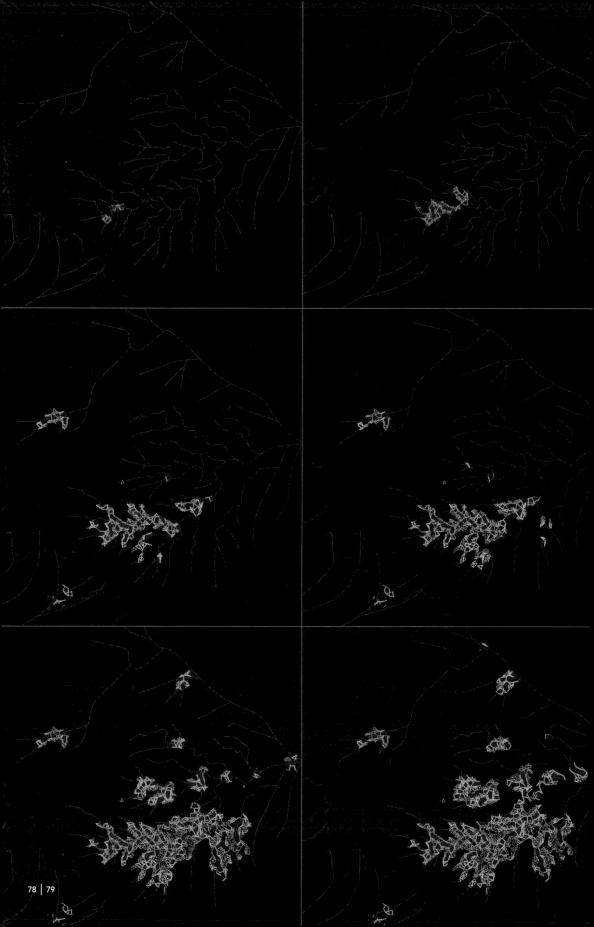

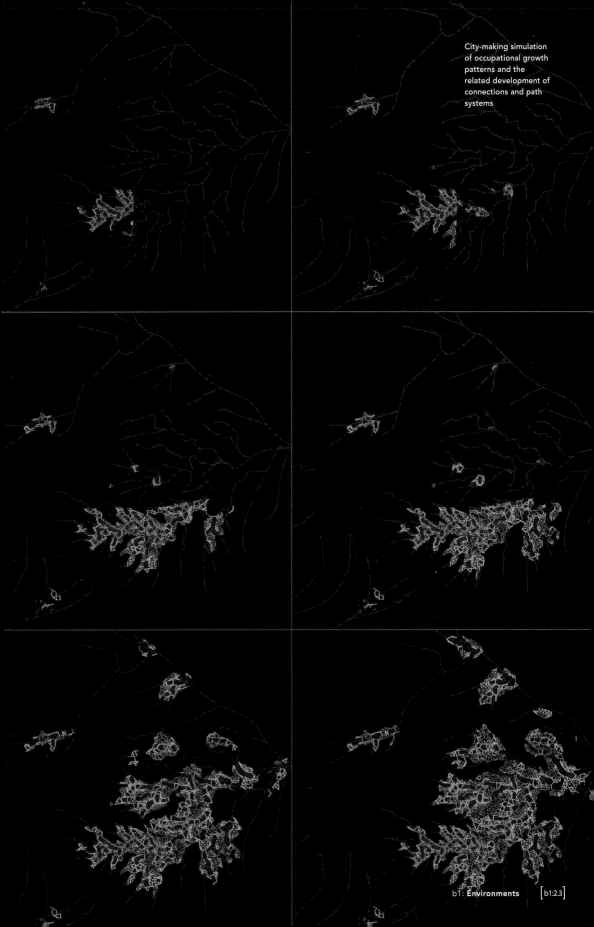

City-making simulation
of occupational growth
patterns and the
related development of
connections and path
systems

b1: Environments   [b1:2.3]

Actions and rules

// The term "algorithm" refers to a list of actions to be performed following
// logical computable rules. Each action takes information (input) from the
// previous step and processes these data following a rule that returns new
// information (output).

Algorithmic operators

{Urban algorithm: rule-based design machine
Action: the design aim of a specific algorithmic rule
Rule: the core of the algorithmic production machine
Input: the information being fed into the rule
Output: the information generated by the rule}

Urban design entities

{Court: the cell's soft core
Cell: individual virtual block or ground tessellation unit
Neighbourhood cluster: group of cells framed by main circulation routes
Village prototype: group of clusters defined by topographical limits
Phased city: group of village prototypes defining phases of development}

Network design entities

{Highway: main connection road for all types of traffic with slope less than
10 per cent and connecting different village prototypes
Bridges: main connecting roads for all types of traffic stretching across the
wadi to connect different village prototypes
Roads: network of secondary roads internal to the village and connecting
the various clusters
Path: network of pedestrian roads or ramps internal to the village and
connecting individual cells and clusters
Lifts: types of path to be found on steep slopes connecting main clusters
Stairs: types of path to be found on steep slopes connecting individual
cells}

Macro-input 1: environment

{

    // Data extracted from the site such as landscape morphology, water proximity, solar
    // radiation and wind direction inform the algorithm and connect the development of
    // the city to the opportunities provided by the site.

    Landscape steepness {Landscape steepness affects both the parcelization of the land and the creation of the network system. Areas with less steepness allow the creation of bigger plots and the growth of villages}

    Landscape height {The city grows inside two boundaries imposed by the morphology of the site; the bottom of the wadi, to avoid the damage caused by periodical floods, and the top of the plateau, in order to preserve intact its natural value}

    Natural ventilation {The algorithm uses the prevalent wind direction in the area, north-northwest, in the design of the road network system and in the three-dimensional urban massing to exploit natural cooling power}

    Water proximity {Water is an invaluable resource on site, so the city growth increases close to wadi intersections}

    Solar radiation {The algorithm guides the growth of the city towards parts of the site where the solar radiation is lowest}

}

Macro-input 2: prototypes

{

    // Multiple urban and architectural prototypes inform the algorithm in the process of
    // actualization of the virtual city.

    Building typologies {The city is constructed with courtyard building blocks. The shape of the buildings, their height and the width of their courtyard is adjusted by the algorithm in relation to the environmental fields of the site}

    Connectivity {Connectivity includes the whole organization of the network system, from the local walkways to the main traffic links; each level of the transportation system feeds data and information to the different levels of the algorithm}

    Technologies {The latest technologies are embedded in the design of the city; adaptive and real-time responsive systems are designed to meet the specific needs of each inhabitant. The algorithm takes into account the new opportunities that these technologies afford to the city}

}

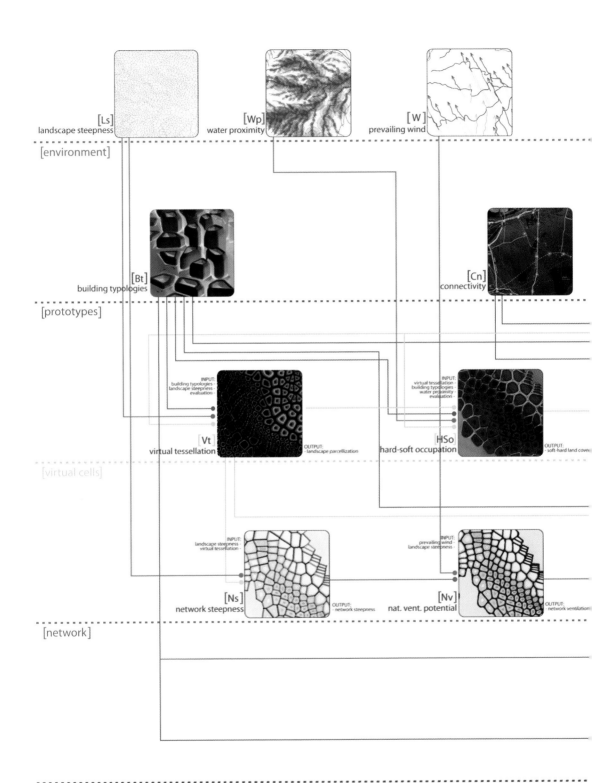

[Ls]
landscape steepness

[Wp]
water proximity

[W]
prevailing wind

[environment]

[Bt]
building typologies

[Cn]
connectivity

[prototypes]

INPUT:
building typologies -
landscape steepness -
evaluation -

INPUT:
virtual tessellation -
building typologies -
water proximity -
evaluation -

[Vt]
virtual tessellation

OUTPUT:
- landscape parcellization

[HSo]
hard-soft occupation

OUTPUT:
- soft-hard land cover

[virtual cells]

INPUT:
landscape steepness -
virtual tessellation -

INPUT:
prevailing wind -
landscape steepness -

[Ns]
network steepness

OUTPUT:
- network steepness

[Nv]
nat. vent. potential

OUTPUT:
- network ventilation

[network]

[neighbourhood]

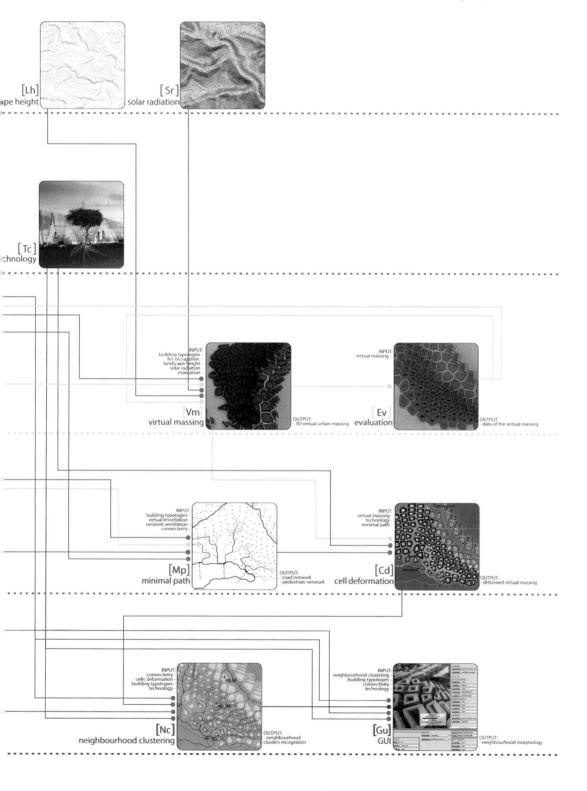

[Vt] Virtual tessellation

// The area is parcellized by means of the Voronoi algorithm. The size of each cell is
// inversely proportional to the ground steepness.

{

    Input:

    {topographic information with a 4 m vertical drop resolution}

    {building prototypes}

    {cell distance and resolution: 20, 30, 40, 50 m}

    Rule 1:

    {Use Voronoi algorithmic tessellation for virtual terracing or cells}

    Output:

    {3D organization of virtual plots or cells}

}

[Hso] Hard–soft occupation

// The percentage of hard and soft occupation for each virtual plot is generated.
// Soft occupation is prevalent in cells closer to the wadi. Moving towards the top of the
// plateau the amount of hard cover increases proportionally.

{

    Input:

    {3D layout of cells}

    {water proximity (topographic axis of wadi)}

    {courtyard block model}

    Rule 2:

    {Compute proximity map from every cell to wadi axis}

    {Define percentage of cells' hard versus soft cover in relation to proximity map}

    {Load courtyard model to percentage of hard versus soft cover for every cell}

    Output:

    {hard–soft land cover and building limits map}

}

[Vm] Virtual massing

// Denser urbanization is generated where the solar radiation is lower and guarantees
// a better living environment. ❶

{

    Input:

    {incident solar radiation on land}

    {layout of hard–soft land cover}

    {courtyard block model}

    Rule 3:

    {Read incident solar radiation field}

    {Define inhabitation density of cells in relation to incident solar radiation field}

    {Load 2D layout of hard–soft land cover for every cell and apply 3D extrusion rule}

    Output:

    {3D virtual urban massing model and urban grid structure}

}

❶ >

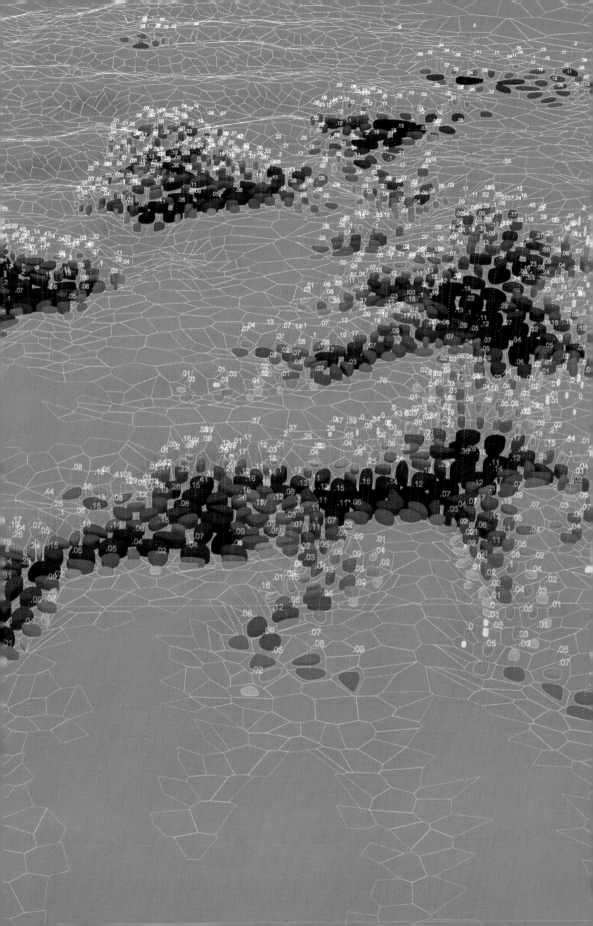

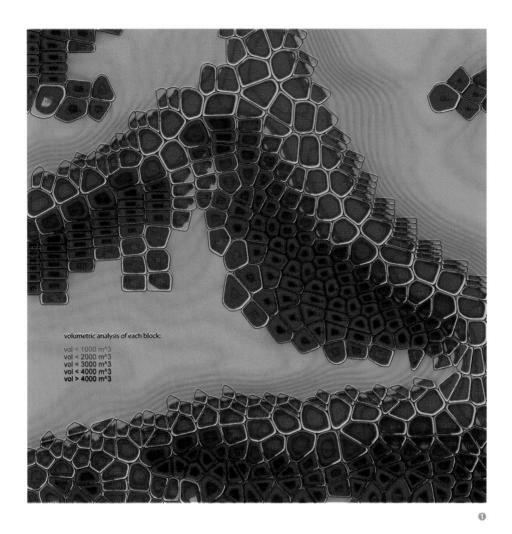

volumetric analysis of each block:

vol < 1000 m^3
vol < 2000 m^3
vol < 3000 m^3
vol < 4000 m^3
vol > 4000 m^3

❶

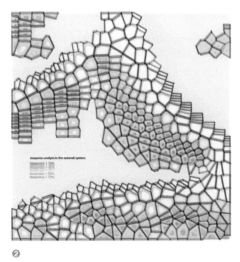

steepness analysis in the network system:

❷

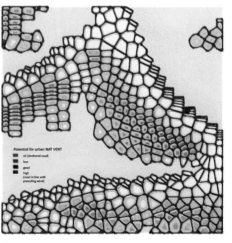

Potential for urban NAT VENT

nil [sheltered road]
low
good
high
[road in line with prevailing wind]

❸

[Um] Virtual Urban Massing evaluation

// The evaluation process represents numerically and visually the output generated
// by the algorithm. It creates a loop that sends back information to the previous
// actions of the algorithm and generates new operational fields for the definition
// of the successive actions within the algorithmic protocol.

{

Input:
{virtual urban massing}
Rule 4:
{Analyse the virtual urban massing}
{Calculate land occupation of each cell}
{Calculate floor area of each building}
{Calculate volume of each building} ❶
{Calculate floor area ratio (FAR) of each building}
{Calculate cut-off angle of each building courtyard}
Output:
{colour-coded maps of land occupations, floor area, volume, FAR and
cut-off angle of each building}

}

[Ns] Network steepness evaluation

// The boundaries of the three-dimensional virtual cells represent the network of
// connections within each village. The algorithm indexes the steepness of each
// road in order to create a new operational accessibility map.

{

Input:
{3D boundaries of virtual cells}
{land topography}
Rule 5:
{Read 3D boundaries of virtual cells and topography}
{Calculate individual edge steepness}
Output:
{colour-coded map of network steepness} ❷

}

[Nv] Natural ventilation potential

// The three-dimensional boundaries of the virtual cells are confronted with the
// prevailing wind direction on site. A natural ventilation potential map is
// produced.

{

Input:
{3D boundaries of virtual cells}
{prevailing wind direction}
Rule 6:
{Read 3D boundaries of virtual cells and topography}
{Read prevailing wind direction}
{Calculate angle of alignment of individual edge}
Output:
{colour-coded map of network natural ventilation potential} ❸

}

[Mpn] Minimal path networks

// "An attempt to produce the connection with the shortest overall length produces the
// minimal path system" (Frei Otto).
// Multiple minimal path networks are generated in relation to ranges of steepness
// of the individual links.
// Links with steepness lower than 10 per cent generate a greenway, integrating a small
// road for leisure and agricultural traffic, trees, cycling and pedestrian paths as well as
// water collection ditches, with a highway that connects all the villages.
// Links with steepness lower than 20 per cent generate the road network system within
// the village.
// Links with steepness lower than 40 per cent generate the pedestrian network system
// constituted by ramps, staircases and lifts.

    {

        Input:
        {3D boundaries of virtual cells}
        {network's steepness map}
        {connectivity}
        {building typologies}
        Rule 7:
        {Read 3D boundaries of virtual cells and cells' centres}
        {Read network's steepness map}
        {Run the minimal paths algorithm on links with steepness <10 per cent}
        {Plot highway paths}
        {Run the minimal paths algorithm on links with steepness <20 per cent}
        {Plot road paths}
        {Run the minimal paths algorithm on links with steepness <40 per cent}
        {Plot pedestrian paths}
        Output:
        {highway network system map}
        {roads network system map}
        {pedestrian network system map}

    }

[Cd] Cell deformation

// The algorithm creates the road network among the buildings with proportional width.

    {

        Input:
        {virtual massing}
        {minimal path: road network}
        {technology}
        Rule 8:
        {Read road network systems}
        {Read 3D boundaries of virtual cells}
        {Modify the vertices of the cells depending on the relevance of the path closest
        to them}
        Output:
        {urban meshwork modified by the network system} ❶

    }

❶ >

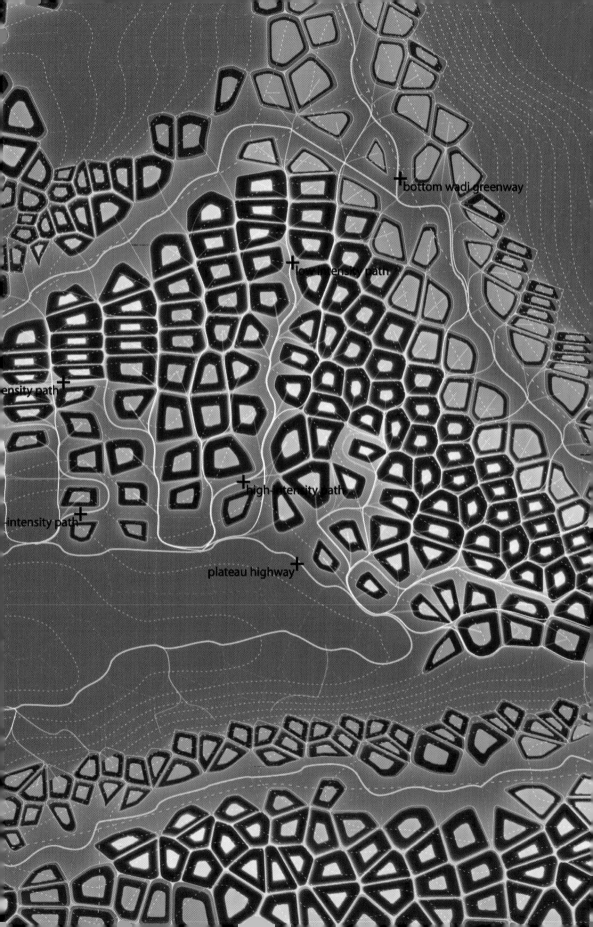

bottom wadi greenway

low intensity path

ensity path

high-intensity path

-intensity path

plateau highway

// Neighbourhood clusters with similar inner features are recognized.
```
{
        Input:
        {3D boundaries of virtual cells}
        {road network system map}
        Rule 9:
        {Recognize neighbourhoods with similar inner features}
        Output:
        { [nh_01] neighbourhood 01: compact clusters of regular blocks crossed by
        pedestrian paths and driveways (schools or research buildings) }
        { [nh_02] neighbourhood 02: blocks of variable dimension on the top of the slope
        (water tank, energy storage) }
        { [nh_03] neighbourhood 03: compact clusters of irregular blocks crossed by
        pedestrian paths and driveways (Western-type residential with large courtyard) }
        { [nh_04] neighbourhood 04: extremely compact clusters of irregular blocks, car-
        free (Eastern-type residential) }
        { [nh_05] neighbourhood 05: highly differentiated blocks in a low slope area
        (research labs, retails, hotels) }
        { [ag_pl] agricultural plot: reed beds, hydroponic culture, water treatment} ❶
}
```

how to 6 : [Gu] GUI: Graphical User Interface

// The Graphical User Interface (GUI) allows interaction with the algorithm before, during
// and after the construction process. Designers, developers, investors and other actors can
// perform a direct manipulation of the parameters affecting the growth simulation. Data
// extracted from areas already built are visualized in the GUI and inform future steps of
// urbanization. From the system of connectivity to the plot size, passing through the
// building typologies and the green areas, each action of the algorithm is thus visually
// negotiable.
```
{
        Input:
        {environment}
        {neighbourhood clustering}
        {building typologies}
        {connectivity}
        {technology}
        Rule 10:
        {Read changing environment and adapt to it}
        {Cccept input from the outside}
        {Give differentiation of choices to developers and investors}
        {Allows freedom of development within a constrained environment}
        {Allows integration of new technologies in a flexible system of norms and
        regulations}
        Output:
        {virtual neighbourhood morphology} ❷
}
```

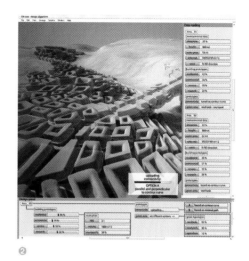

②

①

Digital parametric model
of typical cluster of
neighbourhoods

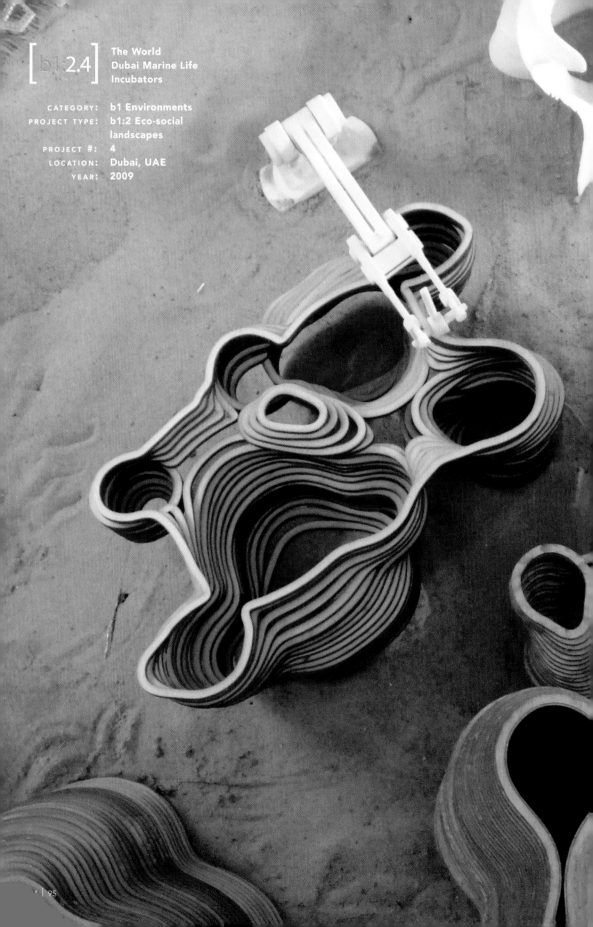

The World
Dubai Marine Life
Incubators

CATEGORY: b1 Environments
PROJECT TYPE: b1:2 Eco-social
               landscapes
PROJECT #:   4
LOCATION: Dubai, UAE
YEAR: 2009

[T]he only true response to the ecological crisis is on a global scale, ... an authentic political, social and cultural revolution, ... not exclusively concerned with visible relations of force on a grand scale, but [it] will also take into account molecular domains of sensibility, intelligence and desire.

Félix Guattari, *The Three Ecologies*

Introduction   Dubai is a unique place; under the visionary leadership of one man, His Highness Sheikh Mohammed bin Rashid Al Maktoum, in nearly 30 years it has transformed from a small fishing village devoted mainly to pearl diving and trading, into a global hub of finance, corporate service and tourism. Built at record speed and without any local socio-cultural or urban reference model, Dubai could only rely on importing existing global types and models of urbanization: the landmark tower, the gated community, the shopping mall, the sports arena, the heritage village, the beach and spa resort, the planted boulevard, the formal garden, the fun park, constitute some of the more diffused examples.

Mechanisms of development   However, the uniqueness of what we can call the Dubai experiment resides in its financial development mechanism; supported by cash-rich Abu Dhabi as part of the UAE, Dubai has used its limited resources to manufacture a sort of media dream able to capture the imagination of the world and attract investments from large corporations, property develop-ment companies, foreign countries and private investors. This simple but effective mechanism is based on a sort of urban hyperbole whereby new types have been hybridized and scaled up to inspire awe and trigger dreams of luxury and grandeur in almost everybody around the globe.

Interestingly, architecture has been marginal to the success of Dubai, possibly due to the lack of reference points within its original landscape. Essentially a flat desert land meeting a flat desert sea along a straight 50 km coast, Dubai had to fabricate its own new scenery, an urban stage able to perform within the vastness of the desert and able to create exciting attraction points visible from almost everywhere. This could only be created through an operation of infrastructural engi-neering supporting vast urban development; single high-profile buildings from known architects may be effective in Bilbao or perhaps even in Doha, but not in Dubai. This new vast urban scenery is then articulated into a series of small-scale chapters, like theatres with small stages for the reproduction of specific environments; these constitute what Koolhaas has defined as mechanisms of good time, essentially providing tourists and the local middle class with endless opportuni-ties to consume, spend and have fun. These two scales of scenery are manufactured with specific apparatuses and are essentially devoted to amaze and attract at the urban scale, and to amuse and capture at the human scale.

pp. 94–95
Co-envelopes – laser-cutted model simulating the tectonic organisation of the bio-cement's living membranes.
By Yuwon Kang

this page
Aerial view of the World Lagoon, Dubai

A machinic utopia   The main apparatus for the design of the large-scale urban scenery is the old fashioned tool of the plan; however, in Dubai the plan shifts from being a tool of description to become a tool of speculation. The cartographic map of Dubai never reflects reality, or, from a different perspective, in Dubai reality is not what you can physically see on the ground. This condition, which might seem absurd within a European perspective (in a map of Paris, for instance, we expect to read exactly what we can find when we get there), is instead deeply ingrained in the mechanism which makes Dubai possible and real; the mechanism of speculative real estate. If we look back at what Dubai was 20 years ago we immediately realize that this mechanism is the only possible one as no pre-existing element is special or unique enough to generate interest and attract investment; the plan of Dubai must always depict a dream so outrageously fantastic as to become real, possible and irresistible. Because the dream is a fantasy it is open to individual contributions; by investing you become part of it, you can shape the dream and at the same time enrich yourself.

The mechanism has, until recently, been working perfectly well: investors came and built, the dream became reality; reality triggered even wilder dreams; many investors made millions and the city grew considerably in population, with 80 per cent of its inhabitants coming from abroad.

Fractal Dubai   As the landscape of Dubai was relatively boring one of the main tricks performed by the plan was to rearrange the city's boundaries in more exciting ways: the waterfront, clearly the main asset for a wannabe dream city, was not only linear and flat but also bounded by the neighbouring emirates of Abu Dhabi and Sharja to an overall length of 50 km. The Ruler recognized this as a tremendous obstacle to his expansion plans and ordered the extension of the coastline and the multiplication and differentiation of waterfront typologies to turn Dubai into an effective waterfront city.

The plan of Dubai suddenly turned into a mathematical experiment: fitting possibly infinite kilometres of waterfront into a 50 km stretch of coast. A fractal-like design was conceived; suddenly land reclamation on one side and artificial water basins and canals on the other extended the coast to almost 500 km, 10 times the original waterfront developable land.

When looked at in plan fractals do have a downside: they look abstract and undifferentiated. The fabrication mechanism of Dubai needed one more ingredient: iconicity; icons have the stickiness factor to become infectious symbols.

Fractal mathematics + iconicity = the palm islands   Three islands were designed, one is complete and two are under construction. After 10 more years of development the dream had grown considerably: 500 km of coastline is not much after all (Italy has got 7600 km of it). A new equation was formulated: algorithmic tessellation + iconicity + max coastline per square km of land = the World Lagoon.

The World Lagoon, Dubai   The World Lagoon is the largest land reclamation project ever attempted; it sits 4 km off the coast of Dubai and is composed of around 300 islands protected by a rocky breakwater barrier. Costing $12 billion just for the land reclamation work, it is four times larger than Venice and the total amount of sandy beach it offers exceeds 1200 km. If you look at it in plan it resembles the real world land masses and each island is named after a real country. Immediately after construction started the World Lagoon became the most talked-about project ever in Dubai; celebrities and billionaires from around the globe flew there for a portrait picture and to book a private island. If the actual Maldives were the development model for the World Lagoon's resorts – luxury secluded beachfront developments – here you could find 100 Maldives within easy reach of Dubai international airport and served by large cruise ships, piers, shopping malls, convention centres, business hotels and so on.

Crisis scenario   Following the success of the World Lagoon, Dubai went on synthesizing dreams: the Universe was conceived and DubaiLand, a fun park as large as the whole of the existing metropolis. Then disaster struck: the global crisis has affected Dubai badly; its dream machine cannot function without a constant flow of cash and suddenly it seemed the global cash flow had stopped. Many lost their jobs and many others had to leave the country in despair, some even threatened by the prospect of imprisonment for their inability to pay their debts.

   The World Lagoon project, being one of the most ambitious, had to stop, as investors and developers were suddenly cashless. Abu Dhabi came to the rescue with a financial bailout and the acquisition of many properties within Dubai, including the new icon of the city, the tallest skyscraper in the world, renamed on its inauguration day after His Highness Sheikh Khalifa bin Zayed Al Nahyan, ruler of Abu Dhabi.

The World Dubai Marine Life Incubators project   This crisis scenario became the opportunity to conceive the World Dubai Marine Life Incubators project. As part of the AA Inter10 research on the systemic architecture of ecoMachines, we began to ask ourselves about the possible new role of architecture within this turbulent context; can architects contribute by developing new spatial and material practices for the re-functionalization of this artificial urban landscape? Can these practices suggest the new mechanisms to synthesize the future of the metropolis?

The World Lagoon is the perfect laboratory in which to investigate what we envision as a global network of centres of urban ecology; the headquarters of the network organizations for the ecological re-development of the globe. It offered a fertile ground for eco-machinic projects because of its combination of iconicity, urbanity, ecological complexity, inherent fragility and sheer size.

Each incubator investigates a specific architectural mechanism of co-existence and co-evolution within the local marine habitat, prefiguring future scenarios of development whereby the lagoon is re-contextualized in socio-economic and technological terms in relation to such phenomena as global warming, coral bleaching, eco-tourism, social networking, workforce global migration, food production, renewable energies, urban well-being and building material flows.

The lagoon becomes a medium through which we can articulate a palette of strategies and engineer related new architectural prototypes.

Intensive difference   The original equation of the World Lagoon was transformed into a new one: algorithmic tessellation + iconicity + max environmental differentiation per square km of land = the World Lagoon marine life incubators.

The project of conversion of the World Lagoon into a marine life and ecology hub starts from Dubai's own developmental mechanism: formulate an outrageously ambitious idea, describe it with the most suggestive set of drawings and models, let the market do the rest. This time, however, the market is constituted by populations of individual ecologists from around the world. The World Dubai marine life incubators are a Mecca for independent ecologists of any kind, pro-fession and race to join forces and manufacture his/her New Eden, extracting value and revenue from a richness and new-found diversity of life to which their activity contributes.

The incubation mechanism in fact operates by systematic cultivation of difference; by unfold-ing value out of the gain of potential diversity it itself produces.

facing page
View of the remaining old quarters of Bur Dubai from the shores of Dubai creek

this page
Artificial coral reef developed with the Reef Ball method

how to 0 : Cultivate coral gardens and develop marine life incubators
{

    // The construction of the World Lagoon has created ecological concerns as the
    // suspended sediment produced by the rainbow blasting of dredged sand used
    // to form the islands is suffocating the local coral reef.
    // Corals within the Arabic Gulf are the only ones in the world known to be
    // able to withstand the climatic extremes typical of this region; studying their
    // mechanisms of adaptation is extremely valuable for scientists as it could
    // reveal secrets that can be transferred to conservation projects elsewhere.
    // Because marine ecology worldwide is threatened by global warming, and
    // because coral reefs constitute the basis of many marine ecosystems, it is
    // clear that every effort should be made to preserve the reefs in this area.
    // Under pressure from many environmental groups, the World Lagoon developers
    // Nakheels have devised a world's first, transferring entire pieces of reef onto
    // the World Lagoon's breakwater barrier, thus protecting them from suffocation.
    // The project, conducted with marine life experts Biorock, became the
    // basis for the marine life incubators projects, starting with the conception
    // of coral gardens, large artificial nursing reefs to be algorithmically distributed
    // throughout the lagoon turning this bare artificial landscape into a laboratory
    // of marine diversity and incubator of new marine artificial ecosystems.

}

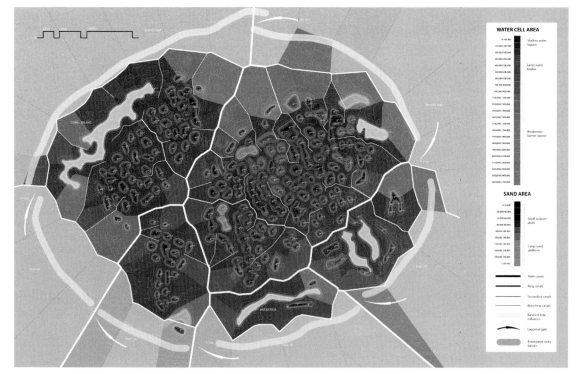

how to 1 : Territories of life frame the artificial marine landscape

{

    // Definition of regions within the World Lagoon favourable to marine life
    // and mapping of the nurturing operational fields.

    1.1 {Define topographical regions on site} ❶

    1.2 {Map operational fields as nurturing gradients; visualize intensity of
           "nutrients" throughout the lagoon}

    1.3 {Trace virtual plots of incubation; each plot identifies a unit of ecological
           incubation} ❷

    1.4 {Compute input and output flows for each virtual plot; these flows constitute
           the capital of matter, information and energy available to each unit of life}

}

❶

BREAKWATER BARRIER LAGOON
This region comprises the part of the seawater just next to the breakwater barrier but not directly involved in the transportation system.

LARGE SAND PLATFORMS
This region comprises the islands that have been joined in the largest sand platforms. Potential for tourism and placement of commercial facilities.

BANDS OF TIDAL INFLUENCE
Positioned around each island, these bands are the most subject to erosion. This region held the highest potential to support marine life.

LAGOONAL GATES
The gates represent the transportation access to the World Lagoon. They are crossed by strong submarine currents that provide flushing to the inner lagoon.

SMALL ISOLATED ATOLLS
This region represents the most scattered upland sand area of the World Lagoon. Potential to create an intense network of eco-touristic activities related to the submarine world.

BREAKWATER ROCKY BARRIER
The region represents a physical rock barrier to protect the World Lagoon from the currents and constant erosion.

MAIN CANALS
The canals comprise the main transportation transfer centre. They go through the main regions of the World Lagoon, constituting a good resource for the development of the site.

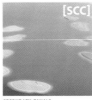

SECONDARY CANALS
They comprise the first bifurcation of the main canals. They start to develop a more capillary system of transportation between the islands.

SHALLOW WATER LAGOON
This region comprises the part of the seawater between the islands. The sea floor is shallow and represents a good resource to develop coral gardens or algae farms.

MAIN CANAL RING
The main canal ring comprises the peripheral transportation system of the site. It goes all around the site just next to the breakwater rocky barrier. It represents a good transportation supply for the main canals.

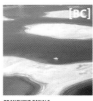

BRANCHING CANALS
They represent the second bifurcation of the main canals. The capillary system ends between the islands allowing a deeper connective network of transportation.

LARGE BODIES OF WATER
These are large patches of seawater just next to the main canals but not directly involved in the transportation system. They could be a good potential site for the construction of ecological material systems.

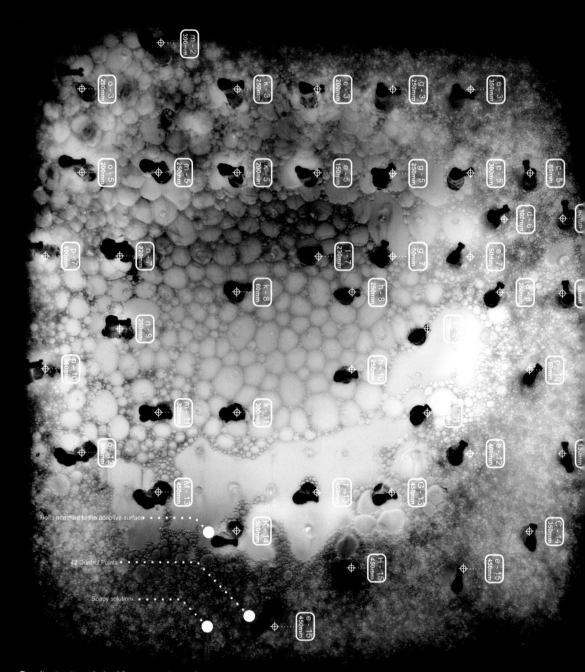

Bolts attached to the adaptive surface • • • • • • •

42 Control Points • • • • • • •

Soapy solution • • • • • •

Resultant pattern derived from current mapping:

The pattern tries to analyse the relations of the context bathymetry and current direction and speeds, in order to understand the reach and proliferation of territories defined by sealife and eco-systems.

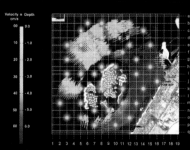

Current direction and speeds

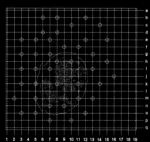

Experiment grid and layout

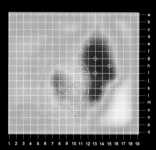

Datascape / speed and bathymetry

how to 2 : Simulate the occupation of territories
{
        // Run time-based simulations of the occupation of the Lagoon landscape and
        // the growth and self-organization of the virtual plots of life.
        // The algorithms to run the simulations and visualize the gardens' plots are
        // first developed empirically by means of specifically developed simulation
        // apparatuses.
        // Based on Frei Otto's theories on the occupation of territories (in nature and
        // human civilization), these models allowed material self-organization to be
        // explored and understood through the production of patterns of colonization
        // and subdivision of the seabed surface in virtual units of life.

      2.1 {Design the testing apparatus} ❶
      2.2 {Load the apparatus with the material and set the starting conditions for
           the experiment}
      2.3 {Run the experiment and video record the results in real time} ❷
      2.4 {Apply operational fields of difference}
      2.5 {Observe the material self-organization and the emergent competition
           among virtual plots} ❸
           Affects → 2.1 and 2.2 Designing and setting starting conditions to achieve
           optimal visualization of material self-organization

}

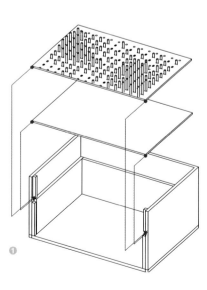

❶

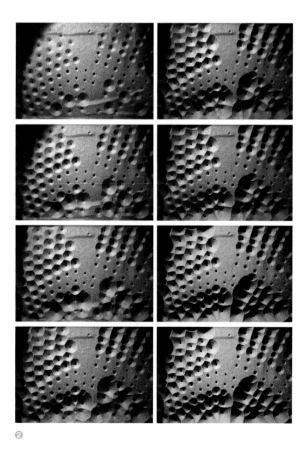

❷

how to 3 : Model the occupation of territories

{

      // Develop algorithmic design techniques to model the patterns of occupation
      // of territories and the time-based processes of self-organization resulting
      // from injection of nurturing substances.

      3.1 {Capture digitally the emergent patterns of self-organization recorded
          during the analogue simulations} ➊
          Refine → 2.3 and 2.5 Observe and record self-organization patterns
      3.2 {Develop an algorithmic design technique to abstract the emergent patterns
          digitally} ➋
      3.3 {Apply changing gradients of nurturing substance}
          <example> Water flow, direct insolation, relative salinity, biological waste
          water concentration </example>
      3.4 {Run digital simulations of occupational layouts in time}
      3.5 {Evaluate behaviours of each plot as competition emerges and as favourable
          plots grow in size and articulation. Compare behaviour to analogue model}
          Affects → 3.2 Algorithmic technique and 3.3 Operational gradients intensity

}

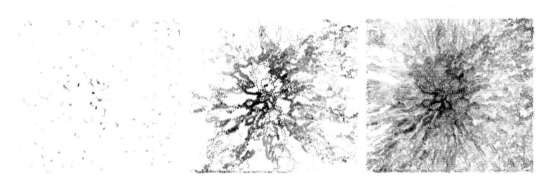

float maxDisp = 6, float maxRad = 7

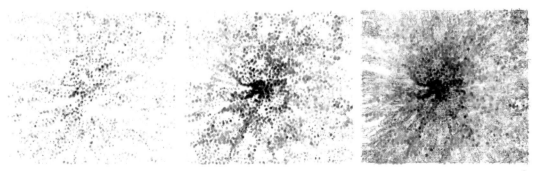

float maxDisp = 10, float maxRad = 10   ➋

how to 4 : Introduce material strategies

{

    // Develop material strategies to manage the process of sand sedimentation
    // and consolidation necessary to form the coral gardens substratum and the
    // marine life incubators' spatial articulation.
    // Introduce the concept of cyber-materials, material systems whose properties
    // co-evolve in time in relation to the surrounding environment.

    4.1 {Define a material system}
        <example> Interlocking sticks, bundled rods </example>
    4.2 {Define the accretion process}
        <example> Biorock mineral accretion, bacteria induced bio-cementation,
        mangrove plantation </example>
    4.3 {Test accretion in time}
        Refine → 4.1 Material system
    4.4 {Define rules of accretion on site in relation to the self-organizational
        behaviour of each living plot}
    4.5 {Run accreting scenarios} ❶
        Affects → 4.1 Material system and 4.2 Accretion process
    4.6 {Draw and render accreted spaces}
    4.7 {Define strategic protocols of accretion and phase the evolution of the
        coral garden plans and the emergence of the marine life incubators} ❷
        Affects → 1.3 Tracing of virtual plots and 1.4 Flows of nutrients

}

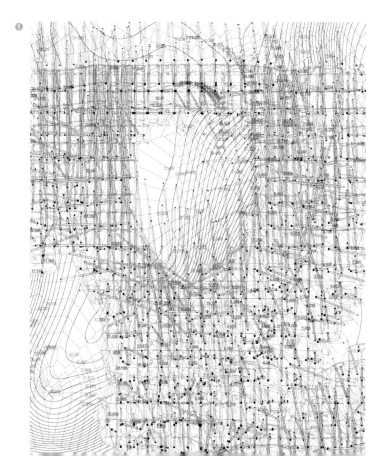

❷ >

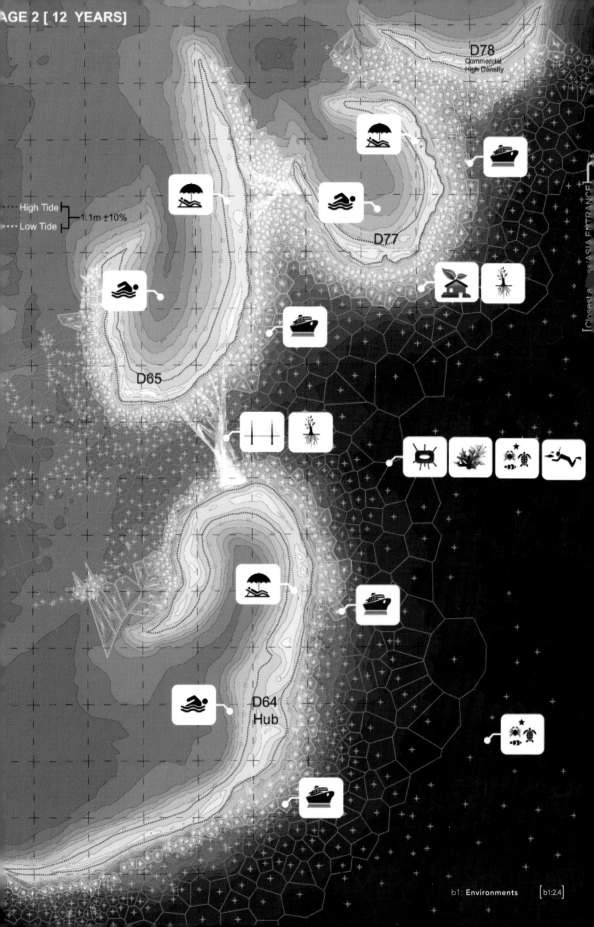

D78
Commercial
High Density

D77

High Tide
Low Tide   1.1m ±10%

D65

D64
Hub

Closest a es/ASIA ENTRANCE

how to 5 : Model architecture as a marine life incubator

{

    // Develop the three-dimensional articulation of the marine life incubators;

    // build physical scale models to choreograph the architectural and spatial

    // effects inherent in the incubators' material and ecological strategies.

    5.1 {Select a cluster of plots to model}

    5.2 {Define scale, resolution and consistent material definition}

        Refine → 4.6 Drawings of accreted space

    5.3 {Define rules of articulation in the three dimensions}

    5.4 {Test material properties} ❶

    5.5 {Run the accretion process} ❷

    5.6 {Record results and spatial effects}

        Affects → 4.7 Marine life incubators strategic phasing and planar organization

}

❶

❷ >

Testing model of Dolphinatoll: a land sedimentation machine for the production of an artificial atoll operating as a dolphinarium in the Arabic Gulf

fibrous structures

[b2:1.1]
From Fibrous Room to
Aqva Garden
p. 118

ecoMachines

[b2:2.2]
The STEM series
p. 146

Prototype

1. In the field of product or industrial design the term "prototype" is typically related to a testing model developed to engineer or refine new design solutions belonging to a certain product's category. **2.** In architecture such a definition has evolved since the advent of rapid prototyping technologies and the automation of building construction to indicate an experimental approach to the development of unique building components. However such a definition operates within the technical domain and is marginal to the conception of architecture and the urban environment.

3. In this conception "prototype" refers to an original type, form or instance of something serving as a typical example, basis or standard for other things of the same category. As such the term acquires a more challenging character than the alternative definition offered by architectural typology.

As De Landa points out:

> For the typologist the type (eidos) is real and the variation an illusion, while for the population thinker, the type (the average) is an abstraction and only the variation is real.
>
> Manuel De Landa, *Intensive Science and Virtual Philosophy*, London/New York: Continuum, 2002, p. 48

As such typologies are absent from the conception of the self-organizing city and are substituted by proto-types. **4.** Prototypes are here defined as contingent assemblages of a large number of components organized via multiple relationships. The emergent properties of these assemblages exceed the sum of their constituent parts. Regulated and evolved through feedback loops of interaction, prototypes differentiate in lineages that progressively develop specialist and dedicated behaviour, form and actual material organization.

Material system

1. When the matter of architecture is freed from the essentialist conception that considers it as a formless entity regulated by transcendental geometric rules, forms and proportions, it suddenly acquires potential for self-organization and becomes generative.

This generative potential can be harvested as a form of analogue computation to generate spatial and architectural solutions out of defined design problems.

Such a possibility however implies a conceptual shift from the understanding of buildings as the rational assemblage of discrete components to their formulation as self-similar structures made up of multiple discrete elements; we define these kinds of structures as material systems. **2.** Within this paradigm material organization becomes prominent as the overall capacity of the structure to self-organize will depend on the organizational principles controlling the relationships among the discrete elements. These principles will promote communication across scales, in which the particular is able to affect the general and vice-versa.

3. The overall material properties of such a system will then emerge from an iterative dialogue with the surrounding context, will evolve and adapt to change; moreover this adaptation will be mostly gradual, at least until a tipping point is reached.

Such a continuous understanding of material properties is crucial to the development of the self-organizing city and its prototypical structures whose articulation is no longer seen to produce a difference in kind but is redefined as a progressive difference in degree.

Diagrammatic design techniques

1. Organizational principles can be translated into diagrams of material organization; such a type of diagram has the ability to function as a design machine when deployed in a specific context and in relation to a specific design problem. In this circumstance the diagram becomes a sort of pre-architectonic platform of negotiation and more broadly, debate; the diagram is a design technique.

2. This specific use of the diagram has created a few misunderstandings as the word "technique" is often confused with the word "tool"; furthermore the confusion has increased with the increased popularity of computational and algorithmic design tools.

A computational design tool is a mere device, it is not inherently diagrammatic or generative; in fact in most cases sophisticated computational design tools are deployed to solve classic optimization or post-rationalization problems.

3. Our use of parametric and computational design tools is instead always devoted to the proliferation of a specific design diagram within a specific design context or environment:

> For the extraordinary diagram no defining routine practice has as yet crystallized. It is instead creatively engaged in the formation of such a (potentially reproducible) practice ... We might thus say that extraordinary diagrams are proto-representations.
>
> Patrik Schumacher, *The Autopoiesis of Architecture*, London: Wiley, 2010, p. 351.

These allow a design technique to operate as a sieve, scanning the environment and generating new operational territories of self-organization.

Soft- and real-time protocols

1. As spatial boundaries are re-described, time frames too need to be qualified with more specificity. Architecture is typically less concerned with time than with space but from the new systemic perspective time becomes an essential ingredient of any algorithmic design protocol. For the conception and evolution of the architectural machines described in this book we have, then, identified two distinct time frameworks: "soft" and "real" time.

In the two projects that follow we consider the design, digital simulation and manufacturing of the structures as "soft-time processes", conceptually separated from the live running of the experiments, defined as "real-time processes".

2. The two are however deeply interweaved and connected; "real time" feeds back into "soft time" and vice versa. In the next chapter we will speculate about the scenarios that could be imagined if this conceptual and practical separation were to be further evolved and blurred.

About ...

The **fibrous structures** are a series of prototypes investigating the architectural potential of rethinking spatial, structural and infrastructural typologies as collections of large numbers of linear filaments; these filaments are organized in a logical way to allow multiple interactions and ultimately to trigger processes of self-organization. Self-organizing fibres are capable of emergent qualities and surprising behaviour; moreover they exhibit adaptive potential to changing environments. Such qualities are well exploited by natural systems as well as by many pre-industrial civilizations that with limited resources have built and are still building fibrous architecture often exquisitely articulated and efficient.

However the history of Western architecture has, possibly ever since Vitruvius, accepted "firmitas" as one of its leading defining qualities; over the centuries this has evolved in the codes of architecture as a form of necessary rigidity, solidity, immobility. Architectural structures are rarely allowed to adapt, fluctuate, evolve over time; material redundancy is often considered wasteful while optimization is performed as a process of determination based on a priori codes and performance criteria.

The Fibrous Room experiment proposes an alternative model through direct experimentation with a prototype for a fibrous concrete structure; a fragment of a possibly very large fibrous architecture made from an innovative chemical mix of cement and polymeric microfibres and ancient weaving and bundling construction logics.

The critical implications of the fibrous experiments are not meant to refer solely to the structural domain; fibrous morphologies are explored in all their material, spatial and sensorial effects. The Aqva Garden project embodies a fibrous infrastructure: a water collection system turned into a water garden sited in a dense urban courtyard. The fibrous space can be experienced through all the senses; the fibrous articulation in fact expands the perceptual games possible with water and its transitional states. Similar spatial effects are explored in other temporary installations such as the Chiuina in La Paz, the Riverside Walk experiment in London or the Tropic Playground installation in Linz.

Recently our research has involved fibrous systems of information; here the fibrous organizational model has been deployed to explore the ability of architectural spaces to

IVY façade system study
model: stereolithography
of the woven structure
designed for the Centre
Point building in Oxford
Street, London

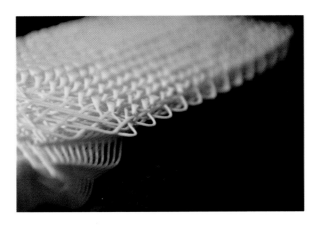

embody in their material organization their function as media interfaces between the multiple urban ecosystems and social subgroups.

The **ecoMachines** series was initiated almost by accident, in London, in the summer of 2006. During a walk in Victoria Park, an encounter with a local botanist triggered curiosity about the proliferating population of algae colonizing the local ponds. These organisms possess extraordinary properties which make them hyper-efficient energetic machines.

Even though algae farming has increasingly emerged as a popular alternative source of bio-fuel, many would consider algae as pests to be eliminated or at least encapsulated within artificial systems to exploit their photosynthetic potential without damage to the surrounding ecosystems.

Many micro-organisms share with algae, unlike flowers or other plants, regular designation as a threat. This can be ascribed to the fact that their peculiar nature makes them very hard to control, very difficult to choreograph or to organize according to our pleasure and convenience.

STEMv1.0 and subsequently STEMv2.0 and STEMv3.0 were conceived as experiments of architectural self-regulation, where architectural components, the Briccole, were engineered to host algal colonies and to turn them into a valuable building material. Algal architectures emerged, revealing unexpected potential in the choreographing of biological systems as part of hybrid architectural prototypes.

As the architect turned mediator of bio-machinic processes, architecture appeared transformed into a living system, embedded with potential for evolution and interaction, both within the environment and with an excited public. This realization was then further explored in the more recent versions of ecoMachines: the Urban Algae farms and Biodiversity Workshop projects. These latest prototypes have become real interfaces, mediating between large landscapes and natural ecosystems and the urban dweller, with all his/her curiosities and ecological paranoia. The ecoMachines are now instruments to transform architectural prototypes into new urban typologies capable of enhancing the interaction and mutual affection between the urban dweller and the natural and artificial urban ecologies.

STEMv1.0: living screen system with oxygenating algal capsules of varied density. Prototype model for the Seven Seven Gallery in Broadway Market, London

**From Fibrous Room
to Aqva Garden**

CATEGORY: **b2 Machines**
PROJECT TYPE: **b2:1 Fibrous
                structures**
PROJECT #:   **1**
LOCATION: **Milan, Italy; Venice, Italy; Istanbul, Turkey**
YEAR: **2007–08**

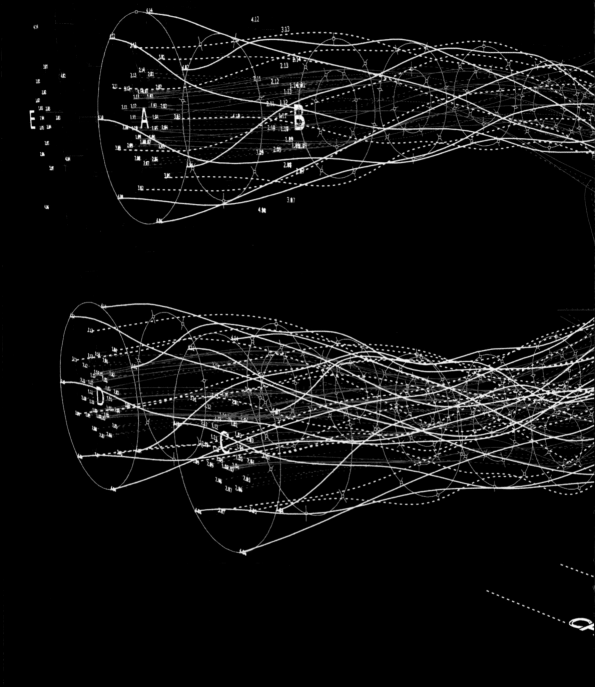

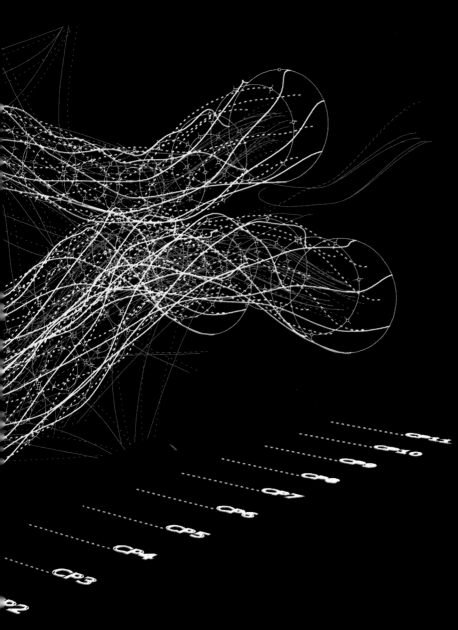

pp. 118–119
Fibrous Room exhibition:
front view of the main
structural prototype of
woven fibres minutes
before commencing the
concrete "pouring" phase
in Garanti Gallery, Istanbul

pp. 120–121
Fibrous structures
workshop: internal view
of woven fibrous concrete
proto-column developed in
ITU, Istanbul

this page
Fibrous Room exhibition:
3D digital associative model
of the complete woven
structure and related
fibrous system

Aqva Garden exhibition:
view of the branching
fibrous tensile structure,
the water percolating fibres
and the counterbalancing
water collection bulbs
during the opening testing
day, in central Milan

The Coral Garden
exhibition: detail of the
self-organized wax corals
developed by iterative
dipping of digitally
manufactured woollen
plaques into liquid wax

Introduction Fibrous structures are the structural and infrastructural skeleton of the self-organizing city; they embody the organizational principles of the city by organizing in space and time its material, informational and energetic flows. Dedicated digital parametric techniques and manufacturing logics enable us to focus on designing the architectural in-formation process. Rather than formal arrangements the "fibrous structures" describe informational protocols and embody their spatial, ornamental, energetic and structural implications.

The Fibrous Room experiment in the Garanti Gallery, Istanbul, was set up as a testing bed for designing a fibrous structural component made of concrete composite: conceived as an experimental "derive" in the field of architectural prototyping, structural design and material ornamentation, the experiment deployed an empirical design method by iterating a new proto-typing protocol guided by strictly defined rules of information.

As such the experiment operated first as a training ground in material disorientation; by means of an international collaborative student workshop it provoked questions such as how wide a series of relevant possibilities can we create in the context of designing, calculating and build-ing a concrete fibrous structure? What kind of new organizational possibilities are generated by recent innovations in the chemistry and material composition of concrete? What kind of new machines and casting procedures will emerge from the materialization of these novel organiza-tional diagrams?

Patterns, performance, prototypes and co-design The concept of pattern, which appears to be antagonistic to randomness, is key to the idea of emergence of coherent structures. In a complex fibrous assemblage a simple set of rules of local interaction triggers the overall system into complex forms of behaviour. Emerging behavioural patterns entail secrets about the overall system of emergent material organization, about the way it handles structural stress and adjusts

Fibrous Room exhibition: detail of the main structural prototype of woven fibres highlighting the weaving logic and the connecting steel discs

to ever-changing spatial configurations. Pattern recognition becomes a form of communication for material systems across scales, from the component to the architectural assemblage to the city.

In the Fibrous Room a 2D ornamental pattern borrowed from the local Arabic tradition defines a simple grid layout which organizes the single structural filaments onto the $x–z$ plane; the same pattern is then allowed to "extrude" and regulate the interaction among the filaments along the y axis. This interaction is then continuously evolved, updating the overall degree of connectivity of the fibrous structure; connectivity becomes the fourth dimension of the room.

Parametric modelling techniques proliferate geometrical rules over many simple entities, enabling large relational models to materialize. These relational structures, in their most diagrammatic form, can be actualized into machinic prototypes; the Fibrous Room is an example of such an architectural machine. The physical embodiment of the digital relational diagram is constituted by a series of processes regulated by related protocols and leads to the liberation of a multitude of material effects and spatial possibilities. This method of prototyping presupposes a form of relational thinking to drive the process of architectural production; as such prototyping techniques and related machineries are deployed as part of a production protocol that aims at maintaining constant openness and poise in the final spatial and material configurations. Parametric design is introduced to support interaction among the fibrous structural system and the other subsystems constituting its environment.

This model involves research and experimentation as the modus operandi for the architectural office, opening up new possibilities in the creation of larger structures of participation and co-design.

The Fibrous Room The Fibrous Room was set up in the Garanti Gallery space opening up onto Istanbul's busiest street, Istiklal Caddesi. The main machinic diagram of a Fibrous Room was directly exposed to thousands of people and tourists, who were encouraged to enter the room and become part of the experiment.

The room frame was a steel structure of approximately 3 x 3 x 8 m, functioning as a constraining device for the fibrous assemblage. Such a device allowed a controlled manipulation of the fibres and a coherent transmission of information from the digital diagram to the physical embodied structure; the frame and its constraining devices were a machinic casting formwork.

In the Fibrous Room the diagrammatic lines were translated into two sets of structural fibre: thick supporting ones, with a hollow diameter of 6 cm, and tendons, thin plastic strips of about 1 cm diameter. The two sets were organized on the $x–z$ plane by a classic Arabic decorative motif visible from the large window of the gallery, connecting the Fibrous Room back to a well-known ornamental language along the streets of Istanbul. However this familiar pattern was deployed in the room to materialize a rather novel and extraneous material organism.

The extrusion of the fibres along the y axis of the room was achieved by means of a weaving operator, not dissimilar to that typical in basket making. This pre-industrial technique and structuring logic was part of the fibrous structure's research protocol, together with bundling, knitting and branching operators. These organizational principles are present not only in human civilization but in many biological organisms, plants for example, allowing them to grow, reconfigure and self-repair. In our socio-technological history they have been used for their ability to achieve resistance together with flexibility and for their applicability to many fibrous materials found in nature independently from their quality and homogeneity; weaving has since remained in the tradition of Islamic culture in two-dimensional representations or patterns that decorate buildings and mosques in Istanbul and elsewhere. Re-addressing this tradition has become possible through digital technologies and, in this experiment, thanks to innovation in the chemistry of cement mixtures; as such the Fibrous Room acquires special relevance as an experiment in post-industrial architectural manufacturing.

Woven structures cannot be defined geometrically with Euclidean exactitude but they can easily be defined locally as parametric relational diagrams to generate virtual fibrous fields.

In the Fibrous Room three sets of large hollow fibres were extracted from the computational field and materialized within the room's frame. These main supporting fibres were woven across the room into three bundles and interconnected in their centre of mass to create a coherent structural component. Special connections distributed the stresses among all the fibres in each bundle and downwards towards the ground while maintaining structural flexibility and geometric adaptability.

Another three sets of fibres, the tendons, were then woven through the main bundles and the connectors and secured to the external frame. This set-up constituted the basic framework for the Fibrous Room machine to function.

Parametric adaptation becomes possible and can be performed to achieve the desired initial deformation of the structure and at the same time give tension to each fibre.

One night, at 2 a.m., a Lafarge truck was granted access to the gallery and the concrete pumping phase started. A specially developed fibre-reinforced and super fluid cement mix was injected into each supporting filament. One by one all the filaments were filled up, radically altering their material status and the equilibrium of forces in the Fibrous Room. This condition of instability liberated the process of material self-organization; novel effects were harvested within the Fibrous Room mechanism; the newly developed plasticity of Lafarge's fibrous concrete actualized as a specific spatial quality in the new configuration of the Fibrous Room. The machinic prototype was able to harness the potential of the fibrous concrete to its structural limits to materialize new spatial and material effects.

Now operating as an analogue computer the Fibrous Room started a process of material computation that continued during the entire curing time of the concrete, constantly readjusting its form to optimize the distribution of internal stresses. As some tendons became loose in the process, re-tensioning of the assemblage was performed regularly by the room staff and visitors until final hardening.

As the solutions were processed in real time, the audience was made aware of and partici-pated in the in-formation process; as the Fibrous Room becomes alive, experimentation equals participation and interaction.

this page
Fibrous Room exhibition: detail of the pivoting joint connecting the main structural fibres to the tendons

facing page
Fibrous Room exhibition: the main woven beams minutes after pouring the fibre-reinforced concrete mix by LaFarge

Aqva Garden The Aqva Garden prototype is a fibrous structure developed by means of an inverse branching operator applied onto a single bundle of 256 tubular netting fibres. The bundle starts in a single point, a water source positioned on the roof of a Milanese courtyard block. After five generations of bifurcations the fibres reach the ground, filling up the courtyard space and ending in 256 water collection bags; as more water flows, the weight of each bag changes constantly with its evaporation and/or collection altering the pattern of tensional stresses within the tenso-structure and as a result redefining the overall configuration of the system.

Bags can be emptied by users and their position changed, causing further readjustments of the overall configuration of the garden in real time.

Microclimatic spaces Aqva Garden operates as an artificial garden that functions as a distributed rain collector and water storage system. Unlike conventional recycling systems Aqva Garden doesn't hide its functional apparatus; rather it embodies it in its structural matrix, the branching system. This allows an expansion of the climatic effects latent within the management of water and its transitional states (e.g. evaporation). Rainwater becomes the protagonist of perceptual games and gardening processes, opening new potentials in the conception of ecological infrastructures for the built environment.

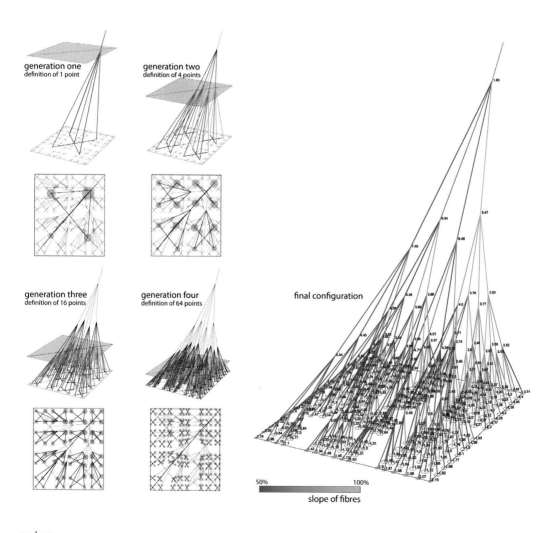

generation one
definition of 1 point

generation two
definition of 4 points

generation three
definition of 16 points

generation four
definition of 64 points

final configuration

50%   100%
slope of fibres

this page
Aqva Garden exhibition:
view of the rainwater
garden and water collection
bulbs after two days of
springtime testing in
central Milan

facing page
Aqva Garden: 3D digital
associative model of the
complete branching tensile
structure and related
rainwater percolation and
storing potential

{

// The fibrous structures protocol describes the design of architectural material
// systems through fibrous components, where the properties of the assemblage
// exceed the sum of the properties of each single component both in terms of
// structural performance and of their capacity to respond to environmental
// stimuli and spatial requirements.
// The protocol includes multiple levels of instructions:

a. Fibrous logic and organizational principles
{The basic component is a generic fibrous lineament}
{Its proliferation produces a generic yet rigorous structural assemblage}
{Its proliferation is organized by means of logic operators such as weaving, bundling, knitting and branching} ❶
{The fibrous assemblages change in time and space, and are functions of human interaction and environmental adaptation}

b. Organizational parameters
{number of fibres in each assemblage}
{length of fibres}
{diameter of fibres}
{relative distance of fibres}
{number and frequency of intersection points}
{relative distance of intersection points}

c. Structural principles
{Stress must be redistributed internally within the filaments of each assemblage}
{Individual filaments must be able to adjust their geometry independently}
{There must be a controlled exchange of forces in each intersection point}
{Filaments need to be under tensional stress at all times}

d. Structural parameters
{stress levels within each fibre}
{deformation of the bundle}
{local curvature variation of each fibre}
{translation in space of each intersection point}

e. Material principles
{Fibres are composite materials}
{Fibres' material properties change in time and space}
{Fibres' material properties are a function of the conditions of the surrounding environment} ❷
{Material properties within the bundle are non-homogeneous}

f. Material parameters
{material density}
{material viscosity}
{material bending moment}
{material tensional resistance}
{material transparency}

❶

❷

g. Environmental principles

{Each fibre is able to sense the environment}

{Each fibre must adapt its properties to minimize environmentally induced stresses}

{Each fibre must produce a perceivable modification of the surrounding environment}

h. Environmental parameters

{microclimatic descriptors (humidity, temperature, incidental radiation) }

i. Interaction principles

{Each fibre must be adjustable}

{Adjustability must be measurable}

{The assemblages are redundant additive systems: more fibres can always be added or subtracted to the assemblage at any time}

how to 1 : Soft time: definition of fibrous logic and organizational principles
{
    // Virtual definition of three-dimensional material organizations.
    // The introduction of logic operators allows the proliferation of
    // relationships among the single fibrous components.

    1.1 {Parametrize a 2D Arabic pattern as an arrangement of connection points on the x–z plane; adjust scale and resolution}
    1.2 {Import a generic fibrous lineament as a basic spline component}
    1.3 {Proliferate the component on the two-dimensional arrangement of points in order to produce a generic non-connected structural assemblage}
    1.4 {Re-arrange the proliferation by means of the weaving logic operator in order to produce an interconnected structural pattern along the y axis} ❶
    Refine → 1.1 Proliferation by adjusting x–z resolution and 1.4 by adjusting y frequency
}

how to 2 : Soft time: introduction of fibre's definition
{
    // Definition of the features of the fibres. Compute individual behaviour and
    // observe overall system's response.

    2.1 {Set the number of fibres in each assemblage}
    2.2 {Determine the length and diameter of the fibres}
    2.3 {Set relative distance of fibres on x–z}
        Refine → 1.1 Resolution
        Refine → 1.4 Logic operator
    2.4 {Arrange number, frequency and relative distance of the intersection points along y axis}
        Plug into → 3.2 Design of stress distribution and stress exchange components and propping elements
    2.5 {Loop back to 2.1 for second set of nested fibres}
}

❶ >

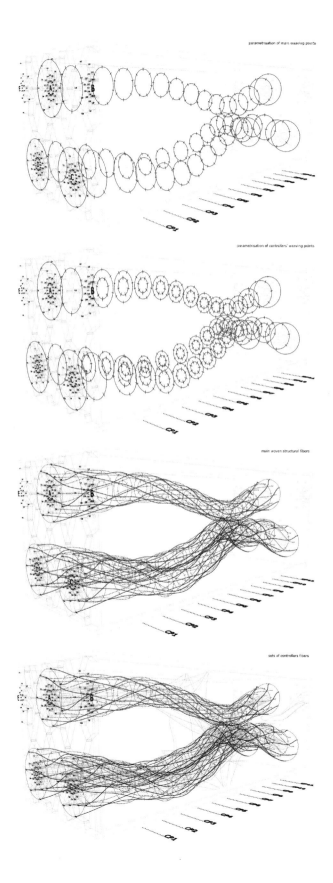

parametrisation of main weaving points

parametrisation of controllers' weaving points

main woven structural fibers

sets of controllers fibers

how to 3 : Real time: experimenting with material systems

{

    // "Soft" diagrams of fibrous organizations are actualized by means of material
    // operators and concrete pouring techniques.

    3.1 {Testing bed: structural and material differentiation by organizational logic.
        Prototypes of 3D woven and bundled structures} ❶
    3.2 {Testing bed: structural and material differentiation by pouring technique.
        Pumping and percolating concrete}
    3.3 {Extract rules of behaviour from prototypical material systems}
        Refine → 1.3 Logic operators and 2.1 Single element analysis ❷

}

how to 4 : Real time: designing the relational machine

{

    // Construction devices for the prototyping of fibrous structures are developed
    // as a new breed of relational frames or machines.

    4.1 {Create a structural frame for fibrous organization} ❸
    4.2 {Assemble the relational system following the digital diagram}
    4.3 {Prop fibres with tendons and nodal connections}
    4.4 {Give tension to the fibres to promote frictional collaboration within the
        woven bundle}

}

how to 5 : Real time: relational adaptation

{

    // Processes of morphological and structural adaptation emerge from the
    // relationships among fibres and tendons; such behaviours are registered and
    // bred to achieve coherent material organization.

    5.1 {Allow individual fibres to adjust their geometry within the overall system}
    5.2 {Tighten tendons} ❹
        Regulates → 5.1 Adjusting of filaments
    5.3 {Overall fibrous layout is modified by the behaviour of each single fibre}
    5.4 {Nodal connections adapt their position to filaments' and tendons'
        behaviour}
        Regulates → 3.5 Propping of the structure
        Refine → 2.2 Fibres' definition

}

❹

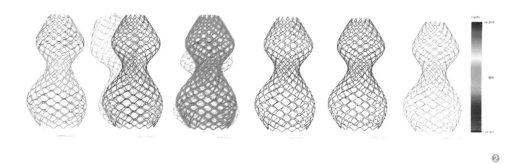

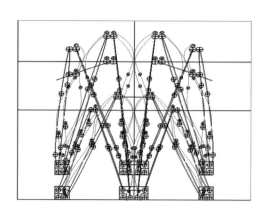

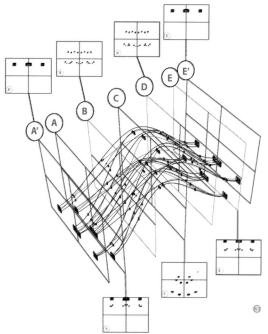

how to 6 : Real time: developing new material definitions
{
> // A new fibrous concrete mixture is developed with Lafarge's chemical experts
> // to achieve maximum pumping/percolating potential while retaining high
> // curing qualities and final flexibility.

> 6.1 {Define mixture of concrete, chemical additives and aggregate microfibres
> to be pumped into main fibres' bundles}  ❶
> 6.2 {Pump concrete mixture into the filaments} ❷
> Refine → 6.1 Concrete mix for easy pumping
> 6.3 {Observe and test density and viscosity of the concrete mixture affecting
> the behaviour of the fibres during and after the hardening process}
> Refine → 6.1 Concrete mix for maximum adherence to hose and maximum
> flexibility after hardening
> Plug into → 8.1 Environmental influence
> Plug into → 9.1 Fibres' adaptability
}

how to 7 : Real time: material adaptation
{
> // The Fibrous Room operates as an analogue computer producing further
> // overall adjustment depending on the properties of the concrete mixture and
> // on the logic operators.

> 7.1 {Fibres adapt their shape during and after the pumping process}
> 7.2 {Bùndles and tendons are deformed by new forces that proliferate across
> the Fibrous Room}
> 7.3 {Tighten the tendons to allow a re-tensioning of the fibres}
> 7.4 {The overall system self-organizes under the pressure of new forces and
> constraints}
> Regulates → 5.1 Overall layout and 5.4 Nodal connection position
}

❷

how to 8 : Real time: environmental mediation
{
// Microclimatic features (humidity, temperature, incidental solar radiation) of the
// environment affect each single fibre that transfers its behaviour to the whole
// system. The Fibrous Room mediates these tensions and adjusts, generating
// novel spatial effects.

    8.1 {Fibres sense the contingent environmental conditions}
    8.2 {Fibres minimize environmentally induced stresses, adapting their properties}
    8.3 {Each perceivable modification of a fibre affects the overall system and the
       surrounding environment} ❶
       Regulates → 5.1 Overall layout
    8.4 {The Fibrous Room environment is, in turn, altered}
       Plug into → 8.1 Fibres sense the changing environment
}

how to 9 : Real time: interaction
{
// Modifications of the Fibrous Room are perceived by the public, who can
// respond by manipulating the tendons, adding/pumping more concrete,
// climbing the main bundles. The fibrous system in turn reacts with a "global"
// behavioural adjustment to the new stress field.

    9.1 {Add concrete to a bundle of fibres}
    9.2 {Manipulate the tendons' fibres}
    9.3 {Climb a bundle of fibres} ❷
       Regulates → 5.1 Overall layout
    9.4 {Add redundancy to the fibrous assemblage at any time by introducing new
       tendons and/or new connecting points}
}

❶

❷ >

STEMv3.0: the Venice Lagoon Experiment for the 2008 Venice Architecture Biennale; manual weaving of the tensional columns of the "Briccole". These algorithmically developed prototypes for the management of the lagoon soil erosion also constitute the nodes of a new bio-fuel infrastructure for the Venice lagoon

[b2:2.2] The STEM
          series

CATEGORY: b2 Machines
PROJECT TYPE: b2:2 EcoMachines
PROJECT #:   2
LOCATION: Seville, Spain; Venice, Italy; Trento, Italy
YEAR: 2008–11

pp. 146–147
STEMv1.0: detail of the
living screen system with
oxygenating algal capsules
of varied density. Prototype
model for the Seven
Seven Gallery in Broadway
Market, London

this page
STEMv2.0: the Guadalquivir
Experiment for the Seville
Architecture Biennale. View
of the oxygenating screen
and the photo bioreactor
bricks containing samples
of the Guadalquivir waters

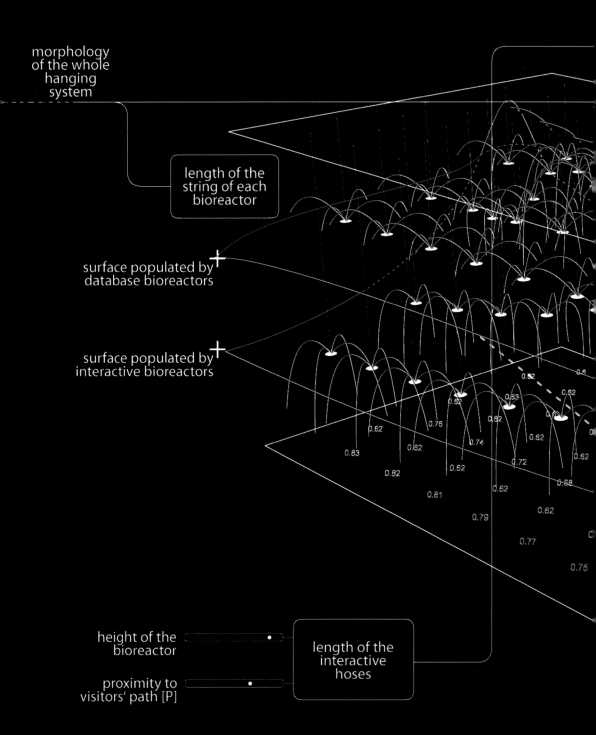

morphology
of the whole
hanging
system

length of the
string of each
bioreactor

surface populated by
database bioreactors

surface populated by
interactive bioreactors

0.52   0.6

0.53   0.52

0.52   0.52

0.52   0.6

0.76   0.62   0.62

0.74

0.62   0.62

0.83   0.62   0.72   0.62

0.82   0.52   0.68

0.81   0.52

0.62

0.79

0.62

0.77   0

0.75

height of the
bioreactor

proximity to
visitors' path [P]

length of the
interactive
hoses

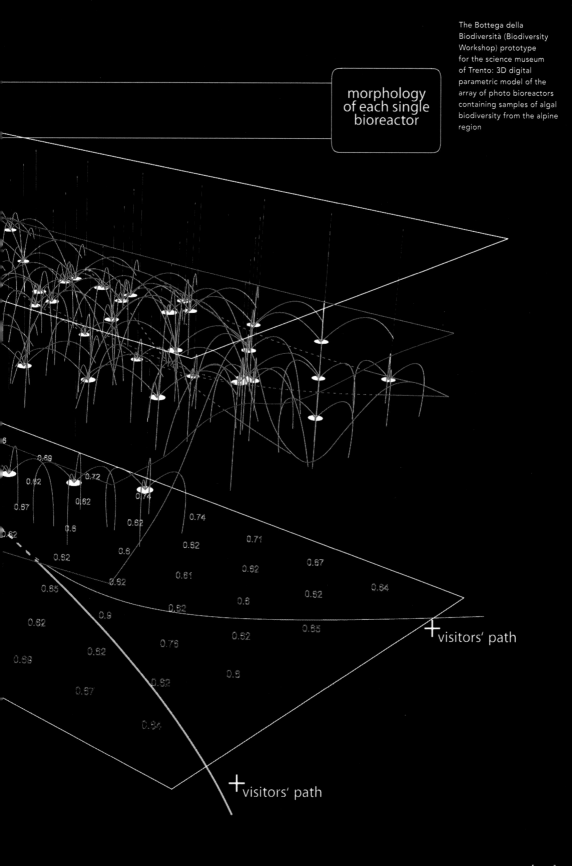

morphology
of each single
bioreactor

The Bottega della
Biodiversità (Biodiversity
Workshop) prototype
for the science museum
of Trento: 3D digital
parametric model of the
array of photo bioreactors
containing samples of algal
biodiversity from the alpine
region

⊹ visitors' path

⊹ visitors' path

STEMv2.0: the Guadalquivir Experiment for the Seville Architecture Biennale. Top detail of the photo bioreactor bricks with oxygenating hairs, LED visual feedback on cultivation frequency and growth monitoring system

Introduction   The STEM series of prototype installations continues ecoLogicStudio's research
into the living material of algae as a potential building component. In common with much of the
ecoMachines oeuvre, the projects aim to reconcile the supposed opposition between ecology and
technology into an instrument of research towards the definition of a new form of hybrid materiality.

The basic building component of STEM, first developed for the 2006 London Architecture Biennale, was a "bioreactor": a contained ecosphere in which algae are supplied with light, nutrients
and CO_2. A cluster of clear plastic bottles containing water from different lakes and rivers in London
were stacked into a wall, and the growth of life within them created a pixilated green screen. This
demonstrated the idea of a "differentiated field", an environment of varying degrees of habitable
space, which is connected to the biological processes occurring within that environment.

The FUNcloud proposal for the 2007 Urbantine Competition suggested this basic idea as a
three-dimensional matrix. Conceived as a simple piece of "furniture", this iteration consisted of
a series of parametrically constructed blocks, the card exoskeleton of which defined the amount
of screening offered, the photosynthetic potential and the structural stability of the individual
components.

Each successive installation has adapted to the particular urban and natural circumstances of
its host city to demonstrate how the architect or engineer can analyse, design, assess and tune
a system which can be applicable in multiple scenarios. This process of refinement necessitates
another central concept of ecoMachines, that of human behaviour: the interactions between the
users and the bioreactors are recorded, allowing visual representation of the multiple levels of
feedback that occur within the system.

Oxy-generation and self-regulation   STEMv2.0, an installation for the 2008 Seville Architecture
Biennale, extended this concept with the invention of an "oxygen-creating interaction machine".
The bioreactors were contained within Briccoles which were treated almost as masonry elements,
stacked to build a curved wall. This performed roles of spatial definition, screening of light and
release of oxygen into the gallery space. At the collective scale the installation was conceived
as a self-regulating screening device. The more light that was absorbed, the greater the bloom
of algae and the greater the screening of the space. The less light each unit received, the

STEMv2.0: the
Guadalquivir Experiment.
Detail of photo
bioreactors during
"feeding"; CO_2 is blown
directly into the block
releasing the oxygen
bubbles generated
during photosynthesis

less photosynthesis occured and the transparency of the wall increased. The "found objects" (environmental factors such as the layout of the wall and the particular micro-ecologies contained in the bioreactors) became integral parts of the conversation between man and ecology.

The concept of communication and interaction exploited the fact that visitors to the exhibition would add CO_2 to the bioreactors, so that the algal bloom – and the variegated environment of light and oxygen created by it – was continually altered by the people who occupied the space. By evolving the design of the bioreactors whereby clear plastic tubes emerged from the body of the machine, a soft, malleable, inviting exterior was created. Users were encouraged to exhale into the tubes, introducing a symbiotic relationship between the permanent and transient elements of the installation.

In order to introduce an element of self-regulation, the blocks were allowed to "talk" to the visitors: the intensity of their LEDs indicated the degree to which they required oxygen. A brighter LED, being more noticeable, would encourage interaction; until enough interactions had occurred and the need for oxygen was less pressing.

Initially, the spread of solar radiation throughout the gallery space and the algorithm used to map the interaction and layout of the installation created the differentiated environment. However, as soon as visitors interacted with the blocks the spread of transparency and screening became unpredictable, resulting in a continuously evolving space. The study and understanding of how this dialogue between user, machine and environment can be tweaked by the designer suggest further applications rich with cybernetic potential.

Within the feedback loops of the system as a whole, several parameters can be adjusted. The physical structure of the Briccole wall, the layout of the installation and the design of the tubes affect the interaction potential, and therefore the amount of CO_2 that is supplied to the bioreactors. This is in turn related to the light and photosynthesis feedback loop, where the positioning of artificial lights and the inbuilt tendency of the algae to create their own shade, thus limiting their growth, create equilibrium within the oxygenation feedback loop. Added to these are the systems of record and memory, where minor changes in software programming or adjustments to the sensitivity of sensors allow the designer to shape the outcome of the experiment while retaining its inherent unpredictability.

Subsequent projects built on other specific aspects of the STEM machinery. The installation for the 2008 Venice Architecture Biennale examined the natural processes of the lagoon and suggested a number of ways in which ecoMachines could "plug in" to such an ecosystem. Referencing cultural and historical elements such as navigational buoys, a catalogue of "lagoon condensers" was developed; these acted as incubators, containers and research tools for the ecology of the region. This jump in scale – from furniture to landscape – represents the continuing development of a provocative attempt to explore the potential of farming, harvesting and extracting biomass within an architectural framework.

The most recent iteration of STEM was installed at the Trento Museum for the 2010 Biennale of alpine and mountain landscapes (ALPS 2010). Based on the same precept of interactivity, the installation allows researchers to monitor the development of the algae colonies populating the project.

From ten lakes of the Trentino region (Garda, Cavedine, Toblino, Santa Massenza, Terlago, Levico, Caldonazzo, Lamar, Serraia and Tovel), samples were collected from three different zones: shore, centre superficial water, centre deep water. Over the course of a month the 70 bioreactors in the installation were analysed at microscopic level to determine the qualitative and quantitative composition of algal species present. As well as a further investigation into how STEM could be extended into the scale of landscape, the Trento installation initiated a dialogue between the work of architects, manipulating natural systems within a design framework, and the more scientific method of laboratory biologists.

Furthermore, the central spatial setting of the Trento exhibition, the Bottega della Biodiversità (Biodiversity Workshop) begins to suggest a physical arena of collaboration where architects and designers who are involved in the more speculative areas of the discipline can meet with other concerned parties. The "Bottega" in this case is a room-within-a-room structure of timber latticework in which the bioreactors are suspended, their position in the matrix representing where each sample was obtained. Depending on the user's requirements, it can be meeting place, display or laboratory. ecoLogicStudio describes this architectural setting as a "prototypical social space", a built structure that questions the role and reach of systemic architecture and its limitations. To what extent must architecture be client-led, and how can it create conditions in which it can become a critical practice? How does experimental design offer its "value" in an industry which defines that term purely economically, in situations where returns may not be immediately evident? By defining a place of exchange where private research can be connected to the public communication on which it increasingly depends, the architect can demonstrate the feasibility of inserting programmatic elements into speculative work.

The "Bottega" suggests a small, independent, practical laboratory where interested members of the public, aspiring students and academic researchers can observe, experiment, analyse and share results. It places emphasis on the active and investigative rather than passive and prescriptive. In a sense, this mirrors the activities (in an architectural sphere) of ecoLogicStudio, which is developing into a forum where material, manufacturing and systemic experiments can take place across a wide range of projects, providing a facility for the ambitious apprentice to hone skills and ideas. This space of production can be traced back to the workshops and guilds of medieval Florence and London, and this reference can be seen as a commentary on current politics of knowledge dissemination. At a time when the role of the state in providing a system of centralized education is under particular scrutiny, the discussion of such a system of reactive, decentralized learning units would seem prescient.

On the larger scale, these experiments ask how, as designers and participants, we interact with the mechanized, hybrid ecological tools which are likely to be increasingly important as we search for a technological fix for our irrepressible need to consume, build, expand and colonize. The systems of control, regulation and equilibrium they investigate fit neatly into a theory of cybernetics which stresses observation and "steersmanship" rather than top-down strategic thinking on landscape and urbanism.

STEMv3.0: the Venice Lagoon Experiment. Detail of the "bio-Briccole" during "feeding"; CO_2 is blown releasing oxygen and triggering oscillatory behaviour in the woven tensional column (designed to increase sedimentation and reduce soil erosion)

The Bottega della Biodiversità (Biodiversity Workshop) prototype: detail of the photo bioreactor with feeding pipes and LED feedback "cultivation" system

how to 0 : STEMv2.0: the Guadalquivir Experiment
{
  // STEMv2.0 is an architectural ecoMachine, a system of multiple,
  // interconnected feedback loops embedded into a spatial matrix. Physical,
  // biological, chemical and design processes occur simultaneously, subject to
  // their own internal regulation and influences from external loops. In STEM2.0
  // the architectural structure functions as a host for algal cultures which are
  // unable to conduct an independent life outside water; conversely algae are
  // extremely efficient oxygen-making and energetic machines and function as
  // active biological components to an otherwise inert artificial structure.
  // Such a relationship unfolds in time and is open to evolution: for the purposes
  // of this method statement, describing the so-called Guadalquivir Experiment,
  // the manufacturing of the structure ("soft-time processes") has been separated
  // from the live running of the experiment ("real-time processes"). The two are
  // certainly connected, but the designer's initial control of morphology and
  // system layout, algae and water testing is run at a different timescale and level
  // to the installation proper. This does not preclude "real-time processes" from
  // feeding back into "soft-time processes", or, in other words, algal structures
  // evolving and absorbing certain functionalities of the Briccoles.
  // The "actions" defined below represent a catalogue of connections between
  // system operations, which overlap the two timescales.

  a. Actions
  {Design actions – choices of planning and control}
  {Systemic actions – automatic physical, biological or chemical processes that
  the designer can initiate but has no outright control over}

  {Plug into: Contributing design action to a successive step}
  {Refine: Recursive design action to a previous step}
  {Affects: Contributing systemic action to a successive step}
  {Regulates: Recursive systemic action to a previous step}

}

STEMv2.0: the
Guadalquivir
Experiment.
Digital parametric
model of photo
bioreactor brick

STEMv2.0: the Guadalquivir Experiment. Wiring the Arduino controllers for the feedback, "cultivation" and memory systems

[feedback to
urban river
ecologies]

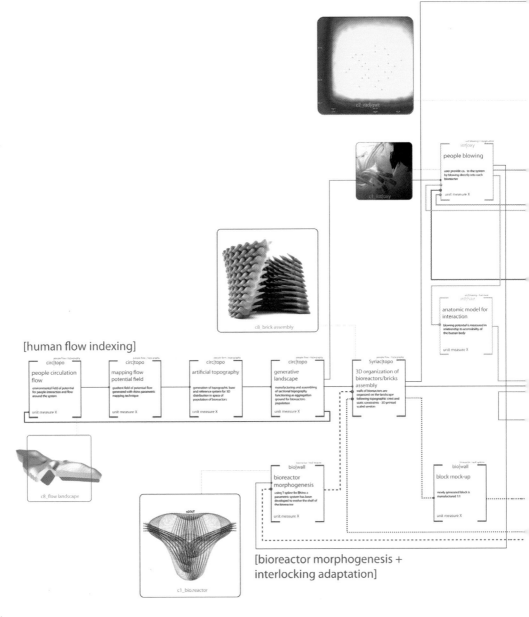

people blowing

user provide co₂ to the system
by blowing directly into each
bioreactor

unit measure X

anatomic model for
interaction

blowing potential is measured in
relationship to accessibility of
the human body

unit measure X

c8_brick assembly

[human flow indexing]

circ|topo

people circulation
flow

environmental field of potential
for people interaction and flow
around the system

unit measure X

circ|topo

mapping flow
potential field

gradient field of potential flow
generated with rhino parametric
mapping technique

unit measure X

circ|topo

artificial topography

generation of topographic base
and reference system for 3D
distribution in space of
population of bioreactors

unit measure X

circ|topo

generative
landscape

manufacturing and assembling
of sectional topography
functioning as aggregation
ground for bioreactors
population

unit measure X

Syriac|topo

3D organization of
bioreactors/bricks
assembly

walls of bioreactors are
organized on the landscape
following topographic crest and
static constraints 3D printed
scaled version

c8_flow landscape

bio|wall

bioreactor
morphogenesis

using T-spline for Rhino a
parametric system has been
developed to evolve the shell of
the bioreactor

unit measure X

bio|wall

block mock-up

newly generated block is
manufactured 1:1

unit measure X

c1_bio.reactor

[bioreactor morphogenesis +
interlocking adaptation]

STEMv2.0: the Guadalquivir Experiment. The overall cybernetic diagram regulating the ecoMachinic prototype installation

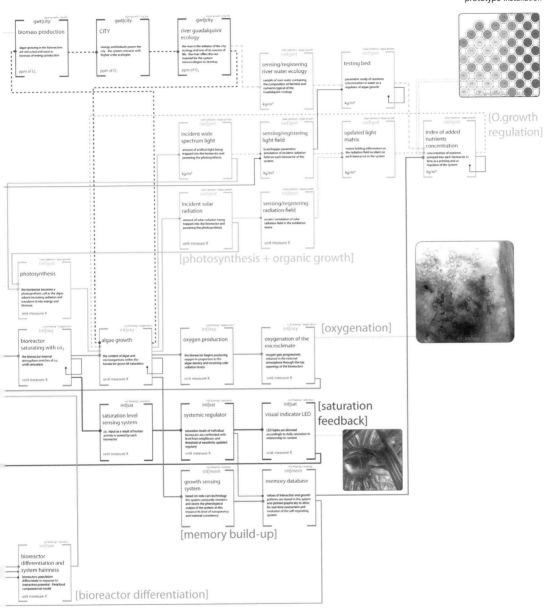

how to 1 : Real time: oxygenation and carbon sequestration

{

// Developed initially as an oxygenating cloud, STEM absorbs CO_2 from the
// atmosphere and produces and releases pure oxygen to the surroundings.
// Rather than simply representational or descriptive, STEM is an
// operational prototype, equipped with systems of mapping, cataloguing and
// annotating that are becoming the essential architectural elements involved
// in the project. The geometric analysis of the environment and the constructed
// elements within it allow the designer to structure the experimental space
// and the flows of matter information and energy in and out of it; continuous
// environmental data are stored in discrete material components that can be
// understood architecturally. The designer's agency in the machinic process is
// essential, as a system of measurement (of nutrient levels, light, interaction,
// CO_2 sequestrated) has to be designed. In other words, what is important is
// not the absolute measuring of energetic flows through the Briccoles but rather
// their levels relative to each other. This concept of relational rather than
// absolute measurement builds in flexibility and points towards a creative,
// designed solution rather than one which relies on the purely scientific,
// analytical approach.

1.1 {User exhalation: contribute CO_2 to the system by blowing directly into each
    bioreactor} ❶

1.2 {CO_2 saturation: bioreactor internal environment enriched with CO_2 to the
    point of saturation}
    Affects → 5.1 Saturation sensing

1.3 {Algal growth: content of algae and micro-organisms within the bioreactor
    grows to saturation} ❷
    Affects → 4.4 Incidence of artificial light
    Affects → 4.6 Incidence of solar radiation
    Affects → 7.1 Biomass extraction

1.4 {Oxygen growth: bioreactor begins producing oxygen in proportion to algae
    density and incoming solar radiation levels}

1.5 {Environment oxygenation: oxygen progressively released in the external
    atmosphere through four vent openings in the bioreactors}

}

❷

❶ >

how to 2 : Soft time: intercepting human flow
{
    // Potential patterns of circulation and occupancy are registered and simulated;
    // such path systems are projected onto an emerging new artificial landscape
    // which sustains the oxygenating cloud; the new topography intercepts and
    // influences the behaviour of visitors as they move around the space, capturing
    // their attention and engaging them in the "cultivation" experiment.

    2.1 {Map circulation of users around environment}
    2.2 {Generate gradient field of potential visitor with Rhino parametric mapping
        technique} ❶
    2.3 {Generate topographic base} ❷
    2.4 {Manufacture and assemble sectional topography to function as aggregation
        ground for bioreactor population}
        Refine → 2.1 Circulation of users around environment
    2.5 {Generate 3D arrangement of Briccoles: design wall to run along crest of
        topographic environment} ❸
        Plug into → 3.5 Hairiness evolution and 4.7 Light matrix
}

❸

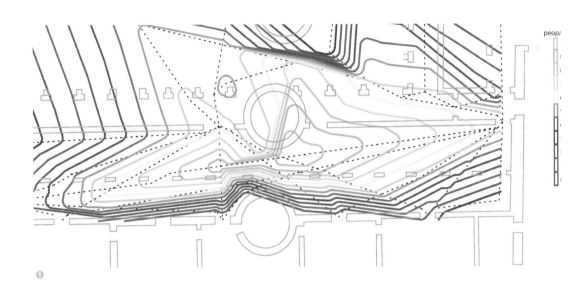

peop/

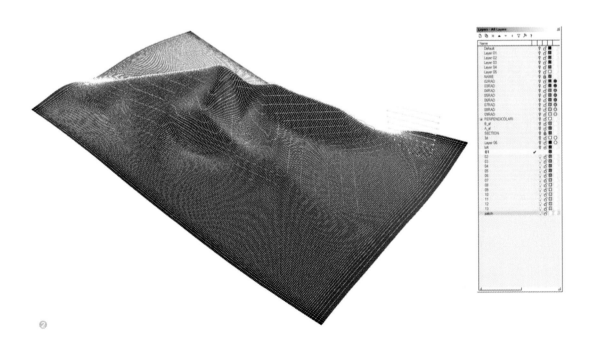

{

// The need for interaction and feeding has induced the Briccoles to evolve into
// interlocking building blocks, with four limbs that would extend and form the
// point of communication with visitors.
// Briccole bioreactors evolve a greater degree of complexity, with an internal
// system of transparent tubes that would be used to add CO_2 to the internal
// chambers of each element. The extent to which the tubes protrude from the
// body of the bioreactor influences interaction potential.

3.1 {Briccole morphogenesis: use Rhino and T-Spline to create suitable forms
for the shell of the bioreactor. Parameters include extension, height and
stacking pattern} ❶
Plug into → 2.5 3D arrangement of Briccoles

3.2 {Briccole manufacture: vacuum-form shells and prepare for installation of
"intestines", LEDs and sensors} ❷

3.3 {Test Briccoles for form and interlocking}
Refine → 3.1 Briccole morphogenesis

3.4 {Anatomic model of interaction: measure potential in relation to the human
body. Interaction potential will increase as the Briccoles near human head
height}

3.5 {Hairiness evolution of Briccoles defined in relation to 3D arrangement: in
addition to the vertical factor in 3.4, define interaction potential according
to the position of the Briccoles along a curve}
Affects → 1.1 People blowing

}

❷

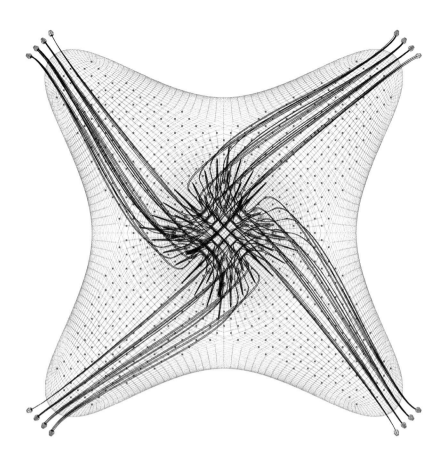

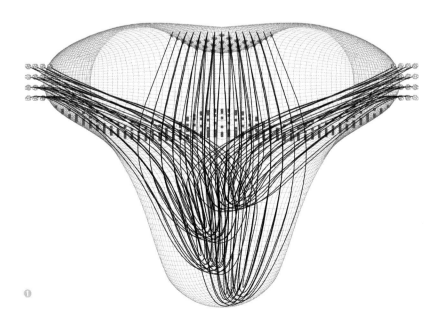

f/2	0,15 ml/l	0,20 ml/l	0,25 ml/l	0,30 ml/l	0,35 ml/l	0,40 ml/l
none						
4x 1cm						
8x 1cm						
8wx 1cm						
8wx 4cm						
8wx 8cm						
8wx 12cm						
8wx 16cm						
8wx 20cm						
8wx 24cm						
8wx 30cm						

how to 4 : Real time: photosynthesis and environmental radiation
{
    // The oxygenating engine of STEM is powered by a biochemical process
    // called photosynthesis that allows algae to synthesize solar energy to grow
    // and "breathe". STEM is informed by a prototype "bioreactor" constructed
    // to measure in a controlled environment the optimal amount of nutrients that
    // would encourage the algae to bloom under certain light conditions. Water
    // from the Guadalquivir River is placed into ten transparent tubes that make up
    // the "intestines" of the bioreactor. A nutrient solution is added in increasing
    // gradations and the bioreactor exposed to 16 hours of "daylight" followed by
    // eight hours of darkness. The results are recorded with a digital camera and
    // time lapsed to demonstrate how the distribution of nutrient levels has
    // affected algal growth within the apparatus.
    // This testing bed is used to fine-tune a digital virtual environment of the
    // gallery and a parametric model of STEM: the model is set up in order to
    // measure the light that each Briccole would receive from the three artificial
    // lights embedded in the cloud in relation to their angle of vertical and
    // horizontal incidence. This predictive mapping allows the designer to place
    // lights and alter nutrient levels in response to predicted and then real-time
    // algal growth.

    4.1 {Existing ecology test: obtain samples of the local water of the region,
          containing pre-existing biological life and nutrients. Analyse water samples
          to determine types of potential algae growth}
    4.2 {Testing bed: perform parametric study of nutrient concentration in water as
          a stimulator of algae growth}
    4.3 {Index of added nutrients: create map to chart results of 4.2 testing bed
          against the 4.9 composite light matrix}
          Affects → 4.8 Photosynthesis
    4.4 {Incidence of artificial light: arrange multiple wide-spectrum lights to boost
          photosynthetic potential of bioreactors}
    4.5 {Artificial light field: use parametric software to calculate how 4.4 will
          affect each bioreactor. Values represent fractions of the maximum artificial
          radiation available reaching the surface of each Briccole} ❶ <overleaf>
    4.6 {Incidence of solar radiation: natural daylight and sunlight enter the
          environment} ❷ <see p. 172>
    4.7 {Solar radiation light field: use parametric software to calculate how 4.6 will
          affect each bioreactor}
          4.4 and 4.6 combined to create:
    4.8 {Photosynthesis: bioreactor receives light radiation and nutrients and
          becomes a photosynthetic cell. Total absorption of both natural and
          artificial light is combined}
          Affects → 1.3 Algal growth
          4.5 and 4.7 combined to create:
    4.9 {Composite light matrix: record aggregated radiation to each Briccole and
          apply nutrient distribution calculation} ❸
          Plug into → 4.3 Index of added nutrients
}

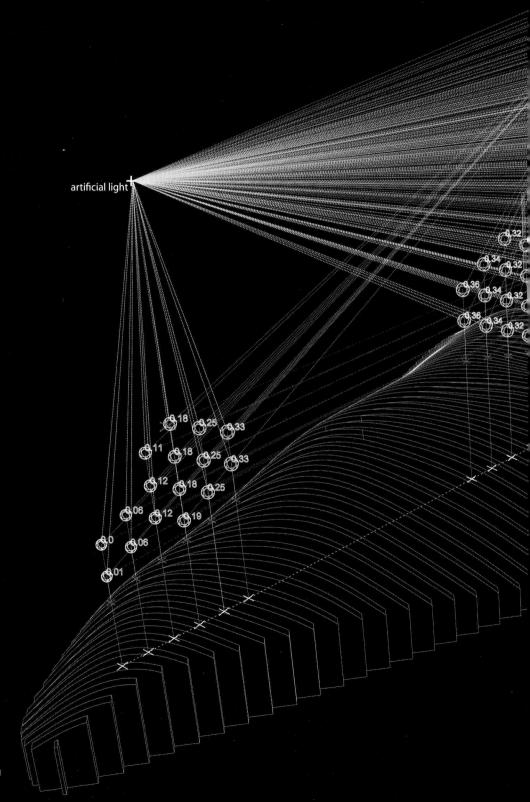

artificial light

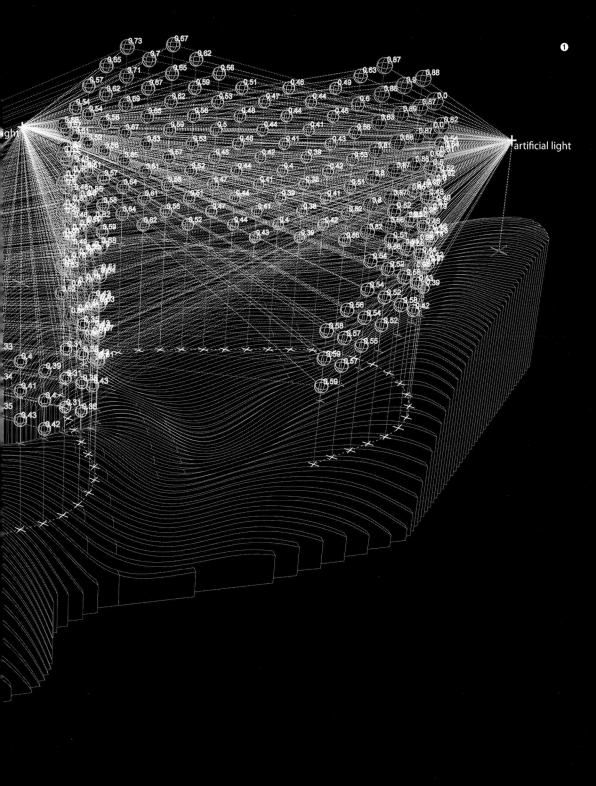

artificial light

how to 5 : Real time: cultivation feedback

{

// As algae grow and interaction/oxygenation increases a new form of cybernetic
// "cultivation" of space emerges. This practice has no precedents and needs to
// be sustained and encouraged; new visitors need to be informed of the past
// and current state of the cloud to choose where and how to intervene, to make
// sense of the cloud behaviour. The Briccoles are then fitted with equipment that
// will allow them to sense, record and display visually the amount of interaction
// they have received in the past.
// Sensors are attached to the protruding tubes used to add CO_2 to the bio-
// reactors. The sensitivity and resistance of the sensors is fine-tuned until kids'
// soft touch is sufficient to send a message to the cloud to record the event.
// Each Briccole than displays its total interactions by means of red LEDs,
// flickering and dimming by one step so that the brightest, most noticeable
// blocks will be those that most require care.

5.1 {Saturation sensing: level of CO_2 added to bioreactor measured by proxy of
     flex sensor manipulation}
5.2 {Systemic regulator: level of CO_2 added to bioreactor compared and ranked
     in relation to other bioreactors, threshold sensitivity updated}
     Affects → 6.2 Memory database
5.3 {Visual indicator: brightness of LED altered depending on ranking in previous
     step. Likelihood of interaction is altered} ➊
     Regulates → 1.1 People blowing

}

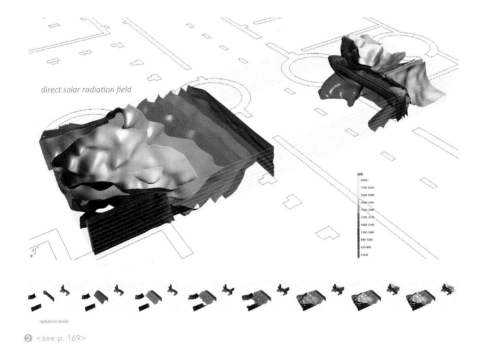

direct solar radiation field

Wh
4300+
3780-4200
3360-3780
2940-3360
2520-2940
2100-2520
1680-2100
1260-1680
840-1260
420-840
0-420

radiation levels

❷ <see p. 169>

➊ >

23B

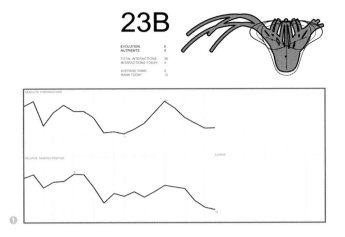

EVOLUTION	6
NUTRIENTS	4
TOTAL INTERACTIONS	36
INTERACTIONS TODAY	4
AVERAGE RANK	8
RANK TODAY	12

ABSOLUTE # INTERACTIONS

RELATIVE RANKING POSITION

23.04.05

❶

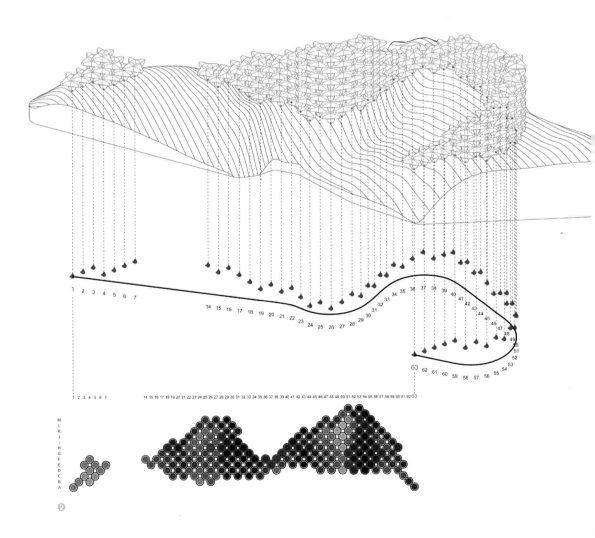

❷

how to 6 : Real time: the development of memory

{

    // The cloud has memory, which in time allows the ecoMachines to evolve
    // behaviour and a more structured interaction with its "gardeners".
    // The concept of the system having a "memory" affords further possibilities to
    // the designer in managing and adjusting the system during its life. Information
    // is sent back detailing how many individual instances of interaction have
    // occurred and the bioreactors are placed in a rank.❶ This is then used to reset
    // the LED brightness settings for the next day and to evolve LED behaviour
    // over time.
    // This record of interactions is paired with a phenotypic record, the
    // physiological development of the algal bloom, so that input can be compared
    // to output. As well as compensating for any local individual imbalance, this
    // systemic memory creates a detailed picture of the behaviour of the cloud as a
    // whole. We can determine whether growth progresses in a steady state with
    // each bioreactor generating a consistent quantity of biomass, or whether
    // the system oscillates between periods of intense growth and die-back. By
    // interrogating the data produced we can connect the behaviour of the visitors
    // to the behaviour of the ecoMachines, and allow the designer to mediate and
    // manage this dynamic relationship.

    6.1 {System biological growth: periodically take remote digital images to
        monitor and store the output of the system, level of transparency and
        material consistency} ②
    6.2 {Memory database: values of interaction and growth patterns are stored in
        the system and plotted graphically to allow for real-time assessment and
        evolution of the self-regulating system} ③
        Refine → 3.5 Hairiness evolution and 4.3 Index of added nutrients

}

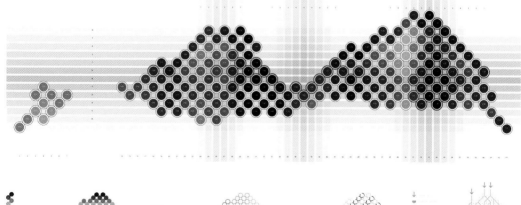

③

how to 7 : Feedback to urban ecologies

{

// As the biological material cultivated within the Briccoles is extracted from
// the natural or urban landscape STEM becomes a sort of incubator of
// biodiversity, a bank of urban species to be cultivated.❶ The richness of
// biological diversity contained in some urban lakes, ponds and rivers is not
// currently experienced by the urban population. Scientists are not operating as
// mediators as most of their research happens outside the urban realm;
// STEM provides a space of mediation, of incubation, a new prototypical
// public room, a workshop of biodiversity in which to craft new mechanisms of
// ecologic co-existence and co-evolution within the city. ❷

7.1 {Existing urban ecologies: the Guadalquivir River has fed the city of Seville as
one of its sources of life – STEM hosts and cultivates the river's biodiversity}
Refine → 4.1 Existing ecology test

7.2 {Biomass extraction: harvest bioreactors to produce energy, food, bio-
chemicals and so on}

7.3 {Information extraction: map biodiversity and cultivate endangered species
within unbalanced urban ecologies} ❸

}

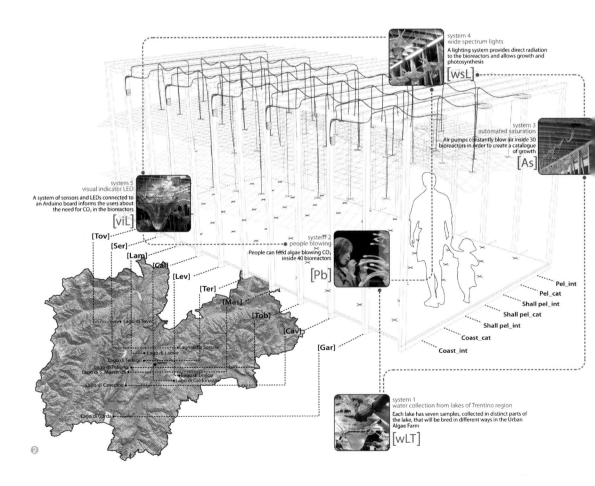

system 4
wide spectrum lights
A lighting system provides direct radiation
to the bioreactors and allows growth and
photosynthesis
[wsL]

system 3
automated saturation
Air pumps constantly blow air inside 30
bioreactors in order to create a catalogue
of growth
[As]

system 5
visual indicator LED
A system of sensors and LEDs connected to
an Arduino board informs the users about
the need for CO_2 in the bioreactors
[viL]

[Tov]
[Ser]
[Lam]
[Cal]
[Lev]
[Ter]
[Mas]
[Tob]
[Cav]
[Gar]

system 2
people blowing
People can feed algae blowing CO_2
inside 40 bioreactors
[Pb]

Pel_int
Pel_cat
Shall pel_int
Shall pel_cat
Shall pel_int
Coast_cat
Coast_int

Lago di Toye
Lago della Serraia
Lago di Lamar
Lago di Terlago
Lago di Toblino
Lago di S. Massenza
Lago di Levico
Lago di Caldonazzo
Lago di Cavedine
Lago di Garda

system 1
water collection from lakes of Trentino region
Each lake has seven samples, collected in distinct parts of
the lake, that will be bred in different ways in the Urban
Algae Farm
[wLT]

❷

❶

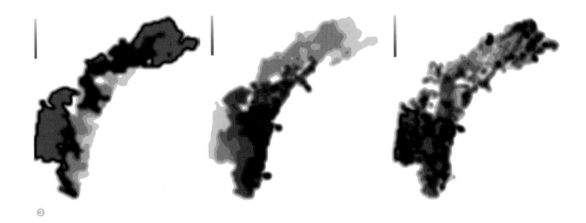

❸

The Bottega della Biodiversità (Biodiversity Workshop) prototype

facing page
Detail of the inoculation procedure where samples of algal specimens from alpine lakes are catalogued and introduced in each photo bioreactor

this page
The scientist in residence using the exhibition as an open lab space of research and interaction with the public

STEMv2.0: the Guadalquivir Experiment. The ecoMachine turning into a playground for the experiencing of urban biodiversity and biologic growth

spaces of co-design

[b3:1.1]
The Cyber-Gardens
(Fish & Chips)
p. 188

[b3:1.2]
Relational Machines: The
Ecological Footprint Grotto
p. 204

spaces of social networking

[b3:2.3]
FUNclouds
p. 222

[b3:2.4]
Social Network City:
Milan 2015 Metropolitan
Proto-Garden
p. 238

Relational ecologic machines

1. Design diagrams can be embodied into material and architectural prototypes; in such a condition architecture performs as an analogue computer, reading contextual forces, loading programmatic and material constraints and feeding back spatial, ornamental and behavioural solutions. Such an architectural mechanism is by definition deeply ecological as it is defined only in relation to a specific habitat, or a specific ecology of materials, forces, information, flows and energetic fields; we call it an ecoMachine, to underline how different such a conception of the term "machine" is when we move away from the mechanical paradigm and embed the mechanism in the milieu. **2.** Such a philosophical shift has a profound material impact on our understanding of the architectural assemblage and on the role of technology within it; it forces a dissolution of the boundaries between the inert (structural frames and envelopes) and active or responsive (mechanical systems), between the user and his/her surrounding environment, between the body and the architectural space, between the furniture and the city. **3.** The Corbusian machine for living becomes an urban-surviving ecoMachine, the Howardian Garden City a cultivated Metropolitan Proto-Garden.

The Metropolitan Proto-Garden for Milan. A virtual gardener accesses the local proto-gardening station remotely via digital cultivation interface

Behavioural spaces

1. As the city becomes embedded with relational mechanisms its conception evolves into a form of simulation. However the simulated virtual city is not a model of a generic digital urban landscape or a reductive abstraction of the real city; rather it is a meta-space in which the contingent and the accidental are absorbed and the generic is developed through the organization of differences and variations. The actualization of the self-organizing city then manifests itself as a progressive acquisition of material and performative specificities in relation to a specific contextualization process. A diverse pool of actors, agents, forces and protocols cooperate to form and reform the urban space. **2.** As such urban space is defined in this book as behavioural as it is the product of processes of co-evolution of multiple agents behaving as a coherent assemblage. It is this coherence that makes new forms recognizable and new urban spaces actual.

Co-design apparatus

1. Within the framework of this book, design is therefore by definition the result of a collaborative effort; however the term "co-design" designates a different practice from what is conventionally referred to as a collaborative design. **2.** It does not imply the simultaneous presence of multiple designers or the direct involvement of the user within the design process of an otherwise conventional building or urban type; rather it defines a design apparatus and related material prototype which involves within its machinic protocol the intervention and interaction of multiple agents, each with their own specific hierarchical position and independent agenda. **3.** In other words, a co-design apparatus doesn't operate via a collection of descriptive opinions from large audiences (as in a public consultation process or in a team of consultants) but it incorporates multiple know-hows to progressively enrich its own machinic protocols and as a consequence increase its intelligence and spatial or behavioural articulation.

About ...

The spaces of co-design are two machinic installations exploring the potential of architectural space to operate as an informational interface.

Recently many examples of media architecture have demonstrated the need to revive architecture's ability to communicate to its audience, to perform a function that can be defined as a hybrid between the billboard and the mirror. If communicating commercial messages is one aspect a new clear feature is the need to mirror nature's variability, its dynamic behaviour.

So we see large roofs animated by waves of flickering LEDs or façades of mirroring paillettes agitated by the wind.

Such manifestations demonstrate the social and economic need for architecture to perform a much more active role of mediator; to turn space and spatial experience into an opportunity to connect to different scales or regimes, ones that may often escape our perception.

The Fish & Chips project is a design interface that mediates the designer's role in choreographing a submarine park with the actual needs and behaviours of the resident fish colonies and ecologies. Through direct interaction with a scale model, presented at the spontaneous schooling exhibition in London, designers, visitors and ecologists alike can co-design the submarine garden in real time, learning how to negotiate their will and intuition with the response and behaviour of real fish.

The Ecological Footprint Grotto, presented at the 2010 Venice Architecture Biennale, takes on the challenge at a larger scale, by turning an immersive grotto into an interactive data map of the world's ecological footprint; spatializing abstract measurements of our society's material exchanges with the biosphere has the potential to shortcut the abstraction of statistical charts and convert the analysis of ecological behaviour into directly experienced spatial and material articulations.

This kind of architectural interfacing calls for a more active and participative user; one who has the ability to read and intuitively interpret global patterns and does not miss the opportunity to react.

Intercalar feedback reaction is the subject of the **spaces of social networking**; these two digital and video projects engage more directly with the urban scale and explore user reaction at the level of emergent social networks: what is the potential of spatially aware, ecologically driven social networking? What are the abilities of self-organized social groups in the shaping of future cities and can we harvest their energy?

The FUNcloud series engages with the concept of public space in London and Milan and questions its current transformation into a privatized corporate landscape by means of a furniture system. This system, composed of a digital planning tool and a material prototype, acts as a catalyst, a body of mediated interaction.

In the Metropolitan Proto-Garden, developed for the Milan Expo 2015 event, the entire city is engaged by the mediating interface. A digital space, a sort of Facebook for ecological urbanism, connects into an ever-evolving network of public and private spaces of interaction; this network is constantly adjusting thanks to both the Milanese and the global citizens of Milan.

Urban rhythms are therefore reflected in the urban interface and become protagonists of a new conception of urban design that features ecological processes and their spatio-temporal articulation. The images of the city will multiply and change continuously, reflecting their ecological cycles, the collective memories of the past, opportunities and sensibilities of the present and feedbacks or projections of the future; network urbanism in real time, intensifying a new ecological brain for the city.

The Cyber-Gardens: Photosynthe-Sense prototype. Students testing lighting levels data being captured by the sensors embedded in the model and flowing to the laptop via Arduino and Processing

[b3:1.1] The Cyber-Gardens
          (Fish & Chips)

CATEGORY: b3 Behavioural Spaces
PROJECT TYPE: b3:1 Spaces of co-design
PROJECT #:   1
LOCATION: London, UK
YEAR: 2010

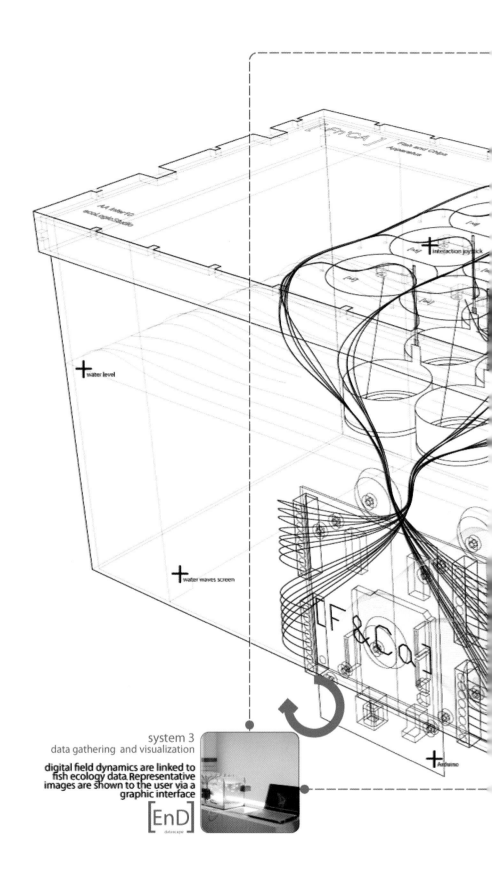

+ water level

+ water waves screen

system 3
data gathering and visualization

digital field dynamics are linked to
fish ecology data. Representative
images are shown to the user via a
graphic interface

[EnD]
datascape

+ interaction joystick

+ Arduino

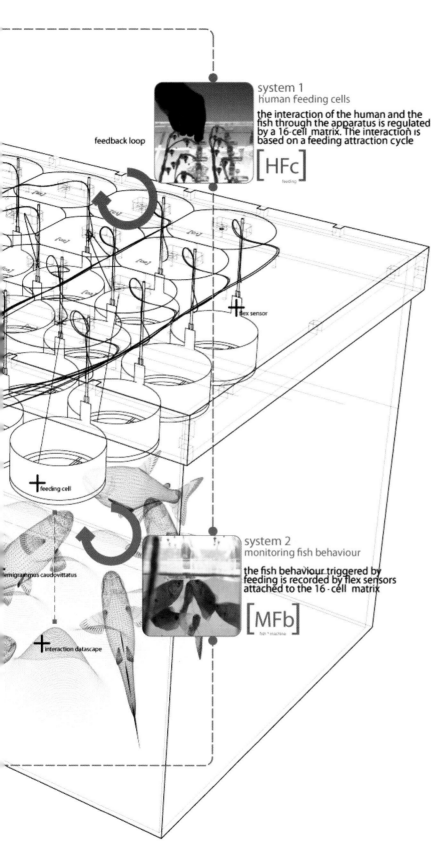

pp. 188–189
The Fish & Chips prototype at the Spontaneous Schooling exhibition in London. The feeding behaviour of the fish in the aquarium is captured in real time and transposed into evolving digital maps on the laptop

this page
The Fish & Chips prototype: cybernetic diagram of machine behaviour illustrating the three main feedback loops within the system

feedback loop

system 1
human feeding cells

the interaction of the human and the fish through the apparatus is regulated by a 16-cell matrix. The interaction is based on a feeding attraction cycle

$$\left[HFc \right]$$

feeding

+ flex sensor

+ feeding cell

emigrammus caudovittatus

+ interaction datascape

system 2
monitoring fish behaviour

the fish behaviour triggered by feeding is recorded by flex sensors attached to the 16-cell matrix

$$\left[MFb \right]$$

fish + machine

The Fish & Chips prototype: detail of the feeders with flex sensing supports, wiring architecture and circuit board

Coral Gardens experiments in World Lagoon, Dubai   Within the context of the AA Inter10 a
series of ecological design experiments, the Coral Gardens, were conducted on the temporarily
abandoned and bare landscape of the artificial World Lagoon in Dubai. Each project investigates
specific architectural mechanisms of co-existence and co-evolution within the local marine habitat,
prefiguring scenarios of development whereby the Lagoon is transformed into urban artificial
coral reefs. Some of these design proposals are featured in b1: Environments as part of the World
Dubai Marine Life Incubators project.

Within this context a series of experimental apparatuses were developed to test novel design
methodologies able to directly engage the ideas of incubation and ecological co-evolution.

Design as "cultivation"   The cyber-gardens apparatus allows us to experience and test design as
a form of cultivation, whereby the designer operates as a cyber-gardener in both choreographing
and breeding new artificial ecologies.

As landscape designer and philosopher Gilles Clement points out in his beautiful description
of the "moving garden", the gardener operates through a process of intensification of difference; his only chance to reconcile his desire of beautification and the natural expressivity of living
processes resides in movement, intended in its biological and physical sense. The formalization of
the garden becomes for Clement a process of formalized transmission of biological messages or,
in our terms, of algorithmic coding.

Such a design process requires a new method that borrows its mechanisms from the social sci-
ences, ecology and cybernetics: the designer's role will expand to encompass that of manager or
moderator, facilitating communication between diverse and heterogeneous systems and ecological regimes. Flows of light and nutrients, human care and physical contact or ecological stress
analysis are allowed to contribute to the growth of a digital abstract garden, the ever-evolving
virtual image of the designer's own experience of "cultivating" his/her project.

The cyber-garden's physical interface is embedded with sensors able to capture and channel
information in real time in order to feed their own virtual/digital image. Emergent digital patterns,

this page
The World Lagoon Coral
Gardens: detail of the
prototype model of a
Biorock reef landscape

facing page
The Fish & Chips
prototype: digital
landscapes generated by
the real-time processing
of data streams from
the prototype model to
the algorithmic design
engine [GH for Rhino]

the garden's plans, in turn influence the way the physical interface is manipulated and upgraded, leading to a sedimentation of design meanings, practices, habits and ideas.

The cyber-gardens are in fact artificial ecologies which share with their biological counterparts their fundamental living principle, the feedback loop; however their augmented nature allows for extended participation and interaction, turning them into tools of systemic design.

Cyber-gardens apparatuses   Three apparatuses are developed and tested leading to diverse gardening concepts:

Photosynthe-Sense   The cloud which draws: a cloud of artificial flowers/floating bubbles actuated by human interaction and by wind generates dynamic shadow patterns >> the shadows are registered by a field of 16 light sensors >> lighting level data are read by Grasshopper and influence the "growth" and differentiation of a parametric digital "garden" >> as in an artificial photosynthesis the digital growth process is proportional to the amount of light reaching the physical "sensors".

CyBraille   The mood board: according to her mood or tone, Leila would stroke the corrugated landscape board in a more delicate, hectic or aggressive way >> the touch is translated in degrees of bending of the flex sensors integrated as nail extensions in Leila's hands >> bending intensity and frequency patterns are read by Grasshopper and evolve the garden plan >> ultimately Leila's mood and conversation patterns influence the design and growth.

Fish & Chips   Designing like a fish: fish swim around floating feeders agitating them and producing small and high-frequency waves >> sensors record the waves' frequency in real time >> wave patterns and therefore fish colony patterns are read by Grasshopper, generating a design output >> which becomes effectively an interactive map of the fish colony's daily behaviour.

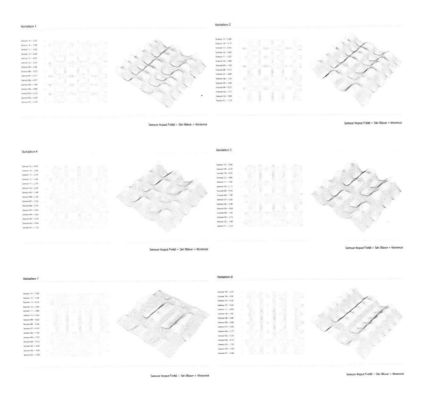

how to 1 : Sense

{

// Fish & Chips must sense and be sensitive to the surrounding environment and
// to human interaction; sensitivity co-evolves with the behaviour of natural and
// social systems part of its environment. The relational act of feeding is
// registered and used as a mechanism to interface natural and digital systems.

1.1 {Define feeding behaviour as mechanism to register and sense systemic
interaction} ⓘ

1.2 {Create an array of coded feeders that operates as an interface to mediate
the relationship between humans and a school of fish}
Plug into → 2.2 Feeders integration

1.3 {Connect sensors to the feeders to sense the Touch–Bending–Vibration effect
that occurs during feeding}

1.4 {Test the sensitivity of the sensors to the chosen stimulus in relation to a
specific fish population. Specific calibration is needed to achieve sensible
readings; repeat feeding to evolve calibration}

}

how to 2 : Structure the cyber-garden

{

// Feeding must be organized spatially by designing the physical organization of
// the "cyber-garden"; individual feeders are also engineered to encourage
// feeding among fish and to facilitate stimulation to feed by humans.

2.1 {A standard aquarium with temperature and water quality control is used as
a testing environment and a custom designed transparent platform/cover is
fabricated to support the feeding/sensing system/process}

2.2 {An array of floating feeders and sensors is attached to the platform. Their
quantity and distribution in space defines the garden's sensing resolution}
Affects → 3.2 Connect the physical to the digital

2.3 {Test the interaction of the feeding platform with the environment. Monitor
and adapt temperature, light and water nutrients in order to achieve good
living conditions for the fish and stabilize feeding patterns}

2.4 {Test physical feeding: activate feeding routines and explore different
feeding behaviours in space and time}

}

② <overleaf>

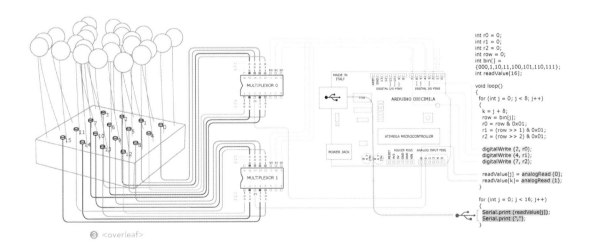

③ <overleaf>

```
int r0 = 0;
int r1 = 0;
int r2 = 0;
int row = 0;
int bin[] =
{000,1,10,11,100,101,110,111};
int readValue[16];

void loop()
{
  for (int j = 0; j < 8; j++)
  {
    k = j + 8;
    row = bin[j];
    r0 = row & 0x01;
    r1 = (row >> 1) & 0x01;
    r2 = (row >> 2) & 0x01;

    digitalWrite (2, r0);
    digitalWrite (4, r1);
    digitalWrite (7, r2);

    readValue[j] = analogRead (0);
    readValue[k]= analogRead (1);
  }

  for (int j = 0; j < 16; j++)
  {
    Serial.print (readValue[j]);
    Serial.print (",");
  }
}
```

how to 3 : Process information and activate real-time mapping

{

// When this stage is reached information is captured from the cyber-garden
// apparatus and must be processed and organized to start producing meaningful
// results. The design of the digital architecture of the cyber-garden allows
// a consistent transposition of this data into multiple formats until ready to be
// visualized through drawings. The writing of multiple script engines is necessary
// to this phase; however equally important is the material organization of the
// informational flows. Specific sensors must spatially connect to equivalent
// digital entities to be able to trace the flow of data and to associate meanings
// to the emergent digital effects produced. The architecture of data flows is a
// crucial component of the cyber-garden.
// Using the Arduino/Processing hardware and software platform combined
// with Grasshopper's diagramming interface it is possible to design such data
// architecture and produce real-time adaptive garden plans. ❶

3.1 {Design data flow into the digital model: information coming from physical
interaction is processed, filtered and organized into streams that feed digital
gardening plans}

3.2 {Connect the physical to the digital: develop a wiring diagram and
design the Arduino board to allow dataflow to reach specific addresses}
❷ <previous page>

3.3 {Generate data flows: physical and digital addresses are identified and
a specific correspondence between the physical and digital data grid is
established} ❸ <previous page>

3.4 {Read data flows into the digital adaptive plan: an associative GH diagram
reads the data flow from the aquarium and updates the garden plan's
drawing. The associative model is refined to cope with the regimes of
variation coming from the aquarium and novel garden patterns start
developing from the initial grid} ❹
Regulates → 4.2 Garden cultivation
Regulates → 4.3 Capture cyber-garden sedimentation

}

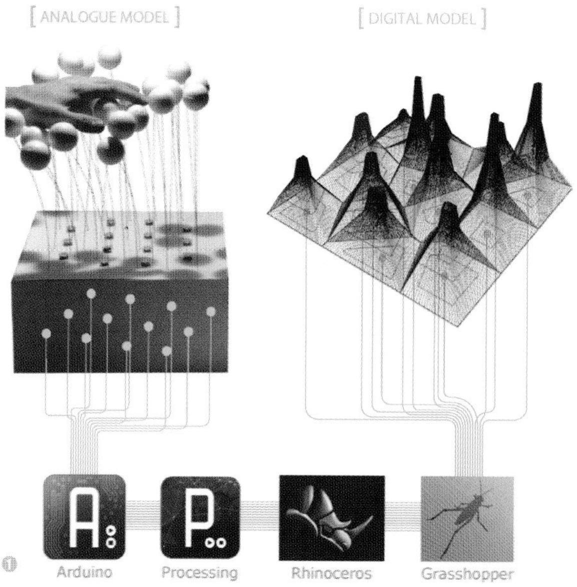

[ANALOGUE MODEL]   [DIGITAL MODEL]

Arduino   Processing   Rhinoceros   Grasshopper

❶   ❹ >

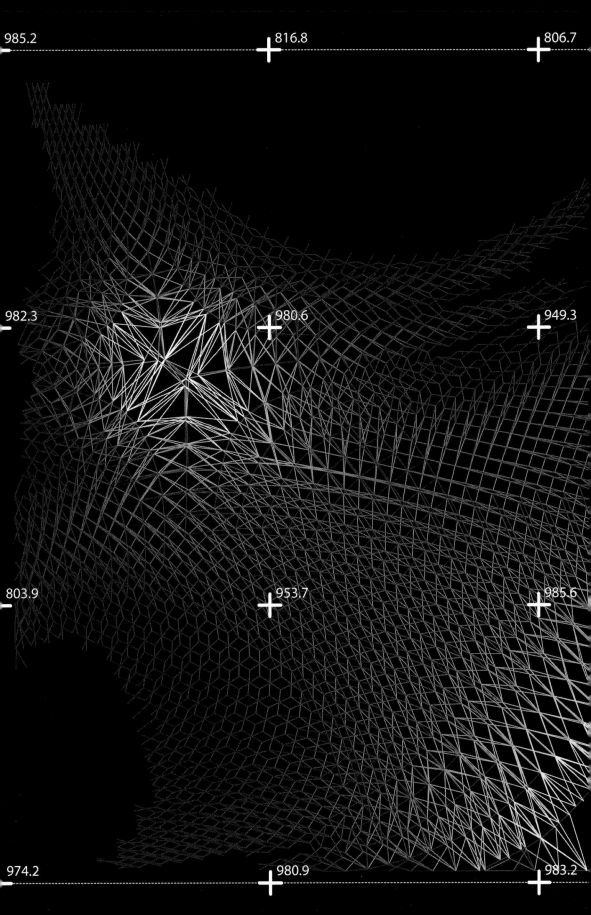

how to 4 : Co-design

{

// As information starts flowing consistently back and forth the process of
// cyber-gardening or of co-designing the cyber-garden begins.❶ Stimuli flow
// from the physical into the digital and vice-versa through a series of feedback
// loops; from the human, to the machine, to the computer, to the
// environment, to the human, to the machine and back again.
// A playful learning process develops whereby the ever-evolving
// configurations of the gardens (and their plans) emerge out of the complex
// interrelations and negotiations of multiple needs. This forces the design to
// be imagined and evolved in a constantly dynamic and mutating fashion,
// always partially "out of control", open to the mediation of ecological as well
// as social and cultural parameters.

4.1 {Define the point at which gardening begins, setting up a zero stage in the
     experiment}
4.2 {Start cultivating the garden through a series of feeding loops while
     adjusting the plans' parameters} ❷
4.3 {Capture, catalogue, sediment and debate the evolution of the cyber-
     garden's plan}
4.4 {Manage the evolution of the garden; induce variations in the environment,
     alter sensing resolution, evolve feeding routines}
     Refine → 2.4 Test physical gardening
     Refine → 3.4 Read data flows into the digital adaptive plan
4.5 {Fabricate new feeding platforms and gardening devices out of the new
     emergent gardening plans}

}

❶

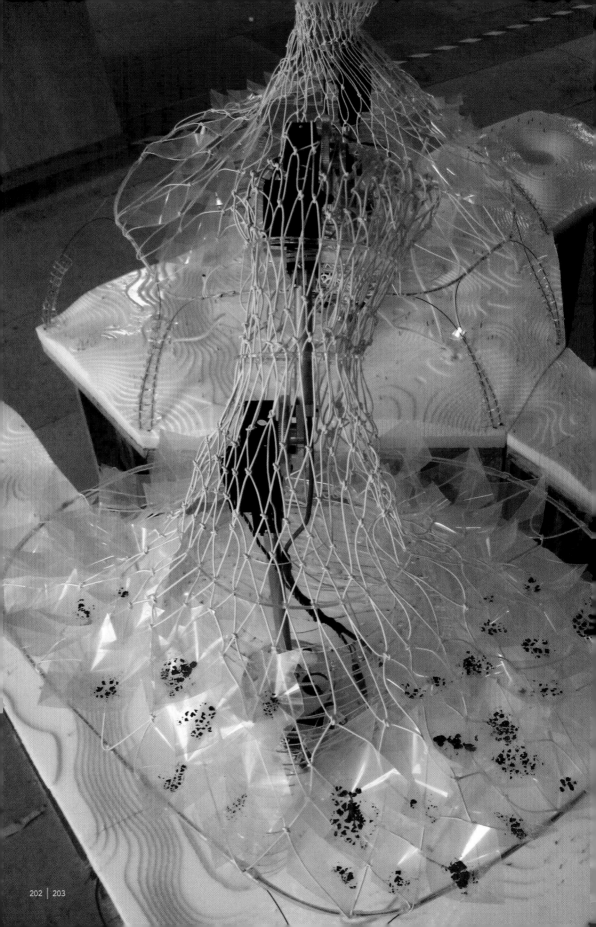

Cyber-Gardens v4 at the
Smart Geometry 2010 in
Copenhagen

facing page
The robotic prototype
model with its central arm
actuated in real time by
servo motors controlled via
digital interface; the arm
behaviour is a function of
radiation data and growth
patterns of the bacteria
cultures on the model's
canopy

this page
The bacteria lab and the
cybernetic diagram of the
machinic model

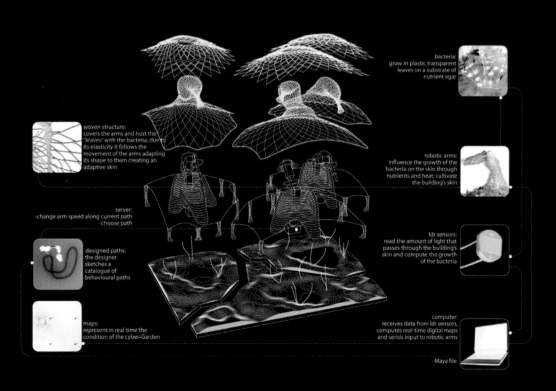

bacteria:
grow in plastic transparent
leaves on a substrate of
nutrient agar

woven structure:
covers the arms and host the
"leaves" with the bacteria; due to
its elasticity it follows the
movement of the arms adapting
its shape to them creating an
adaptive skin

robotic arms:
influence the growth of the
bacteria on the skin through
nutrients and heat; cultivate
the building's skin

server:
-change arm speed along current path
-choose path

ldr sensors:
read the amount of light that
passes through the building's
skin and compute the growth
of the bacteria

designed paths:
the designer
sketches a
catalogue of
behavioural paths

maps:
represent in real time the
condition of the cyber-Garden

computer:
receives data from ldr sensors,
computes real-time digital maps
and sends input to robotic arms

Maya file

Relational Machines:
The Ecological Footprint
Grotto

CATEGORY: b3 Behavioural Spaces
PROJECT TYPE: b3:1 Spaces of co-design
PROJECT #: 2
LOCATION: Venice, Italy
YEAR: 2010

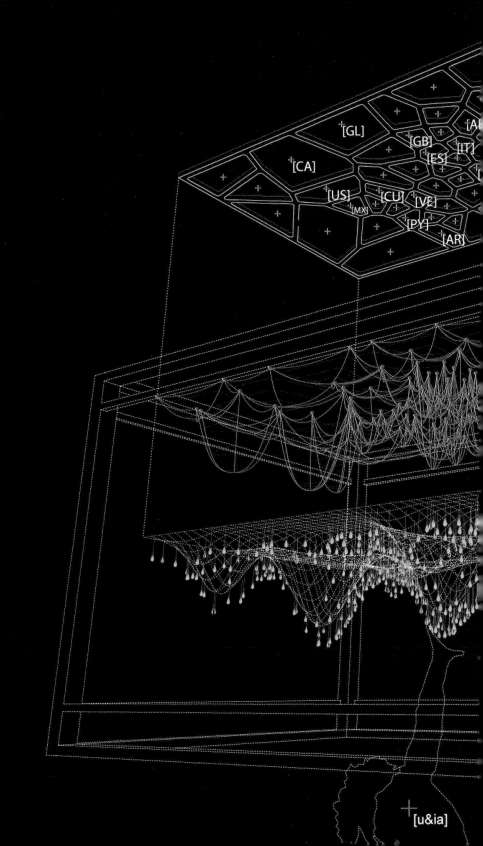

[GL]
[CA]
[US]
[MX]
[GB]
[ES]
[IT]
[CU]
[VE]
[PY]
[AR]

[u&ia]

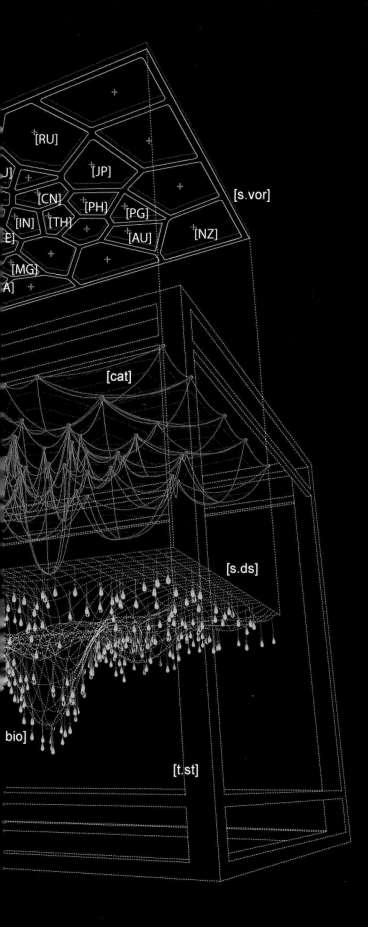

The Ecological Footprint
Grotto for the 2010 Venice
Architecture Biennale

pp. 204–205
View of the self-organizing
hanging ceiling with rice
and clay filled vaults
representing world
countries and their
ecological footprint debit
or credit

this page
3D digital parametric model
of the analogue interactive
ceiling, based on a Voronoi
tessellation of the world
map, catenary vaults and
weighted fabric ceiling

[RU]

[JP]

J]

[CN]

[PH]

[IN]   [TH]

[PG]

E]

[AU]

[NZ]

[MG]

A]

[s.vor]

[cat]

[s.ds]

bio]

[t.st]

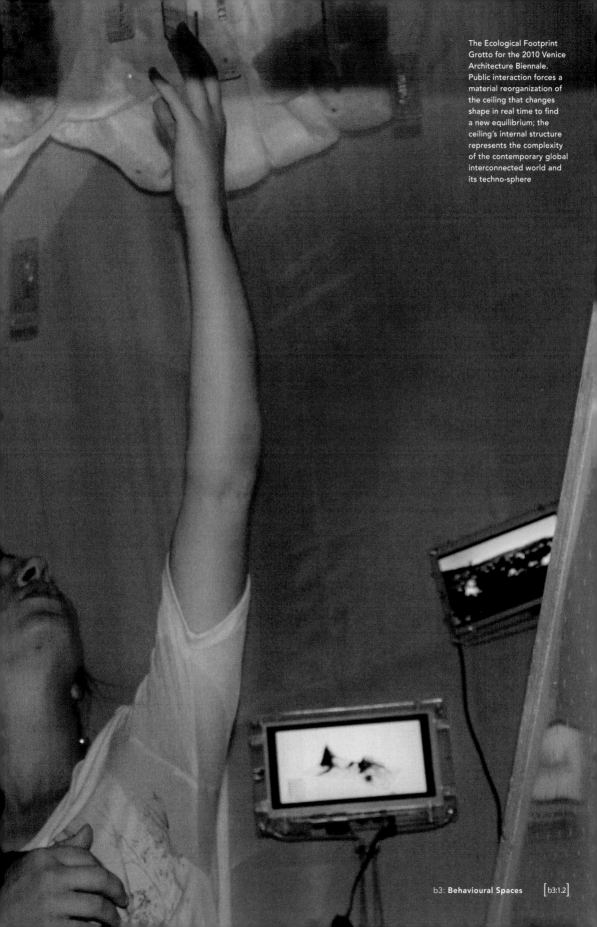

The Ecological Footprint Grotto for the 2010 Venice Architecture Biennale. Public interaction forces a material reorganization of the ceiling that changes shape in real time to find a new equilibrium; the ceiling's internal structure represents the complexity of the contemporary global interconnected world and its techno-sphere

Architectural credos   In the age of ecology the dichotomy between an aesthetic agenda for architectural and urban design, driven by such parameters as coherence, fluidity and elegance, and its ethical counterpart, focused on assessing urbanization's impact on the biosphere, has evolved into a battle of credos (or often brands).

Architecture as a relational machine   The Ecological Footprint Grotto project proposes an architecture that operates as a relational machine, a device able to directly relate and physically connect the personal and intimate space of the grotto with the global human processes affecting the world's biosphere.

As such the Grotto escapes ideological oppositions while seeking to be effective at an intuitive level by interfacing direct material interaction with transmitted or relayed information. The grotto can be ecologically informative, politically engaged, funny, soft, beautifully multicoloured or nuanced and so on, often depending on the contextual moment, specific user and material accumulation.

The Grotto machine reads information from global data collecting agencies that are able to monitor and compute transnational processes and material flows while compiling a chart of national ecological performance. The machine converts data into articulations of an architectural surface in the form of a hanging vault ceiling; process and form, ethical judgement and aesthetic appreciation, irony and political debate are inextricably embedded one into the other by means of machinic interaction.

Cultivating form   Space and form within the Grotto become evolutionary, functions of abstracted material processes and direct ethical and political judgement. Form cannot be designed for blind consumption but needs to be cultivated and harvested. Architecture becomes an incubator of global ecology by means of local material interaction. The machine provides the link, the processing of signals and the blurring of scales. Global and local are no longer two scales of thinking; they become embedded. In this respect relational machines are engines for the production of anti-corporate bodies; networks of local dwellers that are capable of producing spatial and architectural awareness of the global implications of transnational corporate behaviour. Nothing can be hidden when the information travelling the web from sensors distributed around the globe

converge and materialize into intense and inhabitable rooms, sectors where the social organization of a group of people and their actions is capable of influencing the global perception and the material effect of corporate activity. Relational machines are then para-statal apparatuses, opposing the power of corporations that governments fail to control; relational machines are the tools to build a new model of self-organized global urbanity.

The Ecological Footprint Grotto The Ecological Footprint Grotto materialized in Venice, during the 2010 Architecture Biennale, as a small immersive room with an interactive vault ceiling. Inspired in its spatial tectonic aspect by the beautiful diamond vaults in medieval East European architecture and translated into a soft-architecture model by means of Gaudi-like catenary beams, the ceiling adopts some of the devices typical of theatrical machines, such as cables and pulleys, to activate its components in response to external informational stimuli.

The hybridization of these components guarantees a clear spatial and material matrix (hardware) to read and respond to informational stimuli (software); an architecture of bits and atoms, as Negroponte would put it.

The process of activation is like a kind of conversation mediated by the ceiling itself: ecological footprint data are fed to each cell of the ceiling representing countries of the world while the hanging surface is manipulated as a whole by the users of the space. As they push and pull the aggregate filling material national boundaries are blurred and a transnational intelligence materializes within the architectural material system. As stories from around the world populate the screens at the side of the room and modifications on the ceiling materialize a collective ethical response emerges. An ethic of transformation, as Schiavone would put it, triggered by the realization of the unstoppable flows of material information and energy that are shaping our contemporary world, often unseen by the mass media and away from public consciousness.

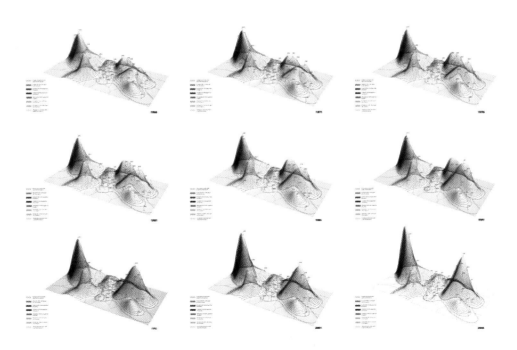

The New Eden: Nature v3.0   True global ecology is a game of collective consciousness, of the self-organization and self-realization of the urban dweller, the only one capable of action. The city is the New Eden, the contemporary incubator of global ecology, where a new form of nature is engineered and exported to the other regions of the globe. If we are to believe that our civilization is on the brink of extinction due to the uncontrolled modifications we are inflicting to our planet then the city is where we can synthesize new models of life on earth that would guarantee our survival in 2050.

Relational machines are architectural models for the implementation of these survival strategies, starting from the dismantling of the technocratic connections that control the axis scientific research–academia–industry which produces hyper-technologic eco-gadgets (eco-chic headquarters, eco-tech plug-ins for renewable energies, eco-sustainable marketing) whose necessity and functionality is fabricated by media brainwashing and diffused anxiety with the sole purpose of reducing the masses to a population of obedient consumers.

Relational machines are platforms for the harvesting of weak and diffused energies, as Andrea Branzi would put it; architectures that operate as open platforms, embedded with cheap open source and reprogrammable technologies, inspired by bio-mimetic logics and systemic philosophy, manufactured with rapid prototyping technologies and self-assembling swarm strategies, woven, knitted and bundled natural fibres, imprecise yet rigorous, effective while redundant, engineered by networks of non-specialized specialists, robust and adaptive social groups.

In a dream from the future   *Nel 2050 l'uomo ha imparato ad intuire e comprendere la complessità del mondo in modo molto approfondito; non cerca più risposte certe e sicure alle sue domande e curiosità, non è più facile preda delle ansie fabbricate dai media, non cercà più rifugio e conforto nella tecnologia, anzi i gadgets tecnologici non esistono più, non crediamo più all'esistenza della natura incontaminata, anzi il concetto di natura come piano di riferimento etico e culturale è scomparso e sostituito da un nuovo EDEN – questo nuovo eden è fondato su una nuova idea di materialità indefinibile con le terminologie che tu conosci perchè prodotta al di fuori dei confini semiotici e tecnologici a cui tu sei ancora legato; infatti la totale esplosione dei confini disciplinari, che è avvenuta in italia intorno al 2025 [un nuovo sesantotto dalla portata ben più devastante] e che rappresenta la fine del sistema accademico classico, ha generato una nuova realtà cognitiva e tecnologico produttiva di tipo catalitico; nuovi meccanismi produttivi stanno emergendo dalla brodaglia residua all'esplosione tramite ignezione di energie straniere o estraee al sistema producendo relatà profondamente globali ma spazialmente e temporalmente legate ai processi materiali locali; i prototipi socio-tecnologici che stanno emergendo hanno identità uniche ed insostituibili, specializzazioni non-specilaistiche emergono oggi in una sorta di neo-rinascimento cibernetico.*

this page
The Ecological Footprint
Grotto: detail of three
vaults corresponding to
three debtor countries
filled with clay particles

facing page
The Ecological Footprint
Grotto: view from
the access stair of the
grotto's ceiling after
two months of
interaction. The biggest
vault represents China

2 The cell depth represents the country's ecologic **debt** or **credit**.

how to 0 : Run the Ecological Footprint Grotto project
    {
        // Develop a new architectural "depth of field" for the concept of informational
        // interface; space and materiality mediate between the human scale and the
        // nature of informational global processes.
    }

how to 1 : Soft time: framing the global ecological footprint
    {
        // Measuring the ecological footprint of the globalized world is a massive
        // undertaking that implies multiple simplifications and reductions to the actual
        // flows of information, matter and energy that fuel individual countries and their
        // internal and external relationships. Such numeric abstraction can be remapped
        // spatially by developing a relational datascape based on the map of the world
        // and on the collected data. This map allows an intuitive understanding of the
        // geography of global ecology. ❶

        1.1 {Read the capital city or geographical centre for each country in the world
              map}
        1.2 {Deploy an algorithmic script to create a two-dimensional relational diagram
              of the world map} ❷
        1.3 {Read global ecological footprint data for creditor and debtor countries}
        1.4 {Transpose data to countries diagram and generate a soft datascape blurring
              the countries' exact national borders and emphasizing ecological footprint
              global tendencies}
        1.5 {Adjust the algorithmic resolution of the world diagram to accurately account
              for peaks of intensity within the datascape}
              Refine → 1.2 Algorithmic script
    }

how to 2 : Soft time: global stories on flows of materials, information and energy
    {
        // It is impossible to capture the complexity of global ecology; however it is
        // possible to frame data on global footprints in order to evidence trends and
        // stimulate discussion on the potentials and limits of global interconnection. The
        // seamless global material flow gives the impression of unlimited availability of
        // resources for some countries but, as the globe is limited, plenty for some
        // means scarcity for others.

        2.1 {Collect case study stories of global flow of material information and energy
              that dodge the ecological footprint global datascape}
        2.2 {Visualize the diagrammatic network of connections underpinning such
              stories, making explicit reference to all the involved countries} ❸ <overleaf>
        2.3 {Refer the network diagram of flows to the map of the world}
              Refine → 1.2 Algorithmic script
        2.4 {Materialize these diagrammatic links into a physical set of connections
              among countries}
              Affects → 4.5 Pulley system
    }

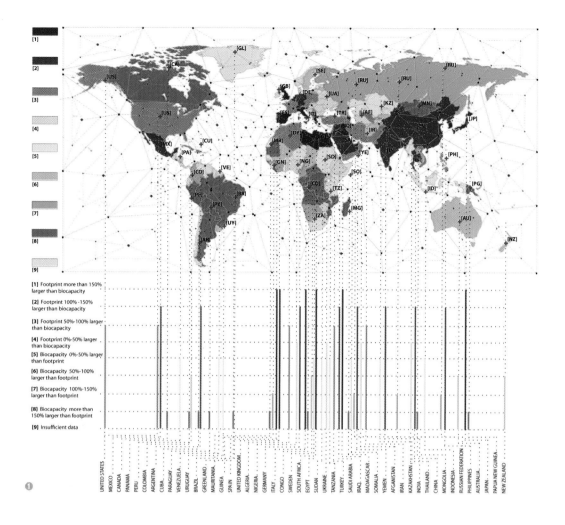

[1] Footprint more than 150% larger than biocapacity

[2] Footprint 100%-150% larger than biocapacity

[3] Footprint 50%-100% larger than biocapacity

[4] Footprint 0%-50% larger than biocapacity

[5] Biocapacity 0%-50% larger than footprint

[6] Biocapacity 50%-100% larger than footprint

[7] Biocapacity 100%-150% larger than footprint

[8] Biocapacity more than 150% larger than footprint

[9] Insufficient data

❶

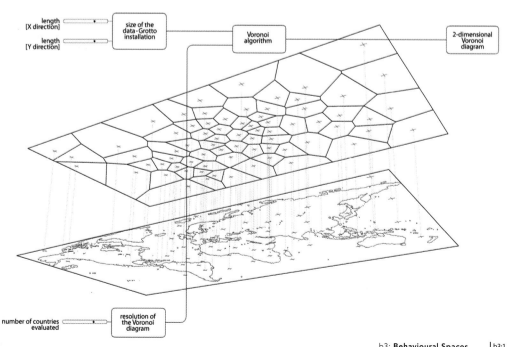

❷

how to 3 : Soft time: an ecological footprint soft ceiling

{

// The ecological footprint datascape is re-described as a soft ceiling,
// providing a means of spatialization to an abstract numeric space.

3.1 {Apply a catenary vault ceiling system to each country's diagrammatic cell}

3.2 {Differentiate the length of each catenary vault to match the datascape
   intensity for that country and/or geographic region}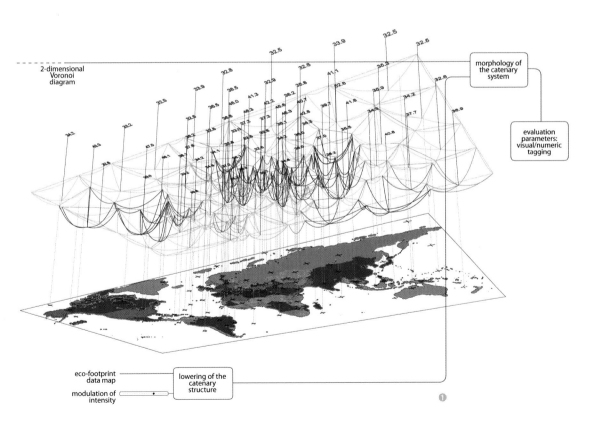
   Affects → 5.2 Material interaction

3.3 {Scale the grotto: use the sensitivity of the digital model to set the height
   of the vault depending on the human body dimension and the level of
   interaction pursued within the structure}
   Affects → 5.3 Re-shaping of the vault

3.4 {Implement multiple affects as emerged in the case study stories and
   related networks among countries through a pulley system} ❷
   Affects → 4.5 Behaviour of non-contiguous cells

3.5 {Fine-tune catenary lengths and connecting string length to achieve
   dynamic response}

}

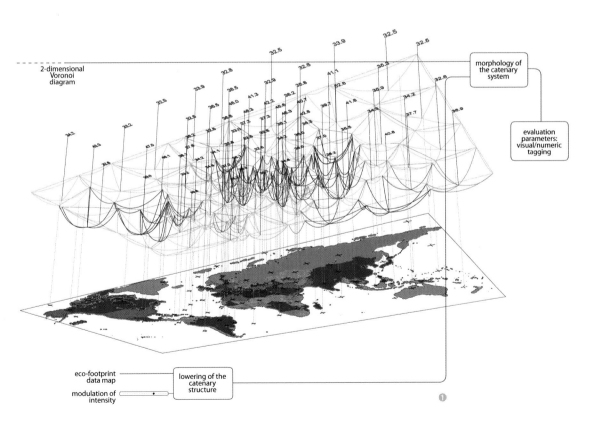

2-dimensional
Voronoi
diagram

morphology of
the catenary
system

evaluation
parameters:
visual/numeric
tagging

eco-footprint
data map

lowering of the
catenary
structure

modulation of
intensity

❶

how to 4 : Real time: the self-organization of the Ecological Footprint Grotto

{

// As the ecological footprint dataset is embedded into the soft ceiling of the
// grotto data begin to trigger processes of material self-organization and the
// grotto becomes alive. As visitors touch and manipulate each country's
// footprint, the world reorganizes in multiple and unexpected ways leading to an
// irreversible process of evolution of the world's ecological status as represented
// by the ceiling. Architecture becomes an interface mediating the individual's
// awareness and aspirations with the world's ever-changing complex behaviour.

4.1 {Set the properties of the fabric that will create the vaulted ceiling. Strength
and elasticity of the fabric will affect the behaviour of the adaptable ceiling
system}
Affects → 5.3 Re-shaping of the vault

4.2 {Dress the catenary structure frame to create a continuous "relational"
surface} ❶

4.3 {Load the hanging ceiling with inert material. Cells representing debtor
countries are filled up with darker clay while creditors are loaded with rice}
Refine → 4.1 Fabric's properties

4.4 {Inert material adds weight to the fabric and creates tension in the
morphology of the vault. More inert material flowing in a cell means more
energy/interaction needed to reverse/modify the situation} ❷

4.5 {Local spillage of inert material constantly modifies the balance of the
world surface while the pulleys system of links materializes non-contiguous
relationships}
Affects → 5.3 Re-shaping of the vault

}

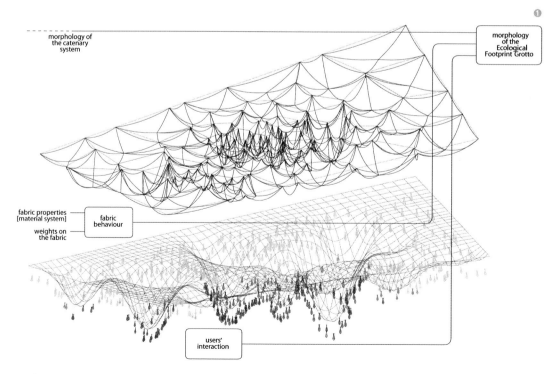

morphology of
the catenary
system

morphology
of the
Ecological
Footprint Grotto

fabric properties
[material system]

fabric
behaviour

weights on
the fabric

users'
interaction

how to 5 : Real time: interaction
{

    // As the public interacts the space evolves its morphology and material
    // quality in time with an irreversible process that is reminiscent of the
    // evolution of global ecology. Data and material flows are reconnected by a
    // mediating architectural structure, the Ecological Footprint Grotto.

    5.1 {Show stories of global flows and related data on the grotto screens to
        trigger an emotional response by visitors}
    5.2 {Let people push inert material from one cell to the contiguous ones}
    5.3 {As visitors re-shape the morphology of the vault a collective emotional
        response emerges, a novel global interpretation of the world as an
        ecological (or illogical) system}

}

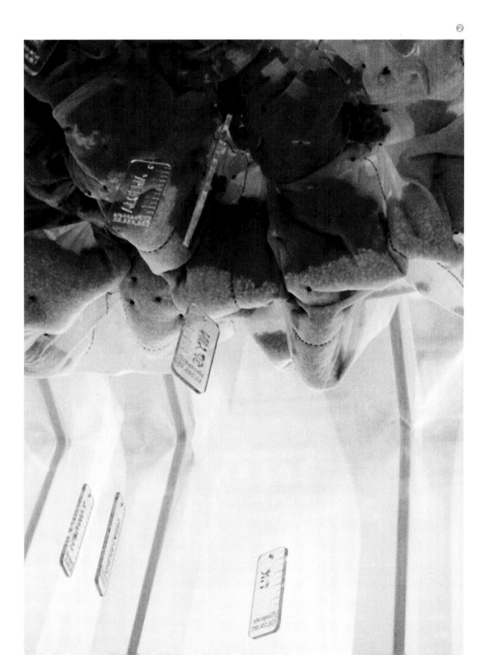

[2.3] FUNclouds

CATEGORY: **b3 Behavioural Spaces**
PROJECT TYPE: **b3:2 Spaces of social networking**
PROJECT #: **3**
LOCATION: **London, UK**
YEAR: **2009**

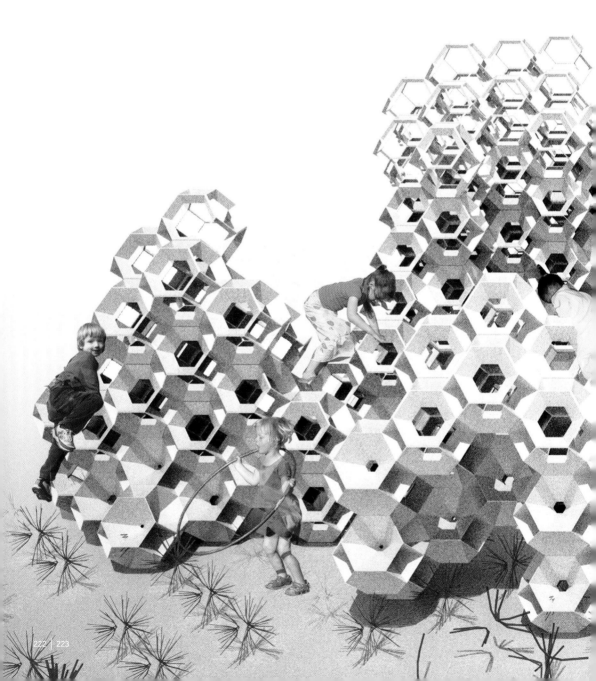

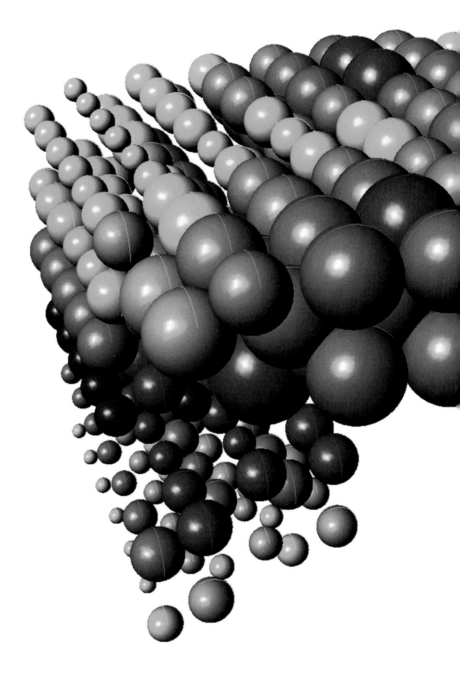

CELL 1: 50%vol AIR
          20%vol H₂O
          30%vol blanket weed
CELL 2: 50%vol AIR
          25%vol H₂O
          25%vol blanket weed
CELL 3: 50%vol AIR
          30%vol H₂O
          20%vol blanket weed
CELL 4: 50%vol AIR
          40%vol H₂O
          10%vol blanket weed
CELL 5: 50%vol AIR
          50%vol H₂O
CELL 6: 50%vol AIR
          40%vol H₂O
          10%vol chlorophyll
CELL 7: 50%vol AIR
          30%vol H₂O
          20%vol chlorophyll
CELL 8: 50%vol AIR
          25%vol H₂O
          25%vol chlorophyll

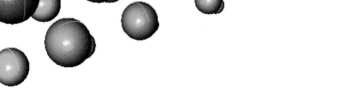

pp. 222–223
The FUNcloud pavilion: rendered view of one of the simulated structures after few days of playful interaction (simulated with 'heavier bricks below lighter ones' rule and 'adjacent bricks must differ no more the 15 per cent in opening')

this page
The FUNcloud pavilion: volumetric diagram of algal growth and related oxygenation potential for each brick in function of its position within the cloud and relative solar exposure

pp. 226–227
The FUNcloud pavilion: internal view of the cloud including photo-bioreactor fibres integrated within the lighter bricks structure

Introduction   The FUNcloud is a prototypical model of development of urban space as a form of participatory "buzz environment". It promotes the generation of space as a dynamic relational process unfolding in time. The potentially direct paths of pedestrian movement in-between relevant urban hubs are confronted and erased by the introduction of disturbance, or resistance, in the form of an interactive field, the cloud. This condition promotes the origination of a new potential field of interaction which in turn transforms the original flow. The transformation is both spatial, with migration from the direct trajectory connecting the hubs, and qualitative, with a programmatic mutation from a merely transitional condition to a fully interactive one. As space becomes more articulated so does the pattern of interaction, from void, to crossroad, to playground, to garden, to leisure centre, to farmland, to residential, to playground again, in a continuous range of intensities, frequencies, durations and climates. It is an entirely computational architectural protocol, where intuitions, material definitions, programmatic requirements, social aggregation, fabrication technologies and chance are registered, processed and fed back at various levels in a continuous chain of cybernetic loops.

The protocol has been applied to multiple scenarios to test and evolve its effectiveness and to re-describe architectural typologies within the new framework of the self-organizing city.

Urban cloud   One such case is the re-configuration of a traditional single-family villa to host a small community of five families. In this project the so-called "Lightwall" ambient cloud operates as a machine for the creative synthesis of global ecological design sensibilities and prototyping technologies with the sedimentation of knowledge within local processes and social contexts. This synergy we believe represents one of the main focuses for a new agenda in architectural design and one of the main drivers of redefinition and transformation of the self-organizing city.

This agenda is pursued further in a project for the re-functionalization of the Truman Brewery parking area in Shoreditch, London. The urban context suits the application of the FUNcloud protocol as the area sits in the middle of a large portion of the east of London, a post-industrial urban expanse which is today bustling with new life thanks to both local Bangladeshi and Indian communities and herds of teenagers coming from all over the world to join the buzz and develop new social and economic networks. The re-functionalization of this area is happening largely as a process of self-organization, often coming from the bottom up, that is, from newly formed collaborative enterprises of young entrepreneurs. Also, while the area has been transformed radically in the last 20 years the architectural framework has remained largely unchanged; it is only in the last

The FUNcloud pavilion:
top view of one of the
simulated structures
composed by truncated
octahedron bricks of
varying porosity and
weight

four to five years (mainly triggered by the opportunities offered by the east London hosting of the Olympic Games) that large corporations have taken an interest in the area and extensive urban and architectural transformation has taken place. As a consequence, re-functionalization has happened through a process of re-furnishing of both public and semi-public or private spaces. The urban cloud is a catalyst for this process of re-furnishing; its protocol is developed with the ambition to improve the quality and efficiency of transformation of the urban environment within this spontaneous and bottom-up model of development.

FUNcloud: urban pavilions   A first version of the cloud was developed for the site as a parametric furniture system able to generate spatial atmospheres by providing light filtration, privacy and oxygenation; this prototype allows an augmented experience of man–nature interaction in dense urban contexts where the presence of traditional vegetative systems is close to zero. A series of plug-ins add functionality and customization to the system, such as artificial lighting, tidy boxes, pin-up surfaces and so on. The parametric nature of the single modules allows for a computational definition of the overall clouds; environmental gradients of solar radiation, people flow intensity and CO_2 emissions can be computed and used as generative environments for the developments of specific clouds/assemblages.

These assemblages have been further investigated for a design competition for an urban pavilion, commissioned as an engine of regeneration. Local flows and interaction potentials on site were measured and are "confronted or resisted" by octagonal material components that, loop after loop, condense and differentiate over the ground. The process gives rise to a catalogue of cellular components varying in porosity, structural resistance, wetness, luminosity and reflectivity. A parametric CAD system allows each component to be coded, charted, geometrically re-described and prepared for direct fabrication with CAD-CAM facilities. The components' relative configuration can adapt to contextual changes and/or new urban or architectural scenarios in the future. The structural cloud supports two other systems and liberates a series of emergent new processes. Rainwater is collected by super-absorbent fibres containing polymers and seeds; more intense rain will result in an increased volume, that is, more collection capacity, and in a faster organic growth. Artificial lighting is provided by another set of fibres, ultra side beam fibre optics, generating a third cloud, dimmed in real time by a computer-controlled system.

FUNcloud: Urban Algae Farm   Re-functionalization by means of augmented man–nature interfacing is also the basis of a larger-scale project, the Urban Algae Farm for the Milan Expo 2015. On a site near San Siro, surrounded by a dense network of farms and canals, the project seeks to re-functionalize an historically active agricultural area currently trapped in a suburban "terrain vague" which has suffocated its original network of activities without providing any valid alternative. The area has, however, been recently the subject of study as part of the "planetary garden" regeneration project connected to the Expo 2015 events.

The main programme of the Expo has abandoned the idea of building a set of wasteful pavilions to instead promote the development of a large garden, called the planetary garden, whereby each country is invited to display food-related issues by means of direct cultivation of typical products. This plan has been extended to the region surrounding the Expo site to encompass a network of farms, some already restored, which the event of the Expo hopes to re-functionalize as a post-industrial farm-scape.

Our site comprises four main farms and seven small ones. The projected direct paths between them re-propose the original network of links connecting them into a deep agricultural fabric; the FUNcloud protocol processes this input information by converting the potential paths into urban disturbance, or resistance, in the form of an urban field of virtual cultivation. This condition promotes the origination of a new potential landscape of interaction which in turn transforms the existing one by means of local intensifications of social and ecological exchange. The transformation is both spatial, with migration of resources and nutrients towards these new local attractors, and qualitative, with a programmatic mutation from a merely transitional condition of suburban terrain vague to a fully interactive one, the Urban Algae Farm. As the landscape grows in articulation so too do the patterns of social interaction and economic investment, from biomass cultivation, to bio-fuel production, to organic food market, to pharmaceutical research, to biodiversity bank, in a continuous range of intensities, frequencies, durations and micro-climates. These feedbacks also influence and determine the volumetric articulation, from the ponds and platforms, to the pavilions and greenhouses, to the larger hydroponic or photosynthetic towers. As in a systemic instant city, phases of development and final configurations of the buildings are in constant fluctuation and self-organization; larger social networks may give rise to larger investment groups and more high-tech solutions, while seasonal variations in harvesting and world food demands will dictate the dimensions of the greenhouses and the intensity of cultivation. Temperature fluctuation will be absorbed by minute adjustments in the sensitive membranes of the bioreactors, while extremely cold winters will increase the demand for bio-fuel harvesting. The richness and biodiversity of the algal world will feed the biodiversity bank sectors and progressively lead to their articulation in centres of research and scientific development.

The FUNcloud protocol opens up the possibility of conceiving architecture as a meta-space of collective endeavour, whereby the actual cityscape actualizes as a consequence of a process of co-evolution of multiple desires, interests, ambitions and agendas. Such a model provides not only a more efficient and robust system of development in a period of such turmoil but also creates the condition of a new model of social participation for the urban dweller. His/her position changes from passive recipient of the services provided by the state (to which he/she pays taxes), to active member of productive urban networks that can be co-financed by the state but that ultimately produce revenue, and power, for the global city.

In an era where national states are losing power and credibility due to their impotence in the face of such issues as global warming, terrorism or human rights, such emergent urban networks and cooperative behaviours could constitute the main global resource for the future transformation of our planet into a systemically integrated whole.

However such a model necessitates larger frameworks and dedicated interfaces to operate globally in an efficient and coordinated way. The next and final project of this book, the Metropolitan Proto-Garden, proposes one such interface and imagines its full implementation in Milan in 2030.

MAXdiv housing project: axonometric and planimetric diagrams of simulated housing complex based on the application of the FUNcloud protocol to a brownfield area near Rho-Pero on the outskirts of Milan; the emerging landscape is interpreted in terms of a differentiated terrain of multiple programmatic intensities and hybrid activities, triggering the conception of novel types of housing clusters

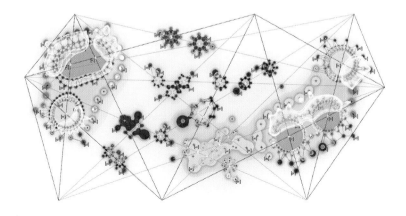

how to 0 : FUNcloud: a playground pavilion

```
{
        // FUNcloud is a pavilion prototype that introduces spatial and qualitative
        // transformation in a pre-existing network of urban paths and relationships.
}
```

how to 1 : Soft time: diagramming potential fields of social interaction and
            urban re-functionalization

```
{
        // A diagrammatic machine is set up to operate as a weighted dynamic model of
        // urban pedestrian paths and connections. The diagram allows simulation of the
        // re-functionalization of the urban landscape based on a series of feedback
        // loops, where the introduction of new instances triggers re-organization of flow
        // and migration of activity to achieve the emergence of novel equilibria.
```

    1.1 {Weigh each of the access points to the urban sector based on the flow of
        people passing through it}
    1.2 {Create a direct path network system among all the main points and extract
        the intersection points among the paths}
    1.3 {Compute for each intersection the weighted intensity}
    1.4 {Extrude the intersection point along Z in proportion to its intensity}
    1.5 {Materialize the flow intensity field and potential for urban interaction} ❶
        Affects → 2.2 Sensitivity to the datascape
    1.6 {Update initial flows as a result of novel urban interaction}
    1.7 {Repeat points 1.1 to 1.6} ❷

```
}
```

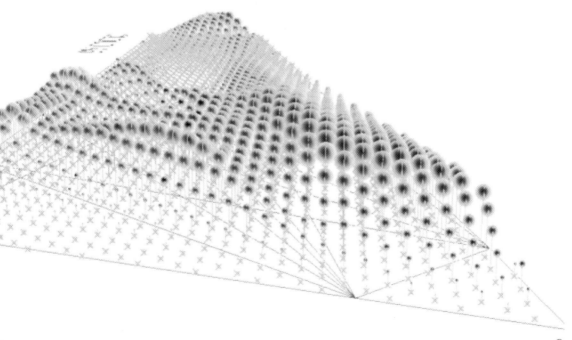

❶

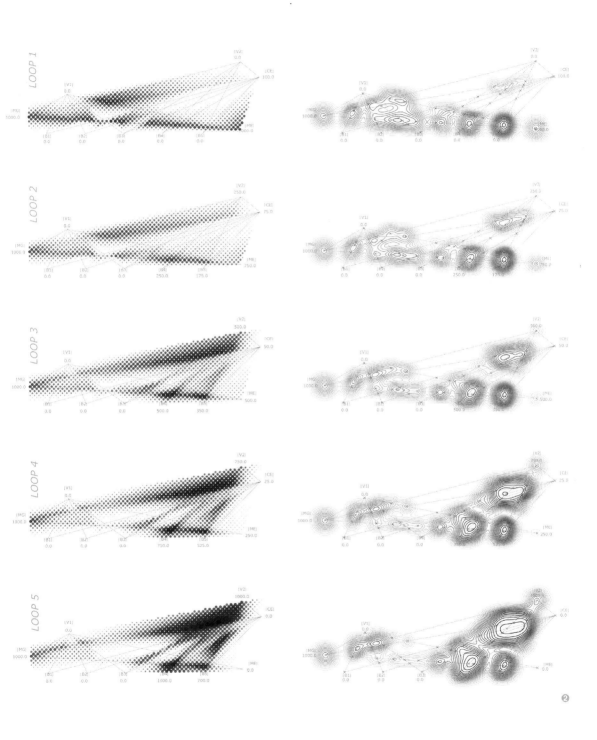

how to 2 : Soft time: condensing the FUNcloud space
{
   // As the new intensity field is generated by the diagrammatic machine a related
   // three-dimensional spatial matrix is described. This spatial definition allows
   // opportunistic programmatic definition and urban re-funtionalization.

   2.1 {Set the resolution of the three-dimensional matrix to a material and
        technological device or component}
        Affects → 3.1 Component's geometry
   2.2 {Define the sensitivity of the matrix to the data cloud describing urban social
        intensity}
   2.3 {Create spatial representations of three-dimensional intensity clouds}
   2.4 {Simulate the potential reconfiguration of the cloud in response to changing
        urban flows and social activities} ❶

}

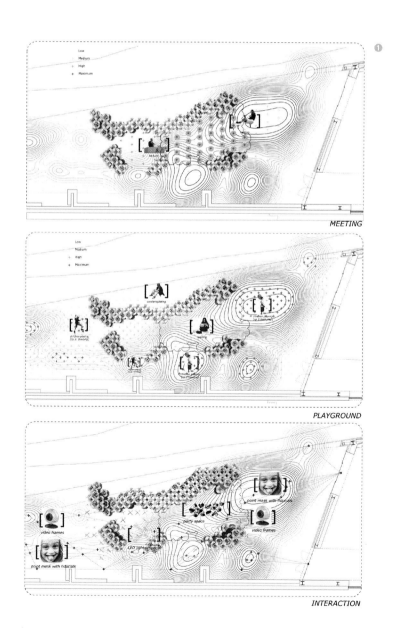

MEETING

PLAYGROUND

INTERACTION

how to 3 : Real time: articulating the cloud's molecules

{

    // A real-time continuous process emerges in which the FUNcloud modifies
    // original urban flows and operational fields through a series of physical
    // and programmatic interventions that grow and become more articulated in
    // time. This physical intervention can be designed by deployment of modular
    // components that can be effectively manufactured and assembled in multiple
    // and ever-changing configurations.

    3.1 {Define the base geometry for the furnishing component, the truncated
          octahedron, and specify differentiating parameters}
          Affects → 4.1 Superabsorbent fibres layout
          Affects → 4.2 Lighting fibres layout
    3.2 {Evolve the range of morphological variations of the component affecting
          their structural resistance, weight and porosity} ❷
          Refine → 3.1 Component's geometry
    3.3 {Engineer the components in a parametric system which allows use of
          sheet materials such as cardboard or recycled plastics, automatic coding,
          charting, unfolding, nesting and CNC cutting of each individual molecule
          for direct and efficient fabrication}

}

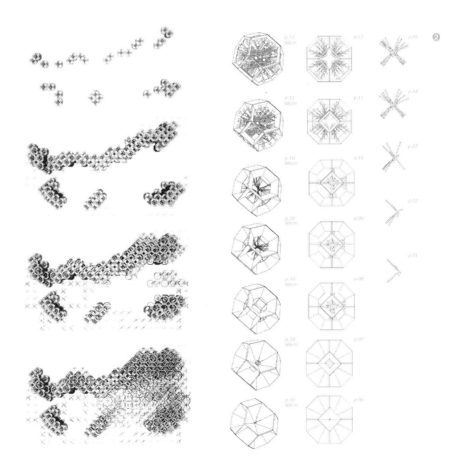

how to 4 : Real time: embedding performance and responsiveness

{

>　// Luminous behaviour and water retention performances are incorporated in
>　// each molecular component of the cloud. These material properties encourage
>　// intensified real-time interaction and responsiveness to emerge; for instance
>　// the cloud will host biological growth in response to weather patterns and
>　// will reconfigure as a dynamic playground in response to social interaction and
>　// playfulness.

>　4.1 {Arrange superabsorbent polymeric fibres and seed bags within the
>　　　components' frame and in relation to their shape and position} ❶
>　4.2 {Arrange lighting fibres inside the components and connect them to a
>　　　tracking camera-driven control system able to turn them on and off in
>　　　relation to the presence and position of the cloud users} ❷

}

how to 5 : Real time: FUNcloud pavilion

{

>　// The combinatorial application of simulated and designed configurations with
>　// on-site real-time reconfigurations gives rise to a new form of urban pavilion
>　// or event space; one that is forever changing but that channels within its
>　// multiple configurations the energies and creativities of its user groups. ❸

>　5.1 {Deploy components on site following the parametric definition}
>　5.2 {Real-time feedback activates the optical fibre regulated by a computer-
>　　　controlled system to generate a layer of luminous gradients that overlap the
>　　　structural one and trigger playfulness and interaction}
>　5.3 {The crowd readjusts the cloud to suit emerging events and trigger novel
>　　　luminous behaviour}
>　5.4 {As rain falls it is collected by the superabsorbent fibres, affecting the growth
>　　　of plants and the creation of an additional ecology on site}
>　5.5 {Articulation grows as social interaction evolves: lack of human response is
>　　　counteracted by intensification of environmental stimuli; unregulated social
>　　　interaction is framed by the pavilion's structural and spatial articulation}

}

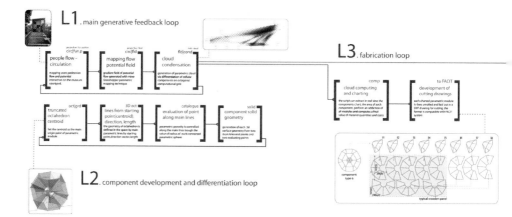

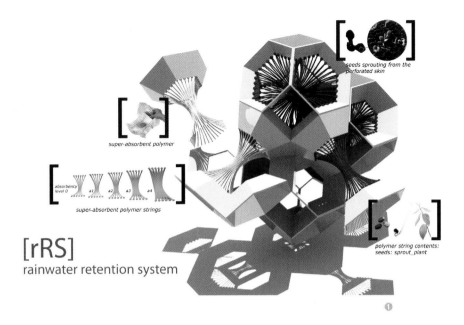

[**L.** **⬡**] seeds sprouting from the perforated skin

super-absorbent polymer

absorbency level 0 a1 a2 a3 a4
super-absorbent polymer strings

[**.** **🌿**] polymer string contents: seeds: sprout_plant

[rRS]
rainwater retention system

❶

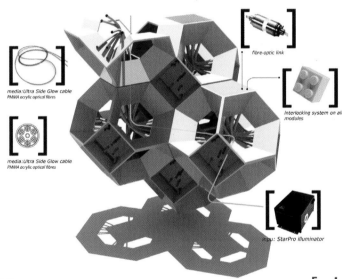

fibre-optic link

media:Ultra Side Glow cable
PMMA acrylic optical fibres

Interlocking system on all modules

media:Ultra Side Glow cable
PMMA acrylic optical fibres

input: StarPro illuminator

fibre-optic lighting system [oLS]

❷

L4. rain screen to organic growth loop

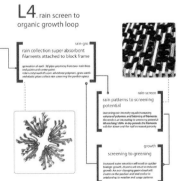

rain-gro
rain collection super absorbent filaments attached to block frame

rain-screen
rain patterns to screening potential

growth
screening to greening

[2.4] Social Network City:
Milan 2015 Metropolitan
Proto-Garden

CATEGORY: b3 Behavioural Spaces
PROJECT TYPE: b3:2 Spaces of
               social networking
PROJECT #:   4
LOCATION: Milan, Italy
YEAR: 2009

[45.49,9.19] [45.48,9.20] [45.48,9.21]

[45.47,9.19] [45.47,9.20] [45.47,9.21]

[45.46,9.19] [45.46,9.20] [45.46,9.21]

[45.45,9.19] [45.45,9.20] [45.45,9.21]

[45.44,9.19] [45.44,9.20] [45.44,9.21]

+ [Shopping]
+ [Hotel]
+ [Sports]
  [Cafè/Restaurant]
+ [Local Info]
+ [Panoramio Pics]
+ [YouTube]

pp. 238–239
Satellite view of central
Milan with indication of
nodal points of urban
activity extracted from
Google Maps database

this page
Map overlay of virtual
plots simulation and Public
Transport Accessibility
Levels [PTAL] for the most
active plots

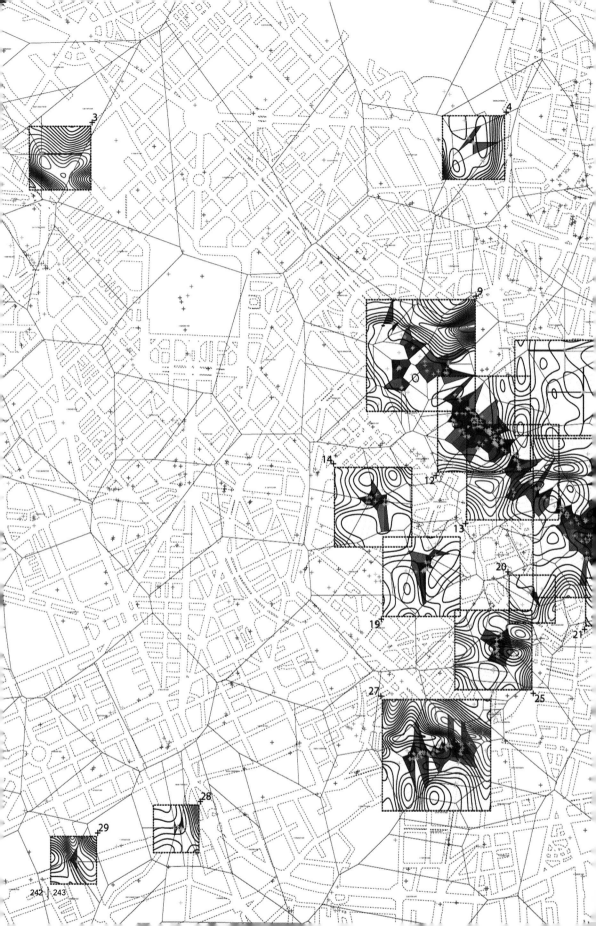

Map overlay of virtual plots
simulation and vegetation
density levels for the most
active plots

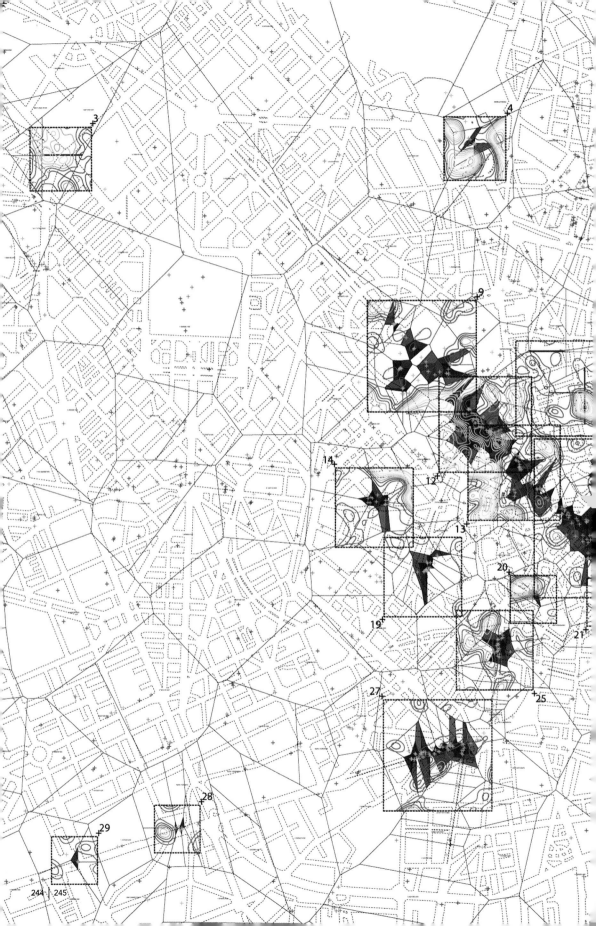

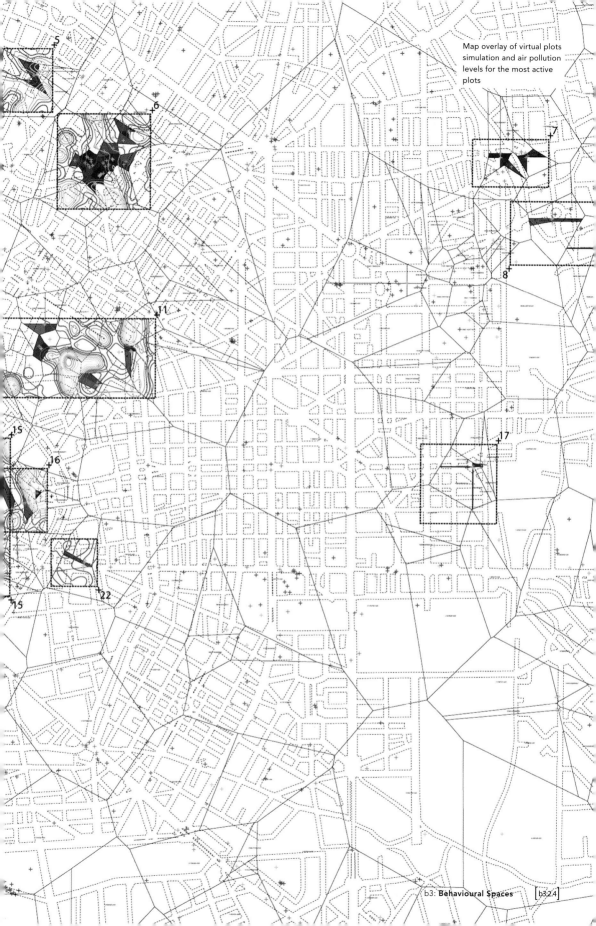

Map overlay of virtual plots simulation and air pollution levels for the most active plots

Artistic behaviour, then, once considered characteristic of small, excluded, marginalized, and unpredictable social groups, once viewed as foreign to the business world,
has now gained a new centrality in the social economy …, a "buzz economy" that
follows discontinuous flows of an energy that is more relational than productive.

Andrea Branzi, *Weak and Diffuse Modernity*, pp. 39, 50

Introduction Milan 2015: Metropolitan Proto-Garden (2015_MpG) is a visionary project – the
projection of a dream for a new kind of cybernetic urban ecology. However, in contrast to fictional
scenarios, the dream is constructed through the systematic and rational hybridization of techniques and technologies that have already entered our daily life: Google Maps and Google Earth,
panoramio, flickr, Facebook on the one side, iPhones, computational design tools, interactive and
robotic devices on the other. In 2015_MpG these instruments are interconnected in novel ways to
read, map and eventually manipulate real material processes as they unfold in the urban environment of Milan: its intensification of public urban life, its global awareness, its concentration of air
pollution, accessibility to its public transportation network, the growth of algae colonies within its
ponds and canals and so on. The 2015_MpG interface extends the reach of digital and networking
technologies to become instruments of communication and "conversation" with the city as a large
complex system.

This video project can be read as a prototype, a proof of concept for a new kind of urban
and architectural interface/infrastructure. This form of machinic architecture is a synthetic hybrid
embedded with biological life (physical proto-gardens), remote sensing and actuating capabilities (control and interaction systems embedded in the proto-gardens), performance (urban
oxygenation, algae farming, microclimatic regulation), computational power (built-in mapping and
simulation engines of the MpG's digital interface) and communication capabilities (online visual
interface and the interactive physical systems).

The 2015_MpG experiment has already started, with the production and testing of temporary installations, and will evolve in time, cultivated by a new breed of proto-gardeners that will
nourish their city with their daily actions: locally and globally, directly and remotely, materially and
conceptually, through sensors or servomotors. The MpG feeds and is fed back by the cultural and
social evolution of global Milan, it is an urban machine for the age of ecology.

Virtual plots The Metropolitan Proto-Garden operates on the subdivision of the city into virtual
plots; a "proto-gardener" must select and register to a plot to start his/her cultivation experience.
The virtual plots are therefore a crucial operational feature of the MpG and are also one of its
more important conceptual elements.

Virtual plots are defined algorithmically and are based on the most diffused form of occupation of territories found in nature: the "distancing occupation". This type of occupation is well
described through the application of the Voronoi algorithm, where the attractor points defining
each plot, or territory of direct influence, correspond, in this case to urban social hubs. The physical location of these hubs is mapped from Google Maps and it therefore updates in real time.
The addition of new hubs, such as cafés, galleries, markets and so on, automatically generates
a new plot of influence and in turn forces the neighbouring plots to reorganize. Virtual plots are
therefore a self-organizing system of sites of occupation of the urban territory by a multiplicity of
urban social groups.

Conceptually each plot can be considered a sort of "liminal body", whose boundaries never
really materialize but are the materialization of zones of transition between different urban
spheres of influence, belonging to different social groups. The power of this description becomes

apparent when the virtual plots are overlapped or made to interfere with the physical urban blocks; this interference forces a re-description of the effective boundaries of the blocks; conventional limits of thought and behaviour are relaxed and new emergent possibilities are liberated.

Within this process "urban cultivation" emerges as a practice with strong spatial, architectonic and urban implications. It goes well beyond the growing of food within small leftover plots of land inbetween consolidated blocks or even beyond the construction of dedicated agricultural blocks.

Moreover virtual plots also provide a dynamic framework for the calculation of a new set of urban parameters, described as operational fields, as well as the structuring of new prototypical cultivation communities, the proto-gardens.

Operational fields   From the systemic point of view the urban environment can be described through the definition of a set of operational fields. These numerical maps or datascapes provide a visual description of the variation and intensity of key descriptor parameters in space and time (now also in real time). The choice of descriptor depends on the project ambition and performative requirements; each social group from within its plot may develop an interest in a specific descriptor as they provide an account of the material processes that are channelled through the plot and directly influence the cultivation process.

Proto-gardens   The proto-gardens are new urban systems whose identity emerges out of a process of actualization of latent social, economic and ecologic potentials. These potentials are recognized through the framework of the virtual plots and the computation and plotting of the related operational fields. Their liberation and actualization in a multitude of forms, spatial conditions and social communities is catalysed by the introduction of new prototypical urban and architectural devices. These devices are characterized by a specific set of performances (evapo-transpiration, photosynthesis, carbon sequestration, etc.), are engineered into specific material organizations or systems (branching fibrous network, woven double curvature surface, octahedral cloud), are embedded with remote sensing and actuating potential (pressure, radiation, pollution, proximity, etc.) and are interfaced with a simulation engine (estimated growth and yield patterns).

Online digital interface for remote cultivation of the proto-gardening stations

Four of them have been proposed for the project Milan 2015: Metropolitan Proto-Garden:

2015_MpG_UH Urban   Hydroponic is a prototype for growing plants in nutrient solutions without the use of soil to provide support. It is highly productive, conservative of water and land and therefore particularly apt to the urban environment. UH integrates an interactive control system that regulates and simulates its growth in time, suggesting cultivation strategies and harvesting patterns to both local and global users.

2015_MpG_AF   Algae Farm represents a new prototype of urban renewable energy power plant. AF is based on the very efficient process of conversion of solar energy and CO_2 in oily compounds performed by algae. From the algae it is then possible to extract bio-fuel, hydrogen and biomass. The prototype can be actualized at different scales, from small installations to large urban farms; larger systems can incorporate research and learning facilities to evolve the technology. A first instance of the prototype is STEMv2.0.

2015_MpG_UO   Urban Oxygenator is a new prototype for dense urban environments. UO is based on the intensification of plants' potential to generate oxygen via photosynthesis. UO will grow and intensify in relation to sunlight and to the concentration of pollutants in the atmosphere (mainly CO_2, CO and thin particulate PM10). More polluted microclimates will benefit by the relative increase in oxygen production and filtering potential. In STEMv3.0 the prototype has been materialized in a cloud-like formation and tested for three months in Seville for the 2008 Architecture Biennale.

2015_MpG_AR   Atmospheric Regulator is an artificial water garden that functions as a distributed rain collector and storage system. Unlike a conventional recycling system, AR doesn't hide its functional apparatus; rather it is embodied in the structural matrix, the branching system. AR operates by expanding the climatic effects latent within the management of water and its transitional states (e.g. evaporation). Rainwater becomes the protagonist of both perceptual games and gardening processes.

this page
Online digital interface
for remote cultivation
showing activity in an
existing prototype

facing page
Map overlay of virtual plots
simulation and proximity
network of cafés and
restaurants for the most
active plots

pp. 250–251
Matrix of the most relevant
urban fields within central
Milan computed by the
Metropolitan Proto-Garden
algorithm. The rows
represent the changing
parameters of computation

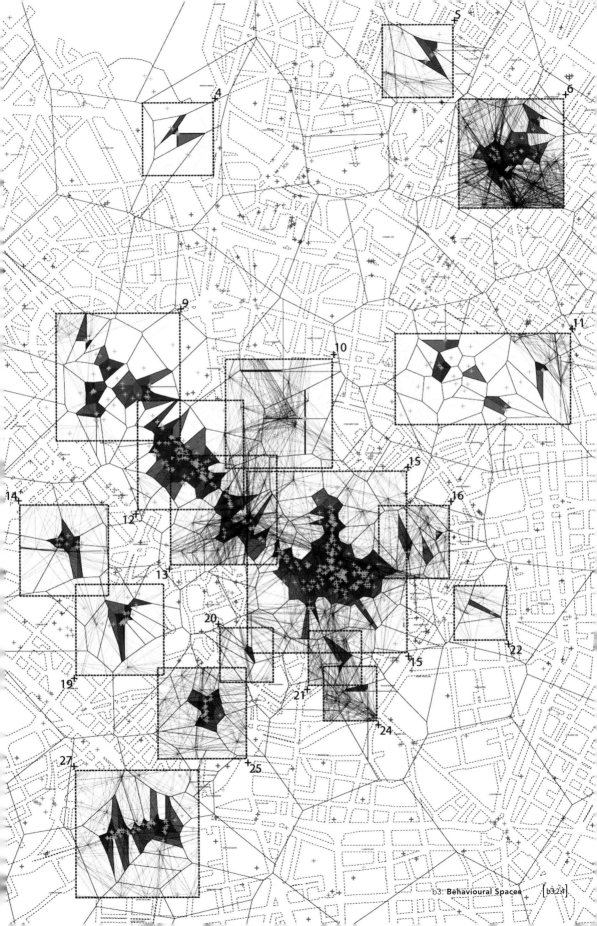

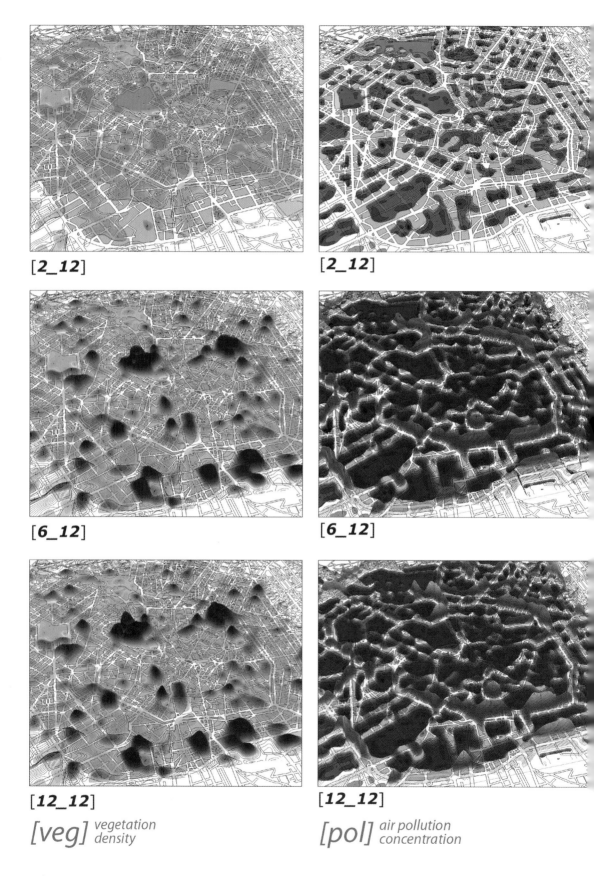

[*2_12*]

[*2_12*]

[*6_12*]

[*6_12*]

[*12_12*]

[*12_12*]

[*veg*] vegetation
density

[*pol*] air pollution
concentration

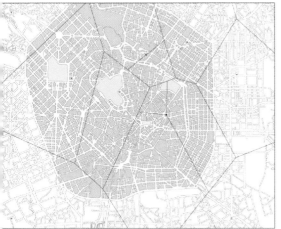

density [*min*]

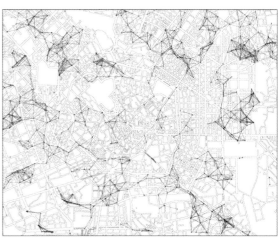

distance [*350m 08:00-12:00*]

[*medium*]

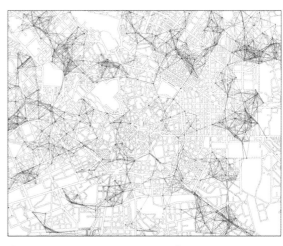

[*400m 12:00-16:00*]

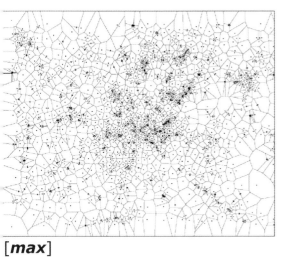

[*max*]

[*gcp*] global cultivation potential

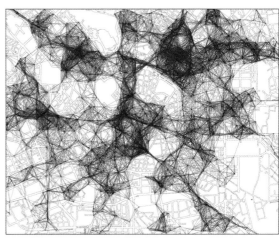

[*400m 20:00-24:00*]

[*ucp*] urban cultivation potential

how to 1 : Run a proto-gardening interface

{

  // The Metropolitan Proto-Garden interface has been presented as a video
  // project. The narrative introduces a dialogue between a cyber-gardener, willing
  // to engage with the remote urban "cultivation" of Milan, and the Metropolitan
  // Proto-Garden, which functions as a mediator between the city, the real urban
  // proto-gardens and the cyber-gardener.
  // What follows is a transcription of this dialogue illustrated by some key frames
  // extracted from the video. We invite the reader to view the full video online by
  // following this link:
  // www.ecologicstudio.com/v2/project.php?idcat=7&idsubcat=28&idproj=46.

Opening titles
Claudia {On one hand there is the virtual
interface (which is almost a Facebook of
architecture) in which the proto-gardener learns
and understands about dynamic processes and
relationships}
*** {CLICK HERE to get information about
Metropolitan Proto-Garden}

Definitions and images of proto-gardens
Claudia {While on the other hand we propose
a series of prototypes which are always related
and fed back to the virtual realm}
*** {REFRESH virtual plots}

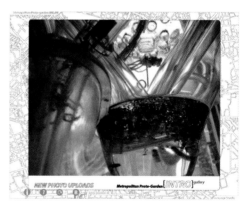

Virtual plots re-computing sequence based on
real-time data
ecoLogicStudio.001 {Pictures uploaded through
Google Earth show real interest in the city even
if it's virtual}
ecoLogicStudio.002 {By applying a Voronoi
algorithm to these data, we can create virtual
plots based on density of interest in the city}
ecoLogicStudio.001 {It's a connection between
the city itself and a new generation of
inhabitants of the global network}
*** {SEE most active virtual plots}
Marco {These are really the global hubs of
Milan}

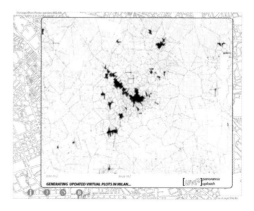

milan 2015 | metropolitan proto-garden
milano 2015 | proto-giardino metropolitano

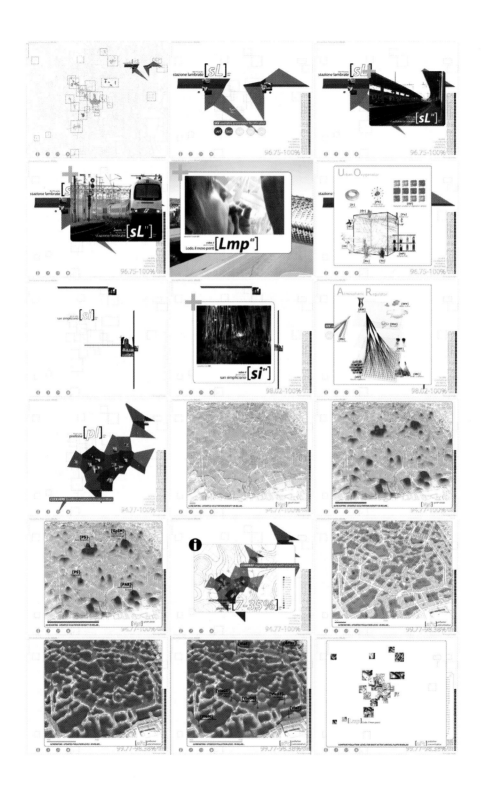

MpG interface proposes prototypes for selected plots and shows active projects

*** {SEE available prototypes for this plot}
ecoLogicStudio.001 {An urban oxygenator is a condensing filter, filtering all the tiny particles that you find in the polluted urban air}
*** {CLICK HERE to see existing Metropolitan Proto-Garden projects}

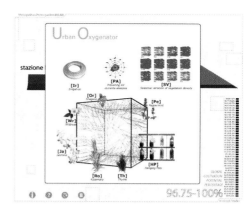

*** {SEE available prototypes}
Claudia {The atmospheric regulator is a prototype that could tackle the entire water cycle and therefore collect water but at the same time use this water collection to create microclimatic effects}

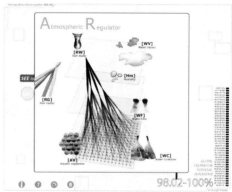

The cyber-gardener selects different ecological filters to visualize relevant environmental fields

*** {CLICK HERE to refresh vegetation density extracting data from aerial photo of Milan}
ecoLogicStudio.003 {The Metropolitan Proto-Garden prototypes become stepping stones between existing green areas}
ecoLogicStudio.004 {They don't act as replacements of green areas but as new interactive plug-ins to the city ...}
Marco {... incubators of new urban socio- and bio-ecologies}
*** {COMPARE vegetation density with other plots}

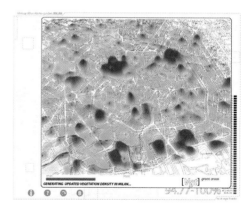

*** {CLICK HERE to see latest uploaded films}
*** {REFRESH pollution levels with atmospheric data extracted in real time}
Marco {From the map it emerges that Milan has got a very high concentration of pollutants ...}
ecoLogicStudio.004 {... which for the proto-gardener could be considered positive ...}
*** {SEE pollution levels for this plot}
*** {COMPARE pollution levels for virtual plots}
Marco {... well ... algae feed on CO_2 and NO_x ... they actually use them to grow and proliferate}

The cyber-gardener selects urban social filters
to visualize the social potential of cultivating a
new proto-garden
*** {CLICK HERE to refresh physical network}
ecoLogicStudio.005 {Each cross represents
the physical attractors in the city ... bars,
restaurants, cafés etc. ...}
Marco {... and this information is available on
Google Maps right now ... an ever-changing
geo-location of social life ...}

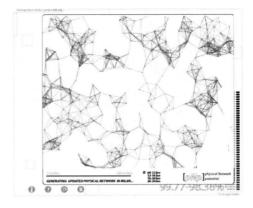

*** {SEE physical network potential for this plot}
*** {COMPARE physical network potential}
Marco {... which gives a visualization of these
network potentials in the city and how they
operate in real life, migrating through the
urban territory ... at different times ... different
seasons}

MpG interface proposes a new bio-energy and
urban agriculture prototype
ecoLogicStudio.004 {Producing energy and
generating new possibilities for the urban
space}
ecoLogicStudio.006 {A world of biosynthetic
hybrids producing biomass and increasing the
interactive infrastructure of the metropolis}

The cyber-gardener checks public accessibility
levels for that plot
*** {SEE accessibility by public transportation}
ecoLogicStudio.001 {The PTAL (Public
Transportation Accessibility Level) shows your
car dependency}
*** {SEE PTAL for this plot}

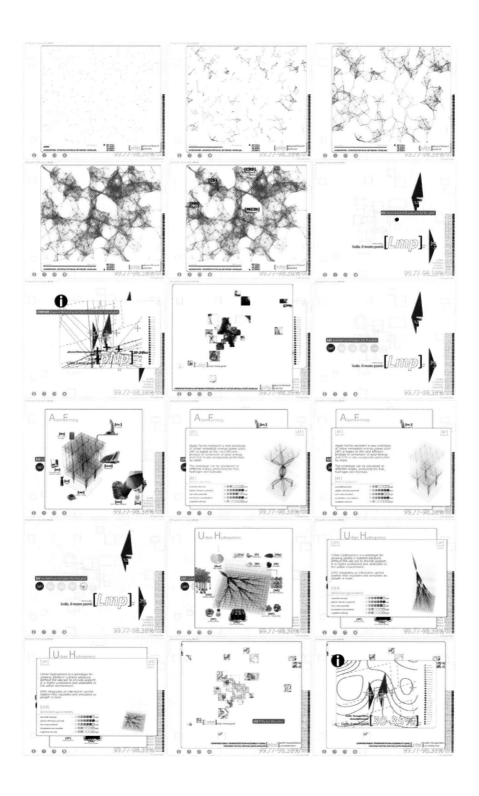

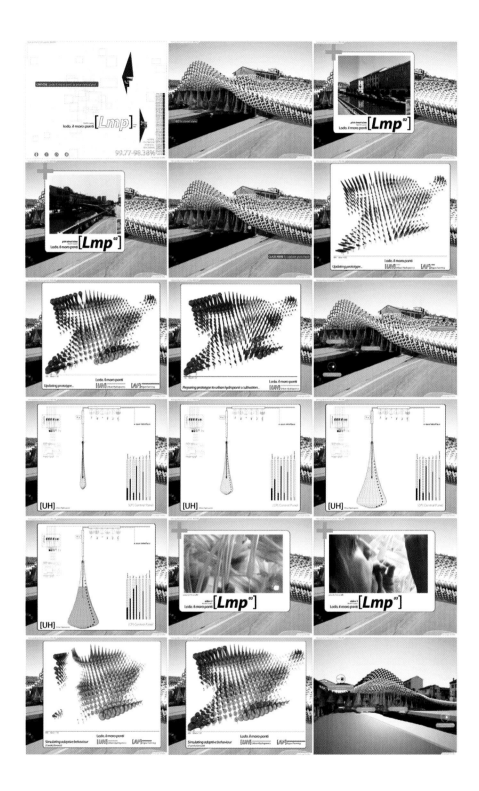

The cyber-gardener is convinced by the
opportunities available and joins that plot to
start cultivating the available prototypes
*** {CHOOSE Lodo Moro Ponti as your plot}
*** {START CULTIVATING urban hydroponics
and algae farming}
*** {GO TO STREET VIEW}
*** {CLICK HERE to update prototype}
*** {CLICK HERE to prepare for urban
hydroponics cultivation}

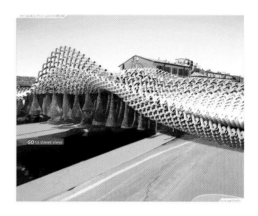

ecoLogicStudio.004 {It's incredible how by
changing the parameters of the environment
you can increase the growth of your proto-
garden}
ecoLogicStudio.006 {From the control panel
the virtual interaction visualizes nutrients and
growth}
ecoLogicStudio.001 {By adding nutrients the
virtual proto-garden can control the real growth
of the urban garden}
*** {SEE physical local interaction}
*** {GET updated prototype behaviour}

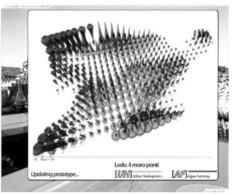

The cyber-gardener uses the digital simulation
engine and the remote control room of the
MpG to cultivate his plot
ecoLogicStudio.001 {The prototype's behaviour
evolves according to both the environmental
and the social conditions of the area ...}
ecoLogicStudio.004 {... social and cultural
events ... church activities ... shops' opening
hours ...}

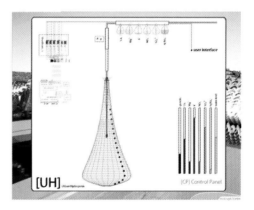

Claudia {It's a visionary project ... it's the
projection of a dream for a new kind of
cybernetic urban ecology ... based on the
hybridization of techniques and technologies
that have already entered our daily lives}

}

Credits

[b1:1.1] Messina 2012: A Regional Proto-Garden

TYPE OF PROJECT: international workshop
YEAR: 2007
AUTHORS: Claudia Pasquero, Marco Poletto, Ivan Valdez, Jorge Godoy
CURATORS: OBR, Tommaso Principi, Paolo Brescia
SPONSOR: Municipality of Messina
SPECIAL THANKS: ICAMP2007 students

[b1:1.2] Regimes of Slowness Caracas: Operational Landscapes

TYPE OF PROJECT: international research think tank
YEAR: 2003
AUTHORS: Claudia Pasquero, Marco Poletto, Guy Lafayette
CURATORS: Caracas Urban Think Tank, Alfredo Brillemburg, Hubert Klumpner
CONSULTING TEAM: Battle McCarthy, Guy Battle
SPONSOR: Cultural Foundation of Germany

[b1:2.3] The Systemic Favela: Design Algorithms for a Social Free-Zone in the Arabic Peninsula

TYPE OF PROJECT: algorithmic urban design
YEAR: 2010
AUTHORS: this project brings together a collection of algorithmic urban design concepts developed by ecoLogicStudio in collaboration with AA Inter10 09/10, for a research project in Abu Dhabi (UAE), and with Carlo Ratti Associati, for KA-CARE invited competition, Saudi Arabia
DESIGN TEAM: Claudia Pasquero, Marco Poletto with Andrea Bugli
CONSULTING TEAM: Prof. Mike Batty, UCL/CASA; Accenture; Atkins; Atmos; ADACH, Abu Dhabi Authority for Culture and Heritage

[b1:2.4] The World Dubai Marine Life Incubators

TYPE OF PROJECT: academic design research
YEAR: 2009/2010
AUTHORS: AA Inter10 2009/2010
UNIT MASTERS: Claudia Pasquero and Marco Poletto
AA INTER10 2009/10 STUDENTS: Wesley Soo, Masaki Echizenya, Noam Hazan, Lola Lozano, Alessandro Bava, Yu Won Kang, Leila Meroue, Wei Hou, Michalis Pastsalosavis, Katerina Albertucci, Zachary Fluker, Wenlan Yuan, Iker Mugarra Flores
CONSULTING TEAM: Maria Arceo, Artist; Dr Abeer Shaheen AlJanahi, British University in Dubai; Brendan Jack, Head of Environment and Ecology at Nakheel property developers
SPONSORS: Nakheel property developers, British University in Dubai
SPECIAL THANKS: Alessio Carta, Manuele Gaioni, Andrea Bugli and Neill Grant

[b2:1.1] Fibrous Room

TYPE OF PROJECT: prototype
YEAR: 2008
AUTHORS: Claudia Pasquero, Marco Poletto, Nilufer Kozikoglu
CURATOR: Pelin Dervis, Garanti Gallery Istanbul
SUPPORTED BY: Adams Kara Taylor; Architectural Association; Istanbul Technical University
SPONSORS: La Farge Turkey
MEDIA PARTNER: Arkitera, Istanbul
SPECIAL THANKS: AA Fibrous Structures Workshop students, v1.0 Istanbul and v2.0 London
PHOTOGRAPHS: ecoLogicStudio and Laleper Aytek

[b2:1.1] Aqva Garden

TYPE OF PROJECT: prototype
YEAR: 2007
AUTHOR: ecoLogicStudio
DESIGN TEAM: Claudia Pasquero, Marco Poletto with Francesco Brenta, Laura Micalizzi
SPONSOR: Tenax srl

[b2:2.2] The STEM series

TYPE OF PROJECT: prototypes

YEAR: 2008/10

AUTHOR: ecoLogicStudio

DESIGN TEAM: Claudia Pasquero, Marco Poletto with Gianluca Santosuosso, Benjamin Fallows, Fabrizio Matillana, Santiago Romero, Kim Bjarke, Liat Marom

CURATORS: Marie Ange Brayer for 2008 Seville Architecture Biennale
Aaron Betsky, Emiliano Gandolfi for 2008 Venice Architecture Biennale
Pino Scalione, Michele Latzinger, Samuela Caliari for Biennale delle Alpi, Trento Science Museum

TECHNICAL SUPPORT TEAM: Nick Puckett [interaction design], Manuela Mantelli [biology], Massimiliano Tardio [algal biodiversity]

PROTOTYPING: Talbot Design Ltd, AA Prototyping Lab, UEL Prototyping Lab, ecoLogicStudio

SUPPORTED BY: Fluid Structures, ZEF Environmental Engineers, MODO Arredo

SPECIAL THANKS: Mirko Daneluzzo, Seville University Team, Trento University Team, Trento Museum of Science

The Cyber-Gardens

TYPE OF PROJECT: prototype/interface

YEAR: 2011

AUTHOR: ecoLogicStudio

DESIGN TEAM: Claudia Pasquero, Marco Poletto with Neil Grant, Nick Puckett, Andrea Bugli, Alessio Carta, Silvia Ortu, Xenia Palaiologou, Manuele Gaioni

SPECIAL THANKS: AA Inter10 09/10 Students, SMART GEOMETRY 2011 Cluster Participants

Relational Machines: The Ecologic Footprint Grotto

TYPE OF PROJECT: prototype

YEAR: 2010

AUTHOR: ecoLogicStudio

DESIGN TEAM: Claudia Pasquero, Marco Poletto with Andrea Bugli, Alessio Carta, Manuele Gaioni, Luca Allievi, Alessandro Bava, Chiara Ferrario, Filippo Fassio, Ponn Laohasukkasem, Gianluca Santosuosso, Fabio Auteri

CURATORIAL TEAM: Luca Molinari with Simona Galateo, Luca Poncelli for the Italian Pavilion at 2010 Venice Architecture Biennale

SPONSOR: SEPA srl

SCIENTIFIC PARTNER: Alessandro Galli, eco-Footprint Network Ltd

SPECIAL THANKS: NABA students of the Master in Interior Design

PHOTOGRAPHS: ecoLogicStudio and Patrick Acheson

FUNclouds

TYPE OF PROJECT: concept

YEAR: 2009/2011

AUTHOR: ecoLogicStudio

DESIGN TEAM: Claudia Pasquero, Marco Poletto with Yota Gotsou, Manuele Gaioni, Anders Nielsen, Chiara Catalano, Andrea Bugli, Daniela de Pascale

Social Network City: Milan 2015 Metropolitan Proto-Garden

TYPE OF PROJECT: concept

YEAR: 2009

AUTHOR: ecoLogicStudio

DESIGN TEAM: Claudia Pasquero, Marco Poletto with Yota Gotsou, Manuele Gaioni, Anders Nielsen, Chiara Catalano

CURATORIAL TEAM: Luca Molinari with Simona Galateo for the Municipality of Milan, Urban Center

CONSULTING TEAM: Mobility in Chain srl

Index

Page numbers in *italic* denote an illustration

AA Design Research Laboratory (AADRL) 17
Abu Dhabi (Systemic Favela) 68–92, *68–73*;
     algorithmic protocol 76, 80–1, *82–3*; brief
     74; differentiations and hierarchies 77;
     endless algorithm for the endless city
     77; Graphical User Interface (GUI) 90;
     hard–soft occupation 84; infrastructural
     systems 75; minimal paths networks (road
     and pedestrian) 88, *89*; natural ventilation
     potential 87; neighbourhood clustering
     90, *91*, *92–3*; network steepness
     evaluation 87; and reverse sustainability
     75, 76; social free-zone 75, 76; and soft
     city 77; urban mechanisms 75; virtual
     massing 84, *85*, 87; virtual plots *70–3*, 76;
     virtual tessellation 84
action plans (Messina) 45
advanced determinism 26
algae/algae farming 117, 154, 158;
     FUNcloud Urban Algae Farm 229–30;
     248; *see also* Metropolitan Proto-Garden;
     STEM installations
algorithm, urban *see* urban algorithm
algorithmic design techniques 11
algorithmic diverseCity 8–9
algorithmic protocol (Abu Dhabi) 76, 80–1,
     82–3
Aqva Garden 116, *124–5*, 132, *133*, *135*;
     microclimatic spaces 132
architecture: engaging unpredictability as a
     creative force 14; fascination with nature
     22, *23*; as systemic design practice 11–12
Architectural Association 74
Atmospheric Regulator (Metropolitan Proto-
     Garden) 248
avant-garde 16

Ballantyne, Andrew 5
bamboo 59, 63, 64
barrios (Caracas) 54, 55, 57
Bathymetric Tissue Proto-Garden (Messina)
     37, 44

behavioural spaces 185 *see also* Ecological
     Footprint Grotto (Venice)
bio-digesting belt (Messina) 37
bioreactors 154, 169
biodiversity 8
biomimetic industrial processes 22
Biorock 100
black water discharge (Caracas) 60
Bottega della Biodiversità (Biodiversity
     Workshop) 156, *178–9*
bottom-up action 18
Branzi, Andrea 9, 16, 212, 246
Briccoles 117, 156, 164, 166, 169, 172, 176
building typologies 81
built environment 16
Bunschoten, Raoul 10
buoneros (street vendors) 55

Caracas (Venezuela) 28, 48–67, *48–53*;
     analysing informal landscape of La
     Vega 60–2; barrios 54, 55, 57; building
     techniques and culture of formality
     56; and buoneros (street vendors) 55;
     contextualization 56–7; designing the
     material system 63; education 57; La
     Vega as testing bed 58; map of informal
     settlement density *52–3*; operational
     fields 58–9; operational landscapes
     59, 65; parasitism in architecture 54;
     prototype's operating manual design 64;
     research hypothesis 56; social dynamics in
     the informal city 57; social empowerment
     as design tool 58
Careri, Francesco 9
Centre Point building (Oxford Street,
     London) *116*
Centre Pompidou 16
Chiuina (La Paz) 116
cities: growth and vitality of 21; liquid 18–20
clean-tech village 74
Clement, Gilles *2–3*, *6–7*, 194
climate change 23
co-design 185, 186 *see also* Ecological
     Footprint Grotto (Venice); Fish & Chips
     project (London)

coding: as gardening 6–7
connectivity 81
control: obsession with 15–16
conurbations 21
Coral Gardens: exhibition 126–7; the World
    Dubai Marine Life Incubators project 29,
    100, 194, *194*
corals 100
creativity: and unpredictability 14
cyber-communities 2
cyber-gardens 194–5; Copenhagen *202–3*;
    CyBraille 195; Fish & Chips see Fish &
    Chips project; Photosynthe-Sense 195
cyber-materials 106
CyBraille 195

De Landa, Manuel 114
Deleuze, Gilles 4–5, 8, 26
"desiring machines" 5
Detroit 8
diagrammatic design techniques 115
diagrammatic machines 42; FUNcloud 232
digital revolution 18
Dubai 96; architecture 96; fractal-like design
    97; impact of global crisis 98; machinic
    utopia 97; Marine Life Incubators project
    see World Dubai Marine Life Incubators
    project; mechanisms of development 96;
    World Lagoon 28, 97–8

eco-social frameworks 28 see also Caracas
    (Venezuela); Messina Regional Proto-
    Garden
eco-social landscapes 28–9 see also
    Abu Dhabi; World Dubai Marine Life
    Incubators project
Eco-Touristic Loom Proto-Garden (Messina)
    37
ecological crisis 3
Ecological Footprint Grotto (Venice) 186,
    204–21, *204–9, 210, 212, 213*; ecological
    footprint soft ceiling 219; framing the
    global ecological footprint 214; global
    stories on flows of materials, information
    and energy 214; interaction 221; self-
    organization of 220
ecological stress 41
ecological sustainability 15

ecology: and material culture 21–3
ecoMachines 17, 117, 184 see also STEM
    installations
economic free-zone 75
edge cities 19
embedded electronics 17
empowerment 58
engineers: close collaboration with 17

Fibrous Room (Garanti Gallery, Istanbul)
    12, 116, *118–19, 120–1*, 128–30, *128*,
    130, 131, 134–42; definition of fibrous
    logic and organizational principles 136;
    designing of relational machine 138;
    developing new material definitions
    141; environmental mediation 142;
    experimenting with material systems
    138; fibrous structures protocol 134,
    136; introduction of fibre's definition
    136; material adaptation 141; public's
    interaction 142; relational adaptation 138
fibrous structures 116–18, 128 see also Aqva
    Garden; Fibrous Room
fibrous structures protocol 134, 136
figurative approach 58
firmitas 116
Fish & Chips project (London) 186, *187*,
    188–203, *188–9, 192–3*; co-design 201;
    processing information and activating
    real-time mapping 198; prototype *195*;
    prototype cybernetic diagram *190–1*;
    sensing 196; structuring the cyber-garden
    196
forecasting, urban 15
forests 8
Frazer, John 16
FUNclouds 154, 186, 222–37, *222–7*,
    228; articulating the cloud's molecules
    235; condensing the space of 234;
    diagramming potential fields of social
    interaction and urban re-functionalization
    232; embedding performance and
    responsiveness 236
FUNcloud pavilion *228*, 229, 232, 236
FUNcloud Urban Algae Farm 229–30

"garden": weakening of conception of
    landscape as 2–3

Garden City 184
gardening: coding as 6–7
geometry 12
Godoy, Horge 37
Google Maps 246
Graphical User Interface (GUI) (Abu Dhabi)
    90
Grasshopper 198
Guadalquivir Experiment see STEMv2.0
    (Seville)
Guattari, Félix: The Three Ecologies 7, 96

hard–soft occupation (Abu Dhabi) 84
Homer: Odyssey 36
human flow: and STEMv2.0 (Seville) 164
Hydroponic 248

"ideology of the process" 11
information flow 21–2
information technologies 19
inheritance 22
interaction, public: and Ecological Footprint
    Grotto 221; and Fibrous Room 142

Koolhaas, Rem 16, 96

lagoon condensers: and STEMv3.0 (Venice)
    155
land instability (Caracas) 62
landscape height 81
landscape steepness 81
Le Ricolais 5
"Lightwall" 228
liquid city 18–20
Luhmann 16
Lynn, Gregg 11

machine for living 184
machines 17; Deleuze's definition of 4–5
Maktoum, Sheikh Mohammed bin Rashid Al 96
master plan 14
material culture: and ecology 21–3
material system protocols 63
material systems 114; articulating (Messina)
    44; designing (Caracas) 63; experimenting
    with (Fibrous Room) 138
MAXdiv housing project 231
memory: and STEMv2.0 (Seville) 174

Messina Regional Proto-Garden 28, 30–47,
    30–5; action plans and subcomponents
    45; articulate material systems 44;
    Bathymetric Tissue Proto-Garden 37,
    44; bio-digesting belt 37; defining
    operational fields 41; diagram operational
    fields 42; Eco-Touristic Loom Proto-
    Garden 37; framing topographic regions
    40; Migrotype Proto-Garden 37, 45; urban
    prototyping and proto-gardening 43;
    vegetation cover of virtual plots 38–9
Metropolis: and eco-social landscape 14
Metropolitan Proto-Garden (Milan) 185, 187,
    230, 238–50, 238–45; Algae Farm 248;
    Atmospheric Regulator 248; Hydroponic
    248; operational fields 247; running a
    proto-gardening interface 252–9; Urban
    Oxygenator 248; virtual plots 246–7, 249
Migrotype Proto-Garden (Messina) 37, 45
Milan: Metropolitan Proto-Garden see
    Metropolitan Proto-Garden
minimal paths networks (road and
    pedestrian) (Abu Dhabi) 88, 89
Modernism 15
mood board 195
multi-functional land use 20

Najle, Circo 8
natural selection, new regime of 22
natural ventilation potential (Abu Dhabi) 81, 87
neighbourhood clustering (Abu Dhabi) 90,
    91, 92–3
network steepness evaluation (Abu Dhabi) 87
networks 18–19
New Eden 212
Niolmeters (Egypt) 4

occupation of territories: modelling of in
    World Dubai Marine Life Incubators
    project 105; simulating of in World Dubai
    Marine Life Incubators project 103
Oosterhuis, Kas 11
operational fields 26; Caracas 58–9; Messina
    41, 42
Otto, Frei 17, 103
oxy-generation: and Metropolitan Proto-
    Garden 248; and STEMv1.0 (Seville)
    154–5, 154, 162

parametric modelling techniques 129
Parametricism 14, 15, 16
parasitism: in Caracas architecture 56
Park, Kyong 8–9
Pask, Gordon 5
pavilion, FUNcloud *228*, 229, 232, 236
Photosynthe-Sense 195
photosynthesis 169
Piano + Rogers 16
planetary garden 3, 229
Price, Cedric 12, 16
proto-gardens 3, 247 *see also* Messina
    Regional Proto-Garden; Metropolitan
    Proto-Garden
prototype's operating manual 64
prototyping techniques 129
prototype 114

rain collection: and Aqva Garden 132; and
    Atmospheric Regulator 248
real-time mapping 198
real-time processes 58, 169, 172, 174
real-time protocols 115
real-time world city 2, 3, 7
Regional Proto-Garden *see* Messina Regional
    Proto-Garden
Reiser + Umemoto 5, 12
relational machines 138, 184, 210, 212
Riverside Walk (London) 116
Riyadh project 28–9

Schumacher, Patrik 11, 14–17
self-organizing city 18, 19; ecology of 2–3
simulated virtual city 185
simulation models 15
social empowerment: as design tool 58
social networking spaces 186–7 *see also*
    FUNclouds; Metropolitan Proto-Garden
soft city 77
soft-time processes 158, 166
soft-time protocols 115
soil stabilization (Caracas) 59, 64
solar radiation 81
STEM installations 117, 146–81; London *117,
    146–7*, 154; Trento 155–6; Venice *144–5*,
    155, *156*
STEMv2.0 (Guadalquivir Experiment)
    (Seville) *148–9*, *152–3*, 154–5, 158–77,

158, *159*, *163*, *178–81*, 248; cultivation
    feedback 172; development of memory
    174; feedback to urban ecologies 176;
    in-forming the Briccoles 166; intercepting
    human flow 164; overall cybernetic
    diagram *160–1*; oxy-generation and
    self-regulation 154–5; oxygenation and
    carbon sequestration 162; photosynthesis
    and environmental radiation 169
style 16
systemic design practice: architecture as
    11–12
Systemic Favela *see* Abu Dhabi

technologies 16, 81
tectonics 17
Thynnie wasp: and wasp orchid 5
Tropic Playground (Linz) 116
Tschumi, Bernard 16

unpredictability 14
urban algorithm 4–5, 6, 7; encoding of the
    self-organizing city 8; key features of 8–10
Urban Oxygenator: Metropolitan Proto-
    Garden 248; STEM 154–5, 248
urbanization 2–3

Valdez, Ivan 37
Venezuela 54 *see also* Caracas
Virilio, Paul 2
virtual massing (Abu Dhabi) 84, *85*, 87
virtual plots 26, *38–9*; Abu Dhabi 70–3, 76;
    Metropolitan Proto-Garden 246–7, *249*
virtual tessellation (Abu Dhabi) 84
Vitruvius 15
Voronoi algorithm 84, 246

wasp orchid: and Thynnie wasp 5
water proximity 81
Wiscombe, Tom 16
World Dubai Marine Life Incubators project
    27, 94–111, *96*, 194; Coral Gardens 29,
    100, 194, *194*; introduction of material
    strategies 106; model architecture as a
    marine life incubator 108; modelling the
    occupation of territories 105; simulating
    the occupation of territories 103;
    territories of life 101